LITTLE HAVANA BLUES

A Cuban-American Literature Anthology

❧ Edited by ❧
Delia Poey and Virgil Suárez

Arte Público Press
Houston, Texas
1996

This volume is made possible through grants from the National Endowment for the Arts (a federal agency), the Andrew W. Mellon Foundation and the Lila Wallace-Reader's Digest Fund.

Recovering the past, creating the future

Arte Público Press
University of Houston
Houston, Texas 77204-2090

Cover illustration and design by Robert Vega

Little Havana Blues : A Cuban-American Literature anthology / [edited] by Virgil Suárez and Delia Poey.
    p.   cm.
Includes bibliographical references.
ISBN 1-55885-160-7 (alk. paper)
    1. American literature—Cuban American authors. 2. Cuban Americans—Literary collections.
    I. Suárez, Virgil, 1962– . II. Poey, Delia.
PS508.C83L58   1996
810.8'0687291—dc20   96-14242
                                     CIP

for Alexandria and Gabriela

CONTENTS

INTRODUCTION

Cuban-American literature, like most ethnic litera-
tures, has seen a resurgence of interest during this decade
of the 90's. Although it is perceived as a new literature, it
has its roots in the nineteenth century. That this literature
has been developing for a hundred years on the periphery
of established literary channels is due primarily to the fact
that many of its practitioners wrote, and in many cases
continue to write, in Spanish. What is "new" about this literature, then, is not its existence, but rather a major shift
among its writers—many of them second generation or
one-and-a-halvers, the term Gustavo Pérez-Firmat has
coined—from the use of Spanish as the language of choice
to the use of English with the occasional "Spanglish."
Cuban-American literature is currently struggling to define
itself within the American literary context, drawing from
rhythms, flavors and landscapes born of a unique experience that has its roots in migration and exile.

The island of Cuba, only ninety miles away from United States shores, is worlds apart. Proximity has made relations between the two nations complex and at times
explosive. In our history, the strained relations have peri-
odically erupted into crisis and conflict, as in the Spanish
American War, the Bay of Pigs Invasion, the Cuban Missile
Crisis and the Mariel Exodus. One only needs to turn to the
newspaper to read about the on-going struggle of *balseros*,
rafters, and more recently the downing over international

waters by Cuban fighter jets of two civilian aircraft flown by Brothers To The Rescue, a volunteer organization that flies over the Florida Straits in search of rafters who need to be rescued.

Relations between these two nations have influenced and at times defined the histories of both the United States and Cuba. Jose Martí, Cuba's foremost poet and liberator, went through periods of exile in the United States and, in fact, orchestrated Cuba's independence movement from these shores, sending the order for the uprising against Spanish domination from Key West to Cuba inside a cigar.

During Martí's time in the late nineteenth century, Cubans migrated and settled in Ybor City/Tampa, Florida and New York, as political exiles and immigrants. In this century, there have been several waves of Cuban immigration that have made an impact through literature. Prior to the Cuban Revolution of 1959, many Cubans emigrated for political and non-political reasons. The largest exodus in Cuban history took place in the years following the 1959 Revolution and culminated in 1965, when Castro proclaimed Cuba a communist country.

In the 1970's, Cubans immigrated to the United States via Spain, when the three governments involved made a pact to make exit and entry visas available. In 1980, after Cubans stormed the Peruvian embassy in Havana, the Mariel Boatlift carried more than one hundred fifty-thousand Cubans through the Florida Straights. More recently, Cubans have been leaving the island on small crafts and makeshift rafts. As this book goes to press, there are more than thirty thousand of these Cuban rafters being detained in the Guantánamo Base and the Panama Canal Zone; migration from Cuba, even this late in the century, is still in progress.

Because the prospect of returning to the island looms over this community but is, under the present regime, an impossibility, current Cuban-American literature springs out of the condition of exile. The implications of this condition are reflected in a longing for roots, a sense of displacement, the persistence of memory, a need to replay history and an idealization of Cuba itself. For many Cuban-Americans, particularly those who left the island as children and those born in the United States, Cuba has become a creation of the imagination, a fictional space pieced together from recollections, fading photographs and family anecdotes. Cuba is always *el allá*, the elsewhere.

It is impossible to discuss Cuban-American literature without including the centrality of Cuban culture. Food, music, religion, and family play important roles as reservoirs of culture. The fact that syncretisms exist in all of these categories, mixing the influence of the Spanish, African, Taíno and Chinese elements, makes Cubans particularly well-suited to absorbing yet another culture, that of the United States, and making it their own. Cuban-Americans are not assimilated; they do not adopt the dominant culture, but rather adapt it. Thus, Cuban-American writers use English, stretching, bending and playing with it, to accommodate their needs—doing whatever it takes to keep the language vibrant and vital, on their own terms.

In general, Cubans are in love with the cacophony of language. We speak every chance we get, and loudly. Whether or not communication takes place is purely incidental. For proof of this, visit the popular Cuban restaurant Versailles in Little Havana, any day of the week and at any time of the day. The din is at times unbearable. Cuban-Americans have retained this boisterousness, even when speaking English. We make frequent use of hyperbole, irony, parody, satire, puns—anything to maintain an audience. Castro himself is a prime example of the Cuban penchant for rhetoric. This love of language completes the list of ingredients, such as rhythm, music, food and family, which make up Cuban-American culture and infuse its literature with life.

The poets, fiction writers, dramatists and essayists gathered here claim a broad spectrum of influences which reflect the complex literary heritage of the Americas. Their works span the temporal, geographic and linguistic borders, shifting from Spanish to English, at times straddling the fence between two languages and two cultures. They affirm as their own William Carlos Williams, Nicolás Guillén, Alejo Carpentier, Lydia Cabrera, William Faulkner, Ernest Hemingway, Jose Martí, Sor Juana Inéz de la Cruz, Langston Hughes, Emily Dickenson and Walt Whitman, to name but a few.

The writers gathered here range from the very young and new on the literary scene, such as Adrián Castro, E. J. Vega, Achy Obejas, Richard Blanco, Gean Moreno and Sandra Castillo to the seasoned and well-established figures such as Jose Yglesias, Cristina García, Roberto G. Fernández, Dolores Prida and Oscar Hijuelos. As Cuban-Americans, they share a certain thematic unity, exploring common ground such as displacement, syncretism, generational conflict and the negotiation of identity. They also approach these themes from positions that are specific in terms of gender, race, class and sexual practices. The Cuban-American experience is not monolithic and demands, after all, to be told through many voices.

The novel excerpts from Margarita Engle and José Barreiro, who through their storytelling revise the historical narrative and bring together the threads which make up Cuban cultural memory in resistance to the plague amnesia which history, as it has been written, has imposed on us. Roberto G. Fernández's excerpt satirizes Cuban society in the U.S., providing us the catharsis of laughing at our own human failings and realizing the tragic-comic nature of our history.

Marisella Veiga's story and Cristina García's novel excerpt present characters who inhabit the domestic space of the home, more specifically the kitchen, where the very process of preparing a meal for a husband or a son becomes the unifying link as each struggles with choices made and their consequences. Dolores Prida reveals the construction of gender and how femininity is played out biculturally in her innovative bilingual play *Coser y Cantar*.

Sandra Castillo and Richard Blanco's poems demonstrate the dynamics of family repression and exile as revealed in the minutiae of the every day, be it teeth marks on a bar of cream cheese or the discovery of the possibilities of peanut butter. Pablo Medina, Ricardo Pau-Llosa, Dionisio Martínez and Silvia Curbelo's work reflect contemporary currents in poetics, exercising a precision of language that distills images to their very essence with a subtlety that leaves the reader savoring every word. But for these poets, language is the medium, not the end in itself. What their poetry expresses, be it deeply personal or projected onto the outside world, is always grounded in the Cuban-American condition.

Adrián Castro, inspired by the Cuban poet Nicolás Guillén and the Puerto Rican poet Palés Matos, has developed a style that is also reflective of the Nuyorican Poets and other "Spoken Word" artists who foreground the performance of poetry and are actively developing new audiences in coffee houses, bars and larger venues, such as the Lalapalooza concert sponsored by MTV.

Oscar Hijuelos, Virgil Suárez, Jose Yglesias and Beatriz Rivera explore life in-depth, using styles which reflect contemporary trends and perspectives in narrative. Oscar Hijuelos, the recipient of a Pulitzer Prize for his novel *The Mambo Kings Play Songs of Love*, has shown that the specificity of Cuban-American experience does not limit its capacity to engage a mainstream reading public.

Ruth Behar, Wasabi Kanastoga and Gustavo Pérez-Firmat produce work that stands as a testament of dislocation, while Carolina Hospital and through their poetry, reterritorialize Cuba in the United States. These poets create interesting distinctions between the mythical, historical and real Cuba.

Omar Torres and Matías Montes Huidobro, all interesting and arresting playwrights, expose us to a diverse stage upon which intrapersonal relationships and the polymics of the Cuban persona intersect.

Rafael Campos, Achy Obejas and Elías Miguel Muñoz present us with narrators and characters who add layers of complexity to the ethnic, in this case a Cuban-American speaking subject, by occupying the space of the multiply marginalized both within the community and externally because of sexual practices. These writers, employing styles and strategies which are radically different from one another, demonstrate that categories of exclusion and inclusion are not mutually exclusive and the Cuban-American experience is as diverse as the individuals who live it and participate in its articulation.

We chose to include all facets of the literature within the categories of poetry, fiction, essay and drama so as to allow the reader to witness the points of connection and divergence in terms of content, theme and style, not only within one particular genre, but across the spectrum of literary expression. Some of the writers included here, such as Gustavo Pérez-Firmat and Ricardo Pau-Llosa, express themselves in more than one genre. Pérez-Firmat in particular has gained distinction as an essayist in both English and Spanish.

As Cuban-American literature grows, writer by writer, poem by poem, it stretches and redefines its boundaries, continually revising its own framework and resisting facile definitions. We interpret this as symptomatic of a literature undergoing a transformation from infancy to maturity, and predict that it will continue to redraw and reshape its own limits as it establishes its own dynamic, though amorphous, place on the American literary map.

LITTLE HAVANA BLUES

A Cuban-American
Literature Anthology

Poetry

THE JEWISH CEMETERY IN GUANABACOA

Ruth Behar

Outside of Havana
are the Jews
who won't leave Cuba
until the coming
of the Messiah.

There is the grave
of Sender Kaplan's father
a rabbi's grave
encircled by an iron gate
shaded by a royal palm.

There is the grave
in Hebrew letters
that speak Spanish
words of love and loss.
Ay kerida, why so soon?

There is the grave
with a crooked
Star of David.
There is the grave
crumbled like feta.

I go searching
for the grave
of my cousin
who was too rich
to die.

I despair.
I've promised a picture
to my aunt and uncle.
They're rich now in Miami
but not a penny for Fidel.

And then I find it—
the grave of Henry Levin
who died of leukemia
at age twelve
and money couldn't save him.

Poor boy,
he got left behind
with the few living Jews
and all the dead ones
for whom the doves pray.

I reach for my camera
but the shutter won't click.
Through ninety long miles
of burned bridges I've come
and Henry Levin won't smile.

I have to return another day
to Henry Levin's grave
with a friend's camera.
Mine is useless for the rest
of the trip, transfixed, dead.

Only later I learn
why Henry Levin
rejected me
a latecomer
to his grave.

My aunt and uncle were wrong.
Henry Levin is not abandoned.
Your criada, the black woman
who didn't marry to care for him,
tends his grave.

Tere tells me she can't forget
Henry, he died in her arms.
Your family left you, cousin,
so thank God for a black woman
who still visits your little bones.

MY GRANDMOTHER IN MIAMI BEACH
WHO SEES EVERYTHING IN BLUE

Blue are the palm trees
with their hair yanked out of their heads.
Blue are the sea gulls
with their wails reduced to whimpers.
Blue are the faces,
the shoe repairman, the bank teller,
the tired girl at the grocery
squashing the eggs and the plátanos
with the bottle of extra pulp prune juice.
Blue, everything is blue.
Blue, blue, blue world.
Bluer since Hurricane Andrew came.
Earth and sky weep, mother and child
divided by an ocean too thick
with the sludge of grief worn bitter
for any boat to cross.

Blue, I see it all in blue.
They tell me it's the cataracts
but I think it's the cannon
that shattered inside my head.
The crazy sailor in La Habana,
I'll never forgive him
just when I was out buying
aspirin for my brother Jaime.
The doctors took out a few pieces.
The rest stayed in my skull.

My bones won't ever forget
I sailed from Poland to Cuba
riding with the cargo and the coal,
my woolen dress stinking
worse than overripe guayabas
I had yet to taste.
My bones won't ever forget
it was me who stayed alone
at our lace shop in Calle Aguacate
with the salesgirl watching
so I wouldn't steal from the state.
My bones won't ever forget
how I almost didn't get out
just to save a few pesos
we lost anyway.

Blue, it was so blue in New York.
When I should have retired already,
I was selling fabric on Saturdays,
not knowing what language I spoke,
Polish, Yiddish, Spanish, English,
under the din of the overhead train.
And before I knew it, I grew old
and came to this little house
with Máximo, expecting a palace,
I don't know why, from this condominium
my brother built with his spare pennies.
Why is it God didn't whisper into our ears
the secret for making money?
Even Andrew didn't think my casita

was worth his time—
the dishwasher rusted by the sea air,
the family pictures faded in the sun,
the bathroom tiles sulking with desire,
they're still there, he flew over it all.

Blue, I am blue and alone in Miami Beach,
my daughters far away, my son busy making money,
my husband in his grave, my bed empty.
I'm old but I miss it,
except for the times he forced me.
I am Noah, stepping out after the flood.
I don't know why I deserved to live so long.
Maybe just so I could find something
that needed to be seen in blue.

RETURNING

I am going home.
I have the passport
with the four names
that once belonged to me
from the country we left

before I knew I had a country
before I knew I had no country.
Kuba, the promised land of jews
krazy to take a boat going anywhere
so long as it let them off in Amerika.

I cannot eat.
I am vomiting up my heart.
I am hearing the voices
of long-dead relatives.
My own life scares me.

I am going home.
Mami has told me
I may not come back.
Papi has told me
not to talk too much.

And then there I am
again, in a small place
made huge by fear and forgetting
the way shadows haunt
when you won't look at them.

I see the two-bedroom apartment
where I would have grown up
as crowded as we did in New York.
I return to streets that don't
remember me, no matter how hard I step.

AMERICA

❧ Richard Blanco ❧

I.

Although *Tía* Miriam boasted she had discovered
at least half-a-dozen uses for peanut butter—
as a dessert topping for guava shells in heavy syrup,
as a substitute for butter on Cuban toast,
as a hair conditioner—
Mamá never quite knew what to do
with the monthly five-pound jars
handed out by the immigration department
until Brian, my schoolmate, suggested jelly.

II.

There was always pork:
on Christmas Eve and birthdays,
on New Years Eve,
the Fourth of July,
and Thanksgiving Day.
Pork-roasted, fried, or broiled,
as well as cauldrons of black beans,
yuca con mojito
and fried plantain chips.
These items required a special visit
to *Antonio's Mercado*
on the corner of West 163rd and Columbus
where the men in *guayaberas* stood in senate
blaming Kennedy—*"ese hijo de puta,"* they would say,

the mixed bile of Cuban coffee and cigar residue
filling the creases of their wrinkled lips—
as they clung to each other
lying about lost wealth
ashamed of their emptiness
like hollow trees.

III.

By seven
I got suspicious.
We were still here.
Overheard conversations about returning
grew wistful and less frequent.
I had mastered a language
my parents didn't understand.
We didn't live in a two story house
with a maid named Alice
like the *Brady Bunch*.
We didn't have a wood panel station wagon
and vacation camping in Colorado.
Dad didn't watch football on Sundays.
None of the girls in the family had hair of gold;
none of my brothers or cousins
were named Greg, Peter, or Marsha.
None of the characters
on the *Dick Van Dyke Show* or *Happy Days*
were named Guadalupe, Lázaro, or Mercedes.
Patty Duke's family lived in Brooklyn, like us,
but they didn't have pork on Thanksgiving.
They went to Grandma's house in Connecticut
and ate turkey with cranberry sauce,
baked yams, cornbread, and pumpkin pie,

just like the pictures I colored
in Mrs. Ross's class
and hung on the refrigerator.

IV.

In 1976
I explained to *Abuelita*
about the Indians and the Pilgrims,
how Lincoln set the slaves free.
I explained to my parents about
the purple mountain's majesty,
the amber waves of grain,
"one if by land, two if by sea,"
the cherry tree, the tea party,
the "masses yearning to be free,"
liberty and justice for all…
And finally they agreed—
this Thanksgiving we would have turkey,
as well as pork.

V.

Abuelita prepared the poor fowl
as if committing an act of treason,
harnessing as much enthusiasm
as possible, for my sake.
Mamá prepared candied yams,
following instructions printed
on the back of a marshmallow bag,
and set a frozen pumpkin pie in the oven.
Dad watched WLTV: "*Lo Nuestro.*"

The table was speared with Gladiolus
and the turkey was set at the center
on a plastic silver platter from Woolworth's.
Everyone sat erect in the green velvet dining chairs
we had upholstered with clear vinyl,
except *Tío* Carlos and Toti,
who were seated in the folding chairs
from the Salvation Army.
I uttered a bilingual improvisation
of a blessing Sister Mary Clare had suggested
and the turkey was passed around
like a game of Russian Roulette.
"DRY," *Tío* Berto said,
and proceeded to drown the lean slices
with pork fat drippings and cranberry jelly—
"*la mierda roja*," as he called it.
Faces fell when *Mamá* proudly presented
her ocher pie; everyone knew pumpkin
was a remedy for ulcers,
not a baked dessert.
Abuelo made three rounds of Cuban coffee
then *Tía* María and Pepe cleared the living room furniture
and put on a Celia Cruz LP.
All the relatives began to *merengue*
over the linoleum of our two bedroom apartment
sweating rum and coffee
until they remembered
it was 1976 and 46 degrees,
in America.
After repositioning the furniture,
Tío Berto was the last to leave.

VI.

In the warm and appropriate darkness
of my room that night
I hung like a chrysalis
realizing I lived in a country
I didn't know,
waiting for a home
I never knew,
and a name
to give myself.

LETTERS FOR MAMÁ

For years they came for you:
Awkward size envelopes
Labeled AIR MAIL (*POR AVION*)
Affixed with multiple oversized stamps
Honoring men from another history.
Monthly, you would peel
Through eggshell pages—
White onionskin sheets
That told you the details
Of Kiki's first steps
And your own Mother's death,
The approximate dates
Recorded by postmarks.

Sometimes there were pictures:
Poor black and white photos
With foreign dimensions
Of children you would point to,
Tell me were my cousins.
I would handle the images,
Look for my resemblance
In an ear, eyebrow or a nose.

When possible
You would parcel
A few pounds of your absence
Into discreet brown packages
Filled with bubble gum,
Baby clothes, hand-me-downs,

A few yards of Taffeta
For your niece's wedding gown,
Which you would later see
Couturiered to her body
In new pictures that would introduce Alfredo,
Her husband, an addition
You would never meet.

Your silent, filed anxieties
Matched the random terrazzo mosaic
Of our porchgarden
Where you sat
Fading into ninety blue miles,
Surrounded by unopened buds of Impatience,
Waiting for the postman,
While gazing at the purgatorial clouds
Swollen with unfallen rain
That would never spew
Through the mouths of coral-faced gods
Into the empty fountains
Of your perched memory.

CRAYONS FOR ELENA

Forget about the enjambment, the precious form of words, the poem, utterly useless and far too complex for this. I do not want to conjure noble lies about you, abstract you with the pen to alter our lives into something far more interesting. This is simple; this is about the $1.98 flip-top box of Crayolas (with the built-in sharpener) we cleverly camouflaged in mother's shopping cart and coerced her into buying for us, capitalizing on the immediacy of her sympathies and the pitying looks of the cashier and customers behind us, shaming her at the check-out counter with our rococo pleas until she yielded. This is about a thunderstormed after-school afternoon when, while cartoons rioted in the screened Florida room, we sat at the dining table, oversharpened and tested all sixty-four crayons on junk mail scraps and blank newsprint, even the colors we hated, the ones that reminded us of freckled Brian Kunkle in the third grade: sienna brown, white, peach, and black. As well as the colors that tickled and thrilled us like dangling live lizards from our earlobes or double-butter popcorn at a Saturday matinee. In those days, when we were far less than a poem. It made sense to us, good sense, to color a prince's hands and nose cornflower-blue and a dog lemon-yellow because they were our favorite colors. These we wore down to stubs, peeling the paper coating further and further, until the name of the color disappeared and we forgot how to pronounce it in English. We (you) left the box in the back of father's brand new Buick. I remember the collage of 64 melted colors, the butter knife we used to scrape the seat, and father's black-leather work belt. Today you called; said you still like to remember the alluring and subtle smell of wax.

EL CURANDERO
(THE HEALER)

❦ Rafael Campo ❦

I am bathing. All my greyness—
The hospital, the incurable illnesses,
This headache—is slowly given over
To bath water, deepening it to where

I lose sight of my limbs. The fragrance,
Twenty different herbs at first (dill, spices
From the Caribbean, aloe vera)
Settles, and becomes the single, warm air

Of my sweat, of the warmth deep in my hair—
I recognize it, it's the smell of my pillow
And of my sheets, the closest things to me.
Now one with the bathroom, every oily tile

A different picture of me, every square
One in which I'm given the power of curves,
Distorted, captured in some less shallow
Dimension—now I can pray. I can cry, and he'll

Come. He is my shoulder, maybe, above
The grey water. He is in the steam,
So he can touch my face. Rafael,
He says, I am your saint. So I paint

For him the story of the day: the wife
Whose husband beat purples into her skin,
The jaundiced man (who calls me Ralph, still,
Because that's more American), faint

Yellows, his eyes especially—then,
Still crying, the bright red a collision
Brought out of its perfect vessel, this girl,
This life attached to, working, the wrong thing

Of a tricycle. I saw pain—
Primitive, I could see it, through her split
Chest, in her crushed ribs—white-hot. Now,
I can stop. He has listened, he is silent.

When he finally speaks, touching my face,
It sounds herbal, or African, like drums
Or the pure, tiny bells her child's cries
Must have been made of. Then, somehow,

I'm carried to my bed, the pillow, the sheets
Fragrant, infinite, cool, and I recognize
His voice. In the end, just as sleep takes
The world away, I know it is my own.

BELONGING

I went to Cuba on a raft I made
From scraps of wood, aluminum, some rope.
I knew what I was giving up, but who
Could choose his comfort over truth? Besides,
It felt so sleek and dangerous, like sharks
Or porno magazines or even thirst—
I hadn't packed or anything, and when
I saw the sea gulls teetering the way
They do, I actually felt giddy. Boy,
It took forever on those swells of sea,
Like riding on a brontosaurus back
Through time. And when I finally arrived,
It wasn't even bloody! No beach of skulls
To pick over, nothing but the same damn sun,
Indifferent but oddly angry, the face
My father wore at dinnertime. I stripped
And sat there naked in an effort to
Attract some cannibals, but no one came;
I watched my raft drift slowly back to sea,
And wished I'd thought to bring a book
That told the history of my lost people.

FOR J. W.

I know exactly what I want to say,
Except we're men. Except it's poetry,
And poetry is too precise. You know
That when we met on Robert's porch, I knew.
My paper plate seemed suddenly too small;

I stepped on a potato chip. I watched
The ordinary spectacle of birds
Become magnificent until the sky,
Which was an ordinary sky, was blue
And comforting across my face. At least

I thought I knew. I thought I'd seen your face
In poetry, in shapeless clouds, in ice—
Like staring deeply into frozen lakes.
I thought I'd heard your voice inside my chest,
And it was comforting, magnificent,

Like poetry but more precise. I knew,
Or thought I knew, exactly how I felt.
About the insects fizzing in the lawn.
About the stupid, ordinary birds,
About the poetry of Robert Frost,

Fragility and paper plates. I look at you.
Because we're men, and frozen hard as ice—
So hard from muscles spreading out our chests—
I want to comfort you, and say it all.
Except my poetry is imprecise.

THE TEST

Singing to himself, waiting for the voice
To call him next, he thought it out again.
He was just an accident. As a boy,
He knew there would be awful things, the men
In hot showers suspecting it was true,
His brothers never loving him again,
A balding man, alone, having Campbell's soup
For dinner. But it wasn't until after when
He'd had the surgery, and then in college
The only love he cared about, that he heard
About the virus. He'd had blood, an acknowledged
Several units—but only that one real love—sure,
There'd been some girlfriends too, two or three…
He laughed to himself. And doctors were surprised to see
The virus, deadly, in the tears. Where else would it be?

LOOKING SOUTH*

❧ Sandra Castillo ❧

The moon followed me,
guided me through the park
from Tía Tere's, past the green bench
where father and I visit each week,
past the darkness, and the chain-link fences
that haunt me in photographs.

Men gathered on 69th Street,
across from the butcher shop
Father traded the military for.
They drank from unmarked flasks
and played dominoes in the dust.
Their laughter made my walk home longer.

"Esta Revolución es verde, verde como las palmas,"
Fidel said, and Tío Casimiro repeated it often.
He said he didn't want Father to forget.
He said Father's ink-stained hands
made the revolution bleed.

Momma doesn't agree.
She dreams of American shopping carts
and bringing Abuela Isabel to America.
But Abuela Isabel reads Echevarría
and knows that "to emigrate is to die."

*From *Red Letters*

ABUELO LEOPOLDO SNEAKS A BITE
OF CREAM CHEESE*

I don't think Mother believed me when I first said
it had not been me who left teeth prints
on the cream cheese Tío Berto got through la bolsa negra.
I remember she approached me twice,
and though I knew she asked because it was my habit
to overuse my adolescent teeth,
I grew scared because I thought it wasn't the cheese
that worried her and this was a mystery
we didn't need: we were suspicious enough.
Carmina and Abraham had just taken el comité
from Ebita's father and Mother was afraid
they knew Tío Berto knew where to get ham, milk, cheese,
and that Tía Estela had worked for Lima
in the '50s and had known Lima's people
had conspired against Batista and would imprison
them both. We were filling out forms,
taking passport pictures, waiting
for our number to come up, hoping our neighbors
wouldn't find out before we were ready to admit
we had been claimed. Mother was worried
one of our relatives would end up in Manga Larga,
La Granja, El Príncipe, Melena 1, Melena del Sur.

*From *Red Letters*

She was praying all our family would have a flight
out in los vuelos de la libertad and that none
of our secrets would spill in juicios populares,
permutas. And because Paulina was cleaning
our house on Saturdays, Mother approached her, too.
Though I am not sure what she said or how she said it.
It wasn't Paulina, I remember her saying,
her fear growing like Abuela Isabel's heart.

SANTERÍA

When Luis Alberto, your first,
couldn't take the steps
in or out of the house without clenching
his fists, his teeth,
and the doctor cut him without explaining,
without making promises,
you took him to Ramón
who shaved him bald
and gave him beaded necklaces
he called elekes.
They were, he said, named
according to their color,
and no one was to touch them,
"no one."

We never asked you about the blues
and reds around his thin neck
because suddenly Luis Alberto
could sit on your hardwood floor
without pain.

After Luis, my cousin, your husband,
pushed you against the cold
of the bathroom tiles to seize you
by the windpipe,

*From *Red Letters*

you thought yourself lucky
to be alive and promised yourself,
your children, they'd never find you
in a puddle again.

And Ramón was glad you were finally
going to let him help you,
though you said you didn't want
to know what he'd do.
"Peace," you said, "peace is all
I need."

You were scared when you
returned to the house
for your clothes, your books,
but Luis was tranquil, yellow,
silent, and you left unnoticed.

IN THE TRADITION OF RETURNING

Adrían Castro

Oye mira meng
listen hear—
do not be astonished
when you see a scorpion
cutting sugarcane…
it is the custom of my country
Don Masayá used to say
his voice full o' rum
perched between mangos and chirimoyas
falling asleep on a hammock.

A cosmic legacy begun by three boats.
Here big and beautiful negras
queens of wind and cemetery
provoke hurricanes
merely flapping their skirts.
negras provoke(can) huracanes
flapping their skirts.
Steel & iron clash
causing bloodshed
causing steel & iron
to feast on blood.

Don Masayá's memory drips the image
of that night
a black cape pis-
tol-whipped him & flew
away with his custom typewriter
with maracas on the keys—
an assassination attempt
on his rhythm.
Don Masayá's memory drips.
Don Masayá's memory drips the image
of many letters he received
already opened
of the echo of his parrot who perched
on his shoulder who sang divine prosody
the echo of his parrot's throat
slit.
Don Masayá's memory drips.
Don Masayá's memory drips as he tumbles
off the hammock
startled by the touch of that colonel's
voice that colonel's
voice
tossing him to foreign soil.

⚜⚜

A brief interruption
to listen to Miguelito Valdés' instruction
& Chano Pozo's percussion
to aid a cultural eruption.

❧❧

The funeral is commencing
what shall we offer the healer of the sick:
17 lavender candles
a half-burned cigar
& a jar
of aguardiente
for tossing him to foreign soil
for tossing him to foreign soil.

❧❧

Do not be astonished
when revolution arrives on a cigar
wearing blue-jeans
& speaking in a trance—
Don Masayá used to say
his voice full o' rum
waking from echoes of abuse
chanting his revenge:
the black cape
shall call me usted
typewriters shall taca-taca in maraca language
envelopes shall be golden
macaws and parakeets will perch on shoulders
& sing a son(g)
the colonel's voice
the colonel's voice shall be a ring of smoke
a memory of ashes—
tomorrow shall be the sweetest sugarcane.

It was the roosters with
throats in full throttle
keek-keedee-croak-ing
in Spanglish…
it was the shores of Biscayne Bay
peppered with tar
with cans of Goya beans
with needles…
it was the belch
of criollo sauces
from mirrored cafeterias…
it was Calle Ocho singing
people screaming
with their hands…
it was Pepe, Carmen, Elena, Miguel
etc., etc…

it was why I shed my guayabera
& grew a tuxedo
shed my guayabera
& grew a tuxedo.
I am of those who chose exile
from exiles.

Yet now here I am
grand marshall of a parade of roosters…
buoying the polluted Biscayne
my Biscayne…
eating enchilada de shrimp…
screaming with my hands…
looking for Pepe, Carmen, Elena,
even Miguel…
etcétera, este se tira.
The tuxedo didn't fit!!!
The tuxedo didn't fit!!!

Ceiba trees
palm trees
Cubano-Dominicano-Americano
& all that comes with it.
I can see them/
those I can see my pearls
bouncing down Eighth Street.
I can see pearls
surfing on Ceiba trees
palm trees
mamá I'm coming home.
Ceiba trees
palm trees
mamita I'm coming home
mamita I'm coming home.

TO THE RUMBA PLAYERS OF BÉLEN, CUBA
...AN INTERPRETATION OF A SONG...

Those drums are committed
are relics
for & de that space
where rumba had its crib.
Legacy of aboriginal cane cutters
traders in spice
the deathly odor
of salted meats.
Sweat sí & yes
that humidity
that humidity ruffled by the sun.

Bongo conga clave
cajón
these are breathing
museums of two cultures
these are the autochthonous
of tone
of rhythm
of speech.

That man leaning on a corner
that woman undulating in a river
that child standing at
a crossroad with
a steel crown
they have not forgotten
the echo of the batá

chiseled into cement
sculptures of hooded monks.
Cobblestone roads hot
as July asphalt
bien caliente because today
September 8th
today tumbadoras are fondled
for La Caridad del Cobre
known around Belén
as Ochún.

Those festivals in plazas presided
by the king Chano Pozo
his fingers aflame
slurrin' hymns in Lucumí
Abakuá
Lucumí Arará
raspy rum rails.
Negras with long yellow
skirts copper bracelets
dancing a sensual shake
twinkling their eyes
in a heavy African ogle
cooling honeydew drops
with fans of peacock feather.

Chickens & roosters walking their struts
oblivious to their sacred blood.
Church and jungle symbolized
Seville and Ile Ife ritualized.
Those rumberos will not
forget the marriage arranged
on high seas.

A new identity writ
in ominous swells. A new
breed of troubadour.
Esas negras will continue
the snapping sway of hips
the tremble of thighs
to the crisp leather
crackling wood
their union
bonded by fingers aflame
responding to burning tongues.

❧❧

Amazing the first tún-tún!
Did Chano Pozo inherit
he whose ears were present
at the first drumming?
Astonishing the first callous!
Oye Chano
are your hands homesick
when not beating on goatskins?
Sobering the first sting of rum!
There are some
who say they saw
his birth in Belén.
Some say he wore colored collares/
necklaces so his congas
could commune with deities.
Some even say he baptized rumberos
with rum.

Oye Chano Pozo
did you have callouses
the size of coconuts?
Did you
wear collares
when you
breathed your
last sigh?

BETWEEN LANGUAGE AND DESIRE

❧ Silvia Curbelo ❧

Imagine the sound of words
landing on a page, not footsteps

along the road, but the road itself,
not a voice but a hunger.

I want to live by word of mouth,
as if what I'm about to say

could become a wall around us,
not stone but the idea

of stone, the bricks
of what sustains us.

These hands are not a harvest.
There is no honest metaphor for bread.

FLOATING

When you have no brothers
you are more than you are.
You carry your own flashlight.
Every oncoming storm brings another
blackout and a hot wind you can feel
from way down the road.
In the dark every stone is
an animal. You learn to touch
things without knowing the
difference. *A silverfish*
is not a rose, and who wants to know?
For weeks the rain is one long prayer.
Some nights the river runs to
your back door with its cargo
of bottles, cigarette butts, stones.
You know the places you're falling
toward, and how to land there,
how in five years your black hair
will float all the way down
your back. The river is old
and deep. The beautiful crimes
of childhood lift you out of
the water, out of your bed at night.
You touch your small breasts
like a benediction. A tender
rain falls over everything you know.

Your grandfather writes elaborate
love letters to the wife of a dead
president. The envelopes drift
out of his shirt pockets when
you think he's asleep, her name
like a cup you drink from in the dark.

FIRST SHIFT AT HERSHEY'S, 4 A.M.

My uncle climbed out of bed before
the alarm and shaved in the
half dark. He'd stand at
the bedroom sink and let the last
of the night roll off his shoulders,
what was left of the moon,
the mirror looking back.

I imagine him when he was a boy
lying in the tall grass in his
brother's farm listening to
the first trains going past
like music playing in a distant
room. *The rest of his life and
the rest of his life.*

In bed his wife kicks
the thin covers to the floor.
I picture him walking towards her
with the straw hat over his heart.
The moon drifting across the
Caribbean. The cold place
where the blade touches the skin.

There are ships pushing off
distant harbors even now.
Cupping the water in his hands
a man knows the hard sleep of
rivers that keep moving and
turn over and wake without light.
Trees remember, stones hold
forth, fish lift the stars
on their backs. Light years before
the first coffee in his mouth

like the first breath, before
the whistle of the sugar
refineries and the hard bread
crumbling down the front of
his shirt, before he wipes
the lather from his face with
the white towel, before the water
in the narrow sink grows dark and
warm when the razor slips, the red
coming off in his hands.

JANIS JOPLIN

There is a song like a light
coming on too fast, the eyes
blink back the static of the road
and in the distance you can almost see
the clean, sweet glow of electric guitars.

Call it the music of the rest
of our lives, a stranger's face
peering through a window,
except that face is yours
or mine. Music like backtalk,

like wind across your heart,
cigarette smoke and bourbon.
Music our mothers must have held
softly between damp sheets,
before taxes, before lay-offs,
before the first door closing,

not piano lessons, not a hymn
or a prayer, or a soft voice
singing you to sleep, but a song
like a green light on summer evenings
after a ball game, after rain,
when the fields finally let themselves go
and we'd drive past the Westinghouse plant,
past Vail and Arcadia. Music
of never going back.

I'm talking about car radios,
about backseats and hope,
and the jukebox at Pokey's
where the local boys tried
their new luck on anyone
and the real history of the world
was going down, nickels and
dimes, the music floating
at the far end of a first kiss,

the first light of the body
that isn't love but is stronger than love,
because it must not end,
because it never lasts.

MY TWO LANGUAGES

❧ Jorge Guitart ❧

for Ken & Dawn

absurdity shoot leaves
disparate tire sale

gift kill monicker
dote mate note

surrender beats father
date late abate

give me reside
dame more

evils marry
males case

swindle steal
time robe

insert i am willow
mets soy sauce

beats look
late mire

FUNK INDIGO

here's bad news
if you hate bad music
the new maldistribution
is the old one
if you pare your nails
your mother dies
and she dies
if you don't
you set the pace
for a lack of cases
superior upper
is inferior lower
everything is wrong
your teachers & crosses
if there is growth
you know the store closes
i am alone
with your doctored self
a shadow with sticks
for arms and legs
you missed the takes
that was a mistake
twenty brands of regret
to choose from.

THE STORY OF L

he asked her to come in acehnese
she asked him to wait in bribri
they shouted at the chef in chechen
they dubbed the spot in dalabon
he complained in enga about the everydayness
she uttered the not so secret name in fore
they described the goggles in guanano
they redacted the heresy in herero
he dictated the innards in ingush
they made the arrangements in jacaltec
they sounded petty in kaluli
they addressed the package in lango
she listed his defects in mande
he spoke to the charmer in nanai
they overwrote the account in otorfo
he dissuaded the husband in pertam
the parakeet orated in quileute
the clerk sounded bright in reto
the offer was made in squamish
they bargained for the accessories in tonkawa
they were not getting through in ulcha
the manager sang in viluma
the porter cried in washo
they asked for the soap in xonol
she told him no in zapotec

GEOGRAPHY JAZZ

❧ Carolina Hospital ❧

Yes! We abandon
the pastel facades,
the curves,
the sculptured towers
on the Beach.
Those glass doors
edged with flamingos
take us, yes
to another city
we recall
only through
second hand
memories.
Yes!

Mongo's hands,
ecstatic pain,
he beats the conga
we rise
we beat the tables
he rises
we sweat
he shouts
we shout
yes!

He succumbs.
His skin is gray
taut
like the old hide
on his drum.

But now I hear
him,
Pérez Prado, yes!
She wants a mambo.
Who?
Lupita.
What's wrong with Lupita?
What does she want?
To dance.
They won't let her dance.
No?
But now she can dance,
here she is dancing.
Yes, yes, yes!
She wants that mambo.
1 2 3 4 5 6 7 8
arms in the sky,
she wants a mambo, a delicious mambo.

A mambo in sax?
It's Chocolate,
a thief in the dark,
playing between chords,
stealing melodies.

Chocolate and synthesis,
syncreticisms,
sin,
sin of the Caribbean, no
limits, no regrets.
One escalating fusion
as sweet as chocolate.

Yes!
I hear them.
Mongo
Dámaso
Chocolate
I hear them all.
It's a bright place
and water sets no boundaries,
and time poses no obstacles.

BLAKE IN THE TROPICS

We leave the Jaragua Hotel
in our stocking feet and shaven faces
to stumble over these bodies
yet to reach puberty.

They have turned dust into blankets
and newspapers into pillows
on a street edged in refuse.
Warm waves break against the sea wall,

never touching their bodies.
We are not in Blake's London and
the black on these boys
will not wash off with the dawn.

FREEDOM

for Belkis Cuza Malé

For twenty years they hid your words
afraid of you,
a young girl from Guantánamo,
the daughter of a cement factory worker.

They silenced poems of
cinderellas and silver platters,
frightened by your beautiful people
and portraits of sad poets.

Now, far from your island and
them,
your poems shout without restrictions.
But the words remain unheard.
Here, a poem
doesn't upset anyone.

HAVANA BLUES

✺ Wasabi Kanastoga ✺

Hey
Old man
Sitting there
Rocking slowly
Back and forth
Front porch.
puffing on your Havana.

Rocking Chair
Singing the blues
Against wooden floor.
chewing on your Havana.

Freshly pressed
Blue guayabera
Exposing your white chest hairs
And red turkey gobbler.
thinking of your Havana.

Behind you
Runs Interstate 10
No palm trees
No mango trees
No swift flowing river
Rising to your second story

Casa de campo
Angered by Cyclone Flora.
crying for your Havana.

So your monthly struggle
Straightens your troubled body
And you check for Uncle Sam's
Once a month visit.
dying for your Havana.

Hey
Old man
Your Havana is about to burn your lips
Just like the ones before
And all the others to come
And all the others to come.

It's been 35 years
and counting
old man.
don't die for your Havana.

FORGOTTEN MEMORY

Abuelita
Dolores
rocks back
and forth
in a daze
and when she laughs
her tongue sneaks through
the front teeth missing.

Occasionally
she'll stand
and run about
like a child
opening and closing
her palms
claiming to catch the wind
playing with icecubes
amazed she's able to hold water
in her hands.

Abuelita Dolores's
hair is gray and unkempt
flattened on the back
from long pillow hours
and her nylon socks
have long ago
lost their elasticity.

In penumbra
her life is a
medicine cabinet
where dreams of
broken elevators
and strewn high heel
spikes
are snapped
by the cold
steel razor
which weekly scrapes
her face.

Once upon a time
flapper-spinster-dancehall girl
your flower beds
lie naked
with petals blown
trampled by
time
love
and unborn children
dying to get out.

LOS DIEGOS

Los Diegos—
two Mexicans
one Chicano
and
a Cuban
brush-stroked
the building walls of
Huntington Park High
with primary
and
secondary colors
on wooden ladders
which
rocked
and creaked
while holding
MJB
coffee cans
for their mixes.

Los Diegos
(after fat-man Rivera),
none had Fridas
on their mind,
borrowed
life
from their imagination
and painted
orange Spartans

and
mustard camels,
replacing
graffiti names
and
numbers
they could not
understand,
re-inventing
cracked walls
waiting to die,
covering
gray
with a barrage
of rainbow
life.

Los Diegos
Muralistas
of my youth
cursing
cheap
brush hairs
attached
to their fingertips.
They
were one
with the paint.
Soon
to become
one
with the grape.

ONLY THE TRULY BEAUTIFUL GO MAD*

❧ Dionisio Martínez ❧

Coming up for air
leaning out of the rain and into
distances only their blue eyes can measure
the suddenly beautiful ones
passing through our lives like time
suddenly there suddenly gone
everything about them a secret
a simple hush
the discreetly beautiful
the ones that come home at night
and tell no one not even themselves
they slip inside and end up
always in the farthest corner
like lint at the bottom of the pocket
delicately beautiful
like a dead language still
spoken for the dead
for the truly beautiful
and mad
because they heard something
a song perhaps and began to take it
apart chord by chord note
by note until there was nothing but

From *History as a Second Language*

the sound of one note
and the note was crushed to bits
and other less human sounds leaped
out
the guts of a single note
the sounds the rest of us refuse
to hear because music is mathematical
and you can't rip
the guts out of an equation
the distantly beautiful ones
wading through the long streets
buck naked and terrified
like children in a river
like God before He gave Himself faith
the absurdly beautiful believers
the ones who will tell you
that the Chosen are not chosen at random
the ones who kneel
and cling to the ankles of the latest anything
the painfully weak and mortally beautiful ones
who come begging to your house willing
to exchange all their beauty and
their elusive madness for the scar on your soul

HISTORY AS A SECOND LANGUAGE*

I grew up hearing the essence
of conversations in the next room.
My father and his friends conspired
in the next room. The new regime
succeeded in spite of their plot.
The next room is usually dark. People
whisper in it. You hear only so much.
Just enough if you know what to listen for.
I thought I heard a murder in the next
room. It was the radio. I thought
I heard a murder long after the radio
had been thrown against the wall and smashed
to bits. It was a whore at the end of
a long day. Families like mine
always managed to have a whore or two
as "good" friends. It made us look
less rich, less whatever being rich meant.
In those days things became
the meanings we gave them and not the other
way around, not like today. The next room
meant the room next door. If you looked
hard enough, you could see through the wall.

From *History as a Second Language*

The specifics of a conversation
were not necessary to understand a plot
or a confession; the blurred
view through the wall was enough
to know more or less how the whores
earned their pay, how a government
might have failed, how a single threat
would keep a family together through war
and sabotage. The room next door
made us what we became with time in exile:
failed lovers, experts in the mechanics
of things we never learned to name.

PAIN*

for Armando Valladares

We all expected to see you lame.
Some *wanted* to see you lame.
When you walked toward us,
we imagined you crawling. It was
like waiting for a train that suddenly
turns into a wolf: it howls
as it runs into the station, its eyes
blind you like headlights, you step
into its mouth as if it were a car, you
think of tunnels and the next stop
as you're being devoured: you expected
a train and can't imagine anything else.
We waited with a wheelchair for a man who
could've used a new pair of shoes.
We asked the obvious questions:
if half a life of torture really
softens the bones until the body falls
like a ruined shack, if rebuilding
the shack is worth the trouble. And when
someone mentioned pain, the word rising
from its metaphors, you tried to laugh.

Your mouth opened like a small wound.

From *History as a Second Language*

CUBA

✄ Pablo Medina ✄

…brillando contra el sol y contra los poetas…
—Heberto Padilla

There it is, the long prow
of the Caribbean, charging to break
the map's complexion.
It is a key, a crocodile, a hook,
an uncoiling question,
a stretch of sinews catching
dribbles from the continent
under which it will, forever, float.

The island mouth is smiling
or frowning, who can tell,
stuffed with waning intentions,
sugarcane and sand.

Such a little place,
such an island listing against sorrow
in the middle of the ocean's gut,
playing make believe
queen of brine, dressing up in green
and calling forth its poets for praise,
its leaders of chesty boasts,

inventing for itself a pantheon
of tropical saints, a vast
and profound literature,
an epic history to rival Rome's.

There it is, pretending it shimmers
over the heads of its people,
denying the terror it feels
when no one listens, denying
that it is always almost drowning,
that it cannot help anyone, least
of all itself, that it is only
a strip of dirt between morning and night,
between what will be and what was,
between the birth of hope
and the death of desire.

FLIGHT OUT OF MIAMI

I am going away.
I am leaving the heat,
the fierce sun,
the spread of concrete
over marshland.
I cannot stand still
and make this home.
Even your slim fingers
and your Cuban eyebrows
speak of displacement,
anguish in control.
I am lost in the fragrance
of gardenias, the palmetto
shadow's dim replacement,
in your face like the city,
roads over water, water
over dreams,
the overwhelming strangeness
of the American landscape,
and your lips
straining to say
what you cannot remember.

WHY I LOOK OUT WINDOWS*

I can hear
the arguments of steel, cranium
of the rains of March,
murmur of petals,
soft milk of love in solitude.
I can feel
my bones disguise themselves
in architecture, flesh and fate:
ripples across oceans
each night more vast, each year
more difficult to wake from.
I can talk to the mirrors of darkness.
They answer flickers
of starlight and ice: a voice,
a breathing across centuries,
the universe made finite in reflection.

From *Arching into the Afterlife*

CUBAN LULLABY*

The throat is tight. Palm trees in the gut.
El borde de la mentira:
memory all the same and laces of laughter.

Try to define it, this search, this
langour between languages, hunger
to leave one's skin, to find freed flesh
prettier than the breeze.
The girl with the wide hips wades into the sea,
coconut milk in her groin, lilac
lips as close to truth as ever were.
The boot black on the boulevard would
spill his rum over that waist the water rings.
She wades into the sea,
lost to the taste-bleared tongue.

From *Arching into the Afterlife*

ETIQUETTE

❧ Gean Moreno ❧

In the end, I could tell them
something that will keep them from sleep.
But what if I do and no one trembles,
what if I tell them that in some countries
a dance could cost them their lives,
and they raise the volume of the music,
they run out to buy new dancing shoes.
What if I tell them a man can lose
his heart to memory and find himself
in a city up in flames, and they
run out to purchase gasoline. What
if I tell them that I've come to show
how, by morning, like a good journalist,
I could have them so convinced of their guilt
for all this that they'll offer me
their hearts and I will ask for more.
And what if they wish to spare me the trouble
and just reach for their wallets.
I can also tell them how from the charred
city all that was left was the building
of the secret police, standing at the center
like a bad joke, but they might begin
to speak American. They might say that
if a man could keep from becoming the ash
that feeds history, then the city would
rise again. But none of these things will
be said because by then I will have mastered

a new language of polite conversation,
every word lacking the hesitation of new knowledge,
my poker face as convincing as grey clouds.

STAND

This photograph is like the sunken pier
down by the lake—they both come up
when least expected. I guess everything
has its own mathematical equation—
the water cycle, the blueprints
of the pier, the meticulous searches
through old scrapbooks. Finding
souvenirs of dead loves has more
to do with probability than accident.
We're always willing to rescue
a good heartbreak, to calculate
our every move. That is why photography
is such an alluring concept—we
can break our hearts a hundred times
with the same image, always altering
the story to make it a bit more
painful. In a world of restless
precision, sometimes remembering
a woman is like taking a stand
for something, or nothing,
like swallowing the moon without
hesitating, like swallowing yourself
in one regretless gulp.

SECOND-HAND

There are things I'll never know—
what to do when the other cheek
is slapped. There are men who favor death.
Others hide in cafes and attempt to prove
that life is like the sea's northern current
that we can step twice upon. Thales was wrong,
heroes will return. Some doors we never open,
some we allow others to open and keep quiet.
There's that conspiracy we always wish to propose,
but night closes in on us. And morning,
everyone agrees, is not a good time.
The sun traces the contours of the face.
Sundays are for leisure. One must rest
after harvesting oblivion for six days.

At the corner of 8th Street and 37th Avenue,
in the Café Versailles, everyone has a cause.
Miró-shocking-blue graffiti, hermetic except
to the trained eye of the juvenile delinquent,
enchants the architecture. Women's crotch sweat
lubricates the motion of leather strangled
thighs and suffocates the winter
like a nymph's song, like the pocketful of truths
everyone has to offer. There, amidst coffee steam,
everyone is tangled in the tree of revelations,
like Dylan Thomas in McKenna's photograph.
But no one offers a compromising phrase.
Cain's fruit was silenced

Overlooking the city from my balcony, I realize
there are things that will never be mine—history
and its epics. Those affairs that come too soon
or too late to engulf me, but, without asking,
mold me. Like seagulls on rowdy beaches, they sway close.
Old men plotted conspiracies over domino games
in exile. I envied them. Now, the park is quiet.
Mozart shook Vienna. Now, Vienna is quiet.
I will never know the odor of correspondence
coming from Montmartre or Madrid in 1936.
I'll never know the taste of the Western Front.
Perhaps my story is a bitter novelist's scribble
on the margin of his manuscript.
I am the dance always danced in the other room.
So I'll die and it'll rain.
Everything else is second-hand.

SUGARCANE

✣ Achy Obejas ✣

can't cut
cut the cane
azuca' in chicago
dig it down to the
roots sprouting spray paint on the
walls on the hard cold
stone of the great gritty city
slums in chicago
with the mansions in the hole
in the head of
the old rich left behind
from other times lopsided
gangster walls overgrown taken
over by the dark
and poor overgrown with no
sugarcane but you
can't can't cut
cut the water
bro'
from the flow and
you can't can't cut
cut the blood
lines from this island
train one by one throwing off
the chains siguaraya

no no
no se pue' e cortar
pan con ajo quisqueya
cuba y borinquen no
se pue'en parar

I saw it
saw black a-frica
down in the city
walking in chicago y
la cuba cuba
gritando en el solar
I saw it
saw quisqueya
brown
uptown in the city
cryin' in chicago
y borinquen
bro'
sin un
chavo igual but
you can't can't cut
cut the water
bro'
from the flow and
you can't can't cut
cut the blood
lines from this island
train one by one throwing off
the chains siguaraya
no no
no se pue'e cortar
pan con ajo quisqueya

cuba y borinquen no
se pue'en parar

¡azuca'!

KIMBERLE

on the stone like white shadows indistinguishable
from the marble the heat the white shadows
the heat of young woman a woman white woman with
cavernous cheeks in a perfect face and the cheeks
are the flaw the error the pain the mistake imperfection
the cheeks with white shadows the stone and the
grain of the stone burning to the touch the white
heat of the stone indistinguishable

kimberle says no to the gods to the marble the
stones to the white heat that courses her veins
the system the muscular arms that hang low with
no purpose (an exile) perfect face imperfect
face kimberle is friends with a specter a black
coat hands that mechanically tease at her neck
at her sex at the holes in her cheeks the sick
yellow dog eyes that respond with enchanted disease
to the shadows and the heat from the stones that
burn to the touch start again start again kimberle

SUNDAY

Love set them going, our mothers,
tiny little wind-up toys
as shiny and urgent as pearls;
later dull and slow, like late model cars,
something bloated about their design.

Love set them going, directed
their noses to the clean cosmetic,
the innocent films.
They married one man;
they made love only once.

It was love that gave them careers,
new wares, made them
dark-haired girls sifting rice,
checking magazines for quick tests titled:
"Do you know your lover?"
"Is your marriage happy?"
Every day the air of nitrous oxide.

They never told the fathers about us,
the daughters standing with arms akimbo.
We were the open secret,
as beautiful and repellent as tattoos.

Now they see themselves the snail on the tank.
We are stone nymphs come to life,
brilliant betas,
too many things at once.

I tell you, if you whisper to me, woman,
it goes no further.
Pain or peace, I cannot take it to them.
If you touch me, your albuminous kiss,
that is between you and me.

It is love, casuist love, a twisted Gabriel
who turns them away:
Our mothers, black veils, votive, orthodox,
gravely whispering to men
misdemeanor sins.

They light dripless, traceless,
invisible candles for penance,
sing prayers like insurance,
dream crashes in station wagons, family cars.
Year after year, the missal for breakfast.

When we become them, a little taller perhaps,
buddha women late in life,
will we be like them,
with our steeples and postulates,
trembling?

Tell me, here, with a tremor of a different sort,
our eyes lidless, your breath cool,
about our mortality.

CHARADA CHINA*

Ricardo Pau-Llosa

Every image in every dream has a number.
Every digit from 1 to 100 corresponds
to several images. Thanks to us *chinos*,
the Cubans are now ready to win at lottery.
If last night you dreamt of a shark,
you must play 45, which is also
the number for President,
Suit, Streetcar, School, and Star,
and often comes up in June drawings.
You heard a phonc ring in your dream?
Then play 70 as well, especially
if you also dreamt a coconut
a shot, a barrel, a rainbow, or a bullet.
A scorpion slid down the terrified leg
of a friend or a cow, play 43 in August.
Monkey, Family, Black Man, Supervisor,
and Dove are 34. And my favorite, 100
for Toilet, God, Broom, Automobile,
Bus Stop, and Collapsed Building.
It usually comes in January.

From *Cuba*

I know what you are thinking:
if these numbers work, why hasn't this *chino*
won the lottery a hundred times?
The wise are robed with poverty.
My dreams have been taken over
by the chart of the *Charada*.
You came to the *barrio chino* for advice
on how to play your dreams. Their free images
evoke a random series of lottery numbers.
Cockroach 48, Rabbit 39, Dark Sun 60, Beggar 91.
But last night I started dreaming
of train tracks and automatically
the other images of 72 came into focus:
an old ox, a saw, a necklace, a scepter
and thunder. Since we all have four dreams
each night, my mind divided 72 by 4 and all
the images of 18 came into focus: a small fish,
a church, a siren, a palm tree, men fishing
and a yellow cat. This last image grew larger
and bared huge teeth, and in came all the images for 92:
a lion, a high balloon, a suicide, Cuba, an anarchist.
All my dreams boil down to one number, 54,
the number for a dream you dreamt having.
You must never play this number!

There is no freedom in wisdom, only order,
and so my dreams are endless jugglings
which have long ago stopped meaning
the pathway to happiness, or riches.
That is why I don't sell the *Charada*
and all its listings. You need your dreams
as they are. You need them to terrify you
and to promise you kingdoms and lotteries.
Let them betray you and laugh at you.
Do not buy those charts on the street!
They are plagued with errors
and it would be a disaster to gamble with them.
I see the birth of a dream swirling in your pupils,
the dream you will have tonight and forget by morning.
No, my ethics prevent me from telling you what it is,
but here are its numbers: 6, 46, 82, 23, 17.

EXILE

"Un pájaro y otro ya no tiemblan."
—Lezama Lima

Let these birds turn into circles,
holding themselves like so much gray,
and let them mean nothing
else than the knot of trajectories.
In the parks of another youth
those other birds trembled branches
into lines that broke the sky,
and from the breeze-drawn shadows
they sang as clouds of leaves
quivered like minnows.

Each bird was a heart in the great
green heart of the tree.
In those parks we would have melted
into the one song of a thousand
brown, dwarfed birds together
composing their gigantic call,
the harmony that guides and loves.
Then we would have made the hours pure
with the hand, the kiss, the word.

From *Bread of the Imagined*

LIME CURE*

❧ Gustavo Pérez-Firmat ❧

I'm filling my house with limes
to keep away the evil spirits.
I'm filling my house with limes
to help me cope.
I have limes on the counters, under the sink,
inside the wash basin.
My refrigerator is stuffed with limes
(there's no longer any space for meat and potatoes).
Faking onionship, they hang from the walls.
Like golf balls, they have the run of the carpet
(but I would not drive them away).

I stash them in flowerpots.
I put them on bookshelves.
I keep them on my desk, cuddling with my computer.
I have two limes in every drawer of every chest
of every room.
I don't bathe, I marinade.

At night, I think of their cores, plump and wet.
I imagine myself taking off the peel and squeezing
until they burst in my hands.

From *Bilingual Blues*

I taste the tart juice dripping on my tongue.
I shudder.
Then I sleep peacefully inside green dreams of lime
and when I wake, I bask in the morning's lime light.

Were it not for limes, I would not know
what to do with myself.
I could not bear this loneliness.
I would burst.
But there is a wisdom in limes, an uneventfulness
that soothes my seething, and whispers to me:
think, be still, and think some more,
and when the night arrives, dream of juice.

ON WHETHER MY FATHER DESERVES A POEM

I will never say
my father used to say.
My father never said
anything
(except dirty jokes
with each phone call).
Scratch idea for poem
with father's words.

My father did not teach
by example.
My father never acted
decisively
(he waffled and gambled
and lost).
So scratch idea for poem
with father's deeds.

Absent words and deeds
what's left me of my father
to write this orphan poem?

WHAT'S WRONG WITH ME

I pick my nose.
I'm shallow.
I spend too much time on my ties.
I get melancholy (baby).
When I come, I don't come cheap.
You can't trust me with matches.
My stomach gives me away.
I wasn't born in Kansas.
I keep my hands to myself.
I pay my debts.
I tremble.

III. BENEDICTION*

❧ E. J. Vega ❧

(for Allen Ginsberg
who asked for poem
about my family)

What remains of the faultless past?
Machetes that sparked through mountain mist
And toppled sugarcane in heavy fields?
And the earthworm—long, pulsing, humble—
That listened intently to the distant plow?
(Which way will it turn? How deep will it cut?)
Grandfather's bankrupt coffee sacks
That once lined busy warehouse walls
Have long turned to cooking fuel.
What say you of this? What say you?
Don Jartín's children flee North,—listen!
So Lidia cut her hair, the less
To haul and Rey buried his poems
In a hill of sickles and cholera, lowering
His head while Jorge squirmed in grandmother's
Lap and placed streams of kisses
On her chin, knowing—it seems now, given
Their urgency—they'd be her last.

From *Teabiscuits with Castro*

VII. MADRID*

At age six, I saw his arm
Of hair and tendon whip round
Her throat and cast her pale back
Across blue cotton sheets.

Behind wood and glass doors,
I sat arching, awestruck
By his callused knuckles
And my photo on the wall.

From *Teabiscuits with Castro*

LITTLE HAVANA BLUES: A Cuban-American Literature Anthology

X. LIDIA, REY, AND JORGE: A SONG*

Mother never measures wool
When she has white cashmere—
She makes of them blouses
Of disoriented cloths—
Stitching blue into autumn
Yellows, she sews often—
Dreaming of flamingoes.

Father never measures spruce
When he has hickory—
He makes of them guitars
Of disoriented hues—
Gluing spruce into Brazil
Wood, he labors often—
Dreaming of ebony.

Brother never measures salt
When he has Rosemary—
He makes of them soufflés
Of disoriented tastes—
Sprinkling sugar on hazel
Nuts, he seasons often—
Dreaming of the *Knicks*.

From *Teabiscuits with Castro*

XIV. NOMENCLATURE*

Sprinkle my heart with cognac and salt,
Feed it to snakes sunning on pine cones,
It has outgrown my chest.
Cast mango skins and lighthouses
Into its sepulcher of bombs and English classes
Before its beating stops and turns into a banker.
Lidia, let us draw our faces in tea leaves, our souls in
    running water.
Rey, let our eyes be clear as mathematics, intense as a
    newborn's.
Jorge, let our words be simple as cannons, bare as canyons,
Rare as the fertilized yolk.
Castro, let us part without suspicion of bars or passports—
As if we could recast our shadows in marble
Or recount our time in Canaan,
Or recognize the bark of the tree that bears our names.

From *Teabiscuits with Castro*

Fiction

THE ADMIRAL IS CURSED*

✖ José Barreiro ✖

It is true the Admiral felt great pressure in his mind to find the nearest source of gold. He said directly to Cacique Bayamo, "In the most powerful land of Castile, my Queen hurts deeply in her breast with a pain most horrendous. Only one thing can cure her: the shiny metal we call gold." I translated the Spanish "oro" for Bayamo as both "guanin" and "caona," copper and gold in our language. "My Queen, and her King will love dearly any people that can provide them with the shiny metal, and they need much of it to quench their hearts' pain," the Admiral said.

Those words I remember distinctly. Since by then I knew how gold is used by the Castilla, what it means to them. I was daunted by this expression. It made everybody wonder just what he meant, and how it could be that the shiny metal might help a sick person, which, interestingly enough, was also our custom. We did not know yet, not even I, the lengths to which the covered men would go to secure the gold.

When Bayamo stood to speak, I also translated his words to the Admiral. Bayamo called the Admiral by a Taìno name, Guamiquina, which means "main chief." He was direct and, again, I remember his words quite well, as they still bounce in my ears.

"Tell the Guamiquina that in these parts we have our kind of people. The good people, Tau-ni-taíno, are peace-

From *The Indian Chronicles*

ful. We share what we have, what the land and the sea give us. As you can see from our many foods, we are a fortunate people. Our spirits are plentiful. Because we are good, our spirits like us. They fortify our plantations. Thus the yuca, thus the maiz, the aji, the beans, fruits of the trees, fish, turtles and iguanas. In the sea, in the kaçi, our eldest Bleeding Mother Moon, guides the women and the snappers…"

"What spirits is he referring to?" the Admiral interrupted, out loud, his voice was accusatory. Bayamo fell deeply silent and looked surprised. I could tell he had never been interrupted in his life. In our people's ways, an elder is never interrupted, and much less in mid-sentence. Young Taíno faces turned away out of respect for Bayamo, who patiently heard my translation. "It is a natural curiosity for spirited men," I added by way of excuse, although I had no doubt by then that the covered men were not spirit beings.

"What spirits would I speak about?" Bayamo responded. "I speak of the grandmothers and grandfathers, the Taíno who are in us. I speak of no one else. I mean only our old ancestor spirits, the spirit of the sea, the spirit of the mountain, the spirit of our incense, and our tobacco, the spirit of our yuca and our corn, those things that forever have helped us…"

I interpreted. The Admiral responded thus: "This that he says is mistaken. Tell him his faith is misplaced. Tell him he would fare better by accepting Our Lord, Jesus Christ, and baptism in the true faith, then he could travel the road to Heaven and Life Everlasting. Tell him those who do not accept Jesus Christ as Lord and Savior will go to Hell, tell them their souls would roast and burn forever and ever."

My translation was more gentle and included an apology for the whole interruption.

"Tell him about Hell. He must understand how the punishment works," the Admiral insisted.

I translated. The cacique peered silently at the Admiral. At that moment I saw Don Christopherens rear back slightly, detecting the intensity of the cacique's *goeiça* or living spirit, which emanated that light hummingbird tremor.

Cacique Bayamo was truly of the elder men of our people, of the ones that spoke to the earth directly, keen with certainty of our Taíno love and common spirit with the living world.

It is true that Castilla have reduced us, have just about destroyed us. I admit that our fighting skills could not match their furious thrust. Truly were they decisive and resolute when we, in our trance, in our habitual and cyclical understanding, took forever to decide anything but what our culture dictated, responses so slow that they still hurt. But I know this, the superb among our people, those most steeped in our traditions, were men and women who could spark response in wind and cloud, could converse with plants and trees, could hear the animals speak, could even be heard by snake and caymán, turtle and manatí.

For generations on generations our Taíno were guided by those conversations, held by our elders with the dreamlike leaders of the reptile and bird nations, with the leaders of trees, the ceiba and the guásima, with the discernible snake motion of the long fish runs, the passing of the flocks, with the very swell of the sea.

Bayamo himself was the snake. His neck and loping shoulders on a thin body, his flattened forehead, carefully manipulated from his birth by grandmothers of his line, a practice for precisely such babies in whose reptile eyes could the great mothers feel the cold, penetrating, never

forgetting, never ignoring, justice of the snake, who can
snatch time from the quickest prey.

Such men and women among our people were extraor-
dinarily powerful. And I can state with certainty that there
never was and never will be even one such as those among
the covered people, whose very best can forge wide roads
out of forest and cross worlds of water and command huge
quantities of death and mayhem, but cannot ever hear the
adjoining voices, the surrounding and constant conversation from our living world.

Cacique Bayamo began the shaking in Columbus'
Christian heart. I saw it, and I was glad to see it, and, now,
to remember it. It was in his look, how he transferred to the
Admiral's eyes his own body's terrifying inner shaking.
Yes, at that very meeting it was that the hummingbird
medicine grasped the Admiral's heart.

"We have guided you in our world," the cacique talked
on. "So you would not be lost. And now you know us. We
are a people that stay on our islands, fishing and visiting,
mindful of the present business of our foods, our bohíos,
our cunuks and our ceremonies. We have been here for a
long time, drinking the same water, eating the same food.
Always, in our gatherings, amongst us, we love the children. And our children, in turn, love and respect us. Even
our dead, our opias who come through the tree-tops from
their Valley of the Dead and have no belly-button, they
stay around us and dance with us. We are good,
Guamiquina. We don't raid. We never raid, we always
build and fish and plant, do for ourselves. In our way, we
feed everyone. If a man comes from other islands, and he
accepts our peace ways, we take him in, marry him into
our people, exchange names with him. In this way, we
extend our houses, our bohíos, and give roof to everyone.

Our chiefs listen to each other. That way we have grown strong and are growing still on these islands." (I translated "islands" as simply "lands" this time).

"The bad men, Kwaib, thigh-eaters, from the south and some raiders from the north, are mean-spirited," Bayamo continued. "They raid for women, raid for our young ones. Among them even, some are very, very bad, caniba warrior bands that leave their women on their own islands—the matininos—and raid for the joy of killing, bent on tasting human flesh. My old people said, 'Watch out when you see those uglies coming!'"

The other headsmen all laughed, out of habit, at the cacique's joke. As I translated, the Admiral smiled, but very lightly. He liked it that our Taíno had their enemies, and made much of it to the King and Queen. I myself always thought Bayamo and other cacique who said such to the Admiral exaggerated their old enemies' cruelties. However, it appeared Bayamo had someone else's cruelty in mind.

"The giant seagulls that carry you across the ocean, your garments and sand-skin, these things I have heard of," Bayamo continued. "Our brother-cousins from cacique Baracoa's villages, over the mountains on our northern coast, they told us about you. Many things were told, when we met them at our common areito, the dance for Yúca-huguama Bagua Maorocoti, Supreme Spirit. They even said you came from heaven and could fly away. They also said that when you left, you took ten of their people, those you put in a cave hole in your own wooden ship."

Columbus stood up with a bound, as I translated the words. Again, he interrupted. "All people are lost without the knowledge of Christ. Those taken are better because of it."

"He is agitated," I said in Taíno, trying to bridge the minds and minimize the insult. "He is a great Captain, but he is not well."

The Admiral spoke hurriedly. "The light of Our Lord had now come to your lands, head man. Innocence cannot save you from eternal torture, the word of God is in your ear now and only the Holy Doctrine will capacitate your people to enter the Kingdom of Heaven..."

Bayamo began to talk to himself. I stopped listening to Columbus, who predicated for another full minute, and listened to Bayamo.

"I have a question of yourself, great lord—are you canoba that your giant seagulls eat Taíno people?" Bayamo asked. "Are you a cousin of thigh-eaters who kidnap our people? I ask the question: Are you good or bad? Because if you are bad to my people, you will go to that hell you have mentioned. If you believe every man answers for his deeds after death, then you will not harm those who do not harm you, or you will certainly go to that fire place of hell."

Having said that, the caciques sat down and the Admiral stopped in mid-sentence. The silence left behind by the sound of Bayamo's voice seemed to dumbfound him.

I translated the cacique's words then, and did not tone down the directness, seeking to maximize the impact. But the admiral had regained his composure. He was not Admiral of the Ocean Sea, Christ-bearer and Grand Navigator, to be without the capability for an answer.

"Tell him again," the Admiral said, looking to his own capabilities and twirling his finger to signify a closure to the parley, "that the people taken are meant to serve us and in return are instructed in the true faith of our Catholic Kings."

I translated this as gently as I could. However, the precision for terms of bartering in our language made obvious the faults of the Admiral's proposition.

The old men of Bayamo understood and did not like the Admiral's reasoning. "What if we don't want to be taught?" one asked. "Why this place of burning?" another one asked. "Why is that necessary?"

An old man who was gnarled and had not aged gracefully, like Bayamo, stepped into the circle in front of the cacique. He looked to a line of elderly women, mostly sisters and aunts in Bayamo's line, standing together behind the seated row of men. The women all had a rearing-back look, fixing weary eyes on the Admiral. The old-timer raised his palm and pointed toward the women with his open hand. "Be careful," he said. "When you counsel your cacique, be careful of the hair faces."

I translated bluntly again, and the Admiral smiled bitterly. "He should fear us more," he said plainly to no one. It was not meant for translation.

The old man had stopped. Now Macaca, the village chief, joined him and they went to stand by a tree. I noticed the old man wore a thin belt of caracol shells around his hips and held a small gourd in his hand. Now he took a plug of rolled leaves from the gourd and put it in his mouth. I could tell he was a medicine man, a behike, and that, like his cacique, Bayamo, there was no fear in him.

The cacique, Bayamo, stood again. "Tell my words to the Guamiquina," the cacique said, and I stood by him to hear him better.

"The fire is sacred to us," the cacique said. "We talk with our sacred fire. In fire we think not of death but of life. As for the Spirit World, as I said, our grandparents await us there." The cacique himself nodded at the Admiral, but warily.

Again, I translated his words and, again, the Admiral was taken aback. Momentarily, his face looked flush and his eyes darted about.

"We are going now," he announced, standing, though with a slight wobble. He stared at the cacique, who stared back.

"The fire is good," the old cacique said. I translated.

The Admiral stared at him. "Tell him that fire burns," he said.

Then the curse was pronounced upon him.

The gnarled old man, the behike of Bayamo standing by the women's council, cleared his nose and throat, then coughed into his left palm. Cupping the thick snot with his right hand, he walked between the fire and the Admiral, suddenly showing the gob directly to the Admiral. "With this I will teach you humility," he whispered harshly in Taíno. "The door to your dreams, I close."

The Admiral turned quickly to face him and our soldiers stepped up too.

The old man had no fear in him at all, his palm and fingers slicing through space at the Admiral. "Hell is in your dreams if you, a far-seeing man, commit the deeds that are in your mind," he said.

A soldier drew his sword, sensing the old man's hostility.

"Don't quarrel here," Columbus told the soldier.

With the growing sense of threat, the Admiral regained his composure. He felt the men of Bayamo might overcome our small troop of not quite twenty. "Our business is over here," he said, and ordered Captain Herrera to organize the troop. The soldiers and sailors surrounded the Admiral and as we began to walk, he asked what the old man had said at the end.

"He said to watch your dreams," I said. "It was a kind of farewell gesture."

The guanguayo had power, I knew, particularly for Bayamo's people. Behike men like the gnarled old-timer meant everything they said. For myself, I knew they would not attack us under the circumstances, and indeed, they lit resin torches and thick, rolled tobaccos and led us down to the shore, singing once again. They carried dozens of baskets full of foods for the ships. But the Admiral had been shown a guanguayo, cohoba medicine, teacher of our people, veil of water between the worlds. Don Christopherens moved stridingly, in measured long steps, but even so, walking to the boats he stumbled several times. Later, climbing on ship, he tripped and had to hang by an elbow from a net while sailors hauled him on board.

We sailed on for many more weeks during this journey, the Admiral intent on proving Cuba a peninsula of the mainland. The weeks dragged on and fewer and fewer of his officers believed him. Twice, out of spite, I reminded him of the words of Bayamo's young chief on the island nature of Cuba. He had me flogged the second time—five swift ones from the many-tailed whip. For that I cursed him myself and intoned the guanguayo of the dark over him as we sailed for long weeks among the islands. And it happened that as the weeks rolled on, he slept less and less and I believe that special curse, which he now and forever carried from the people of Bayamanacoel, blocked the doors between his waking and dreaming selves. Truly, the navigation was difficult through the channels of the smaller islands and the Admiral became extremely nervous. Finally he got sick and brittle. And for weeks, in feverish deliriums, he exclaimed how much the Queen would like it that the Indians believed in a Heaven and a Hell, evidence to push the enterprise of their Christianization. "For the use of their labor," he half-sang sometimes, "we will bring them the true Faith!"

I would add, good friar, that from hearing these ravings (which later became law), Cúneo must have picked up the reference to Heaven and Hell, as he helped nurse the Admiral during that voyage.

ON THE MORNING OF HIS ARREST...*

✖ Margarita Engle ✖

On the morning of his arrest, Gabriel felt a vibrant sun hitting the skin of his machete-hardened fist. He gripped the reins, kicked his stallion and cantered toward the house, where his wife was ringing a cow bell to announce breakfast. Gabriel waved at her, noticing the fullness of her aging body, and the way grandchildren trailed behind her gathered skirts, following her like chicks behind a hen. To Gabriel, the sound of her cow bell was both mournful and welcoming, like the sound of a conch-shell trumpet, a century earlier, on one of the big plantations, calling the slaves in to dinner.

Today he would tell her what he'd heard from Alvaro. He would tell her the rumors from town about troops being stationed on all the big farms to keep the new Alzado rebels from coming down from the mountains in search of food and other supplies. They would need medicines, boots, ammunition. If it turned out like before, no one would refuse to help. No guajiro would refuse to feed boys who were fighting against a new tyrant, especially if the new one planned to start seizing ordinary farms, small farms along with the foreign-owned sugar giants.

Gabriel cantered toward his bohío remembering his wife the way she looked when he first met her, the great-granddaughter of Basque shepherds, a woman accustomed to living on harsh land, a good strong country girl who

From *Singing to Cuba*

didn't waste time longing for plumbing or electricity. For her, their outdoor shower stall with its bucket of cold water was more than enough luxury. Someday Gabriel planned to build her a stone house with a stone floor. In that floor he planned to inlay many small cross-sections of the stalactites from the caves by the sea where once the timid Siboney had lived peacefully, with nothing to fear but the hurricanes, sharks, and raids by cannibals in their big canoes. Those caves had served the cimarrón African slaves well, long after the last Indians had been slaughtered. The caverns were big, yellow glowing chambers filled with mysterious underground streams, even waterfalls, and inexplicable specks of light which somehow reached into the depths from tiny hidden openings above, openings revealing intensely blue sky and explosive black clouds. Underground, practically the entire island was connected by caves.

Once there had been so many bats in the caves that guajiros made a regular business out of harvesting the guano and selling it to foreigners as fertilizer for their big sugar fields.

Gabriel rode toward his house still thinking about his wife and the rumors and the caves which could someday help him build a glowing golden floor for his imaginary stone house. You couldn't tell how beautiful the stalactites were until you got them out of the caves, where they could find the sunlight and really begin to radiate, like underground stars brought up into the sky. There were no dangerous animals in the caves, only a few majá boas too small to hurt a person. Escaped slaves had believed that one of those small boa constrictors could kill you with its poisonous breath, like the fiery breath of a dragon. The cimarrónes said that after a thousand years each boa would turn into a sea serpent and swim out of the caves and into the ocean to swallow Spanish ships, the ships which brought slaves across the immeasurable sea from their African homes.

The slaves believed certain trees could get up at night and dance. They believed people could fly away from slavery, just get up out of the fields and barracoons and enter the sky, flying back to Nigeria or the Congo. When Gabriel was young there were still many men and women who had been born slaves and had only been free since the last days of Spanish rule. These people had sworn to Gabriel and the other children that at one time so many slaves flew away that entire plantations were crippled and had to close down their sugar mills because no one was left to load them with the heavy burdens of raw cane.

One of Gabriel's uncles married the daughter of a Congolese woman who had only been freed a few years before giving birth to the girl who would later become the wife of a guajiro. When Gabriel was a child, he thought his light uncle and dark aunt were the two happiest people he'd ever met. They acted like people who had found a way to trick the devil, laughing all the time, and singing, ignoring the pale town children who threw rocks at them when they rode into Trinidad on Sundays and feast days.

They had been the ones who took Gabriel and his brothers into the mountains and showed them the ruins of cimarrón villages buried deep in the shadowy, enigmatic forest. When Daniel saw the remains of false trails, and the deep pits covered over with leaves and armed with erect, sharpened bamboo stakes, he decided he would someday move away to Havana and study history and find out how the slaves figured out such ingenious ways of hiding and protecting their secret villages.

Years later, Daniel actually did it. He went away and became a historian and came back talking about rebellion and survival. He went up into the mountains and tried to live like a cimarrón, hunting wild pigs and harvesting wild honey and roots and tubers. He invited Gabriel up to his hideout to see how the cimarrónes buried their gold in secret places, gold they obtained by trading food and wild honey to pirates who landed on the secluded beaches near Trinidad, rich but hungry. That was in the days when every treasure fleet had to pass through Cuba on its way from Mexico and South America to Imperial Spain, delivering the wealth of conquered Aztecs and Incas into the royal treasuries.

When Daniel told him about the cimarrón gold, Gabriel had thought it strange that escaped slaves who could never live out in the open would treasure a mineral which could only be spent in town. What good would it do them? Wasn't the wild honey itself more precious to a forest dweller than any amount of gold?

And Daniel had explained that the runaways always guarded a secret reservoir of hope. They had to hide in the forest in total silence, never singing or whistling, in case bounty hunters might be roaming the forest with their muskets and trained dogs, searching for escaped slaves to sell back to the planters.

"If a cimarrón traveled through the forest at night and saw a light," Daniel said, "then he might think it was a witch, and he would spread wild mustard seeds in his path as he walked, to paralyze the witches, because the cimarrónes believed that once a witch stepped on a mustard seed, her feet would freeze to the spot and she could never move again.

"Runaways even had to be afraid of birds. In the forest there is a bird which whistles exactly like a man. A cimarrón could never be sure whether he was hearing the song of a bird or the whistle of a bounty hunter calling his dogs.

"Cimarrónes were also afraid of the tocororo, that pretty bird with a stripe across its chest. The Spaniards said tocororos looked like they were wearing the uniforms of the King of Spain, green with a scarlet sash. Any slave caught looking at a tocororo could be accused of disrespect, and would be whipped or sent to the stocks. Even after they were free and in hiding, the runaways kept on dreading these birds, with their short monotonous song, co, co, co, co.

"The cimarrónes were afraid of sleep. They believed majá boas could suck out all your blood while you were sleeping. They believed the soul could wander away from a sleeping body and, if the body was awakened before the soul returned, a terrible sickness would result. But they said the sickness only affected the body, which stayed in the forest dying of fright, while the soul roamed free."

Gabriel approached the house, deciding that he would not tell his wife how sleepless he had been lately. He would not tell her he had been getting up at night, wandering around the farm, chasing the devil and shaking his fist. He would not tell her that he had developed a fear of sleep which overwhelmed him every night, when he lay awake thinking about the rumors, about Alvaro with his reptile-green uniform, and Alvaro's brothers Omar, Emilio, and Adán, trekking up into the mountains, becoming Alzados—rebels—like so many guerrilla warriors before them, like Alvaro himself when he fought with Castro. Gabriel had been terrified of sleep, thinking that maybe the troops would come at night, and maybe among them he would find relatives and what would God think, brother fighting brother again, so soon, when a war had just ended. Worst of all, during those long dark hours when Gabriel's fear of sleep was profound and all-consuming, there was the gnawing rodent-like fear eating at Gabriel from the inside out, the fear that something might happen to his family and his farm.

Gabriel ate breakfast with his wife and sons and their wives and his daughters and their husbands and all his grandchildren, with the many people who all lived together under the single small thatched roof. Yes, one day they would need a bigger house, a stone house with a stone floor, a floor like gold, like cimarrón gold received from pirates in exchange for wild honey, gold you could bury and save as a reservoir of hope.

They ate, a fine meal of papaya with lime juice, and corn meal spiced with anise. They ate together in the open air, seated on stones and logs tossed about the farmyard like toys thrown by a giant. Gabriel sat on a four-legged Taíno stool, with its comfortable concave stone seat. Thousands of years old, Daniel had verified, when Gabriel found it intact under the protective branches of a ceiba tree in the mountains. A stool some chieftain sat on hundreds of years earlier, while eating a meal much like this one, shared with all his family.

Gabriel finished his breakfast rapidly, then sat about telling his grandchildren stories about the Indians and escaped slaves. He told them how the runaways liked to raid their old plantations on Christmas, during the dry season when it was easy for them to ease back into the mountains with looted weapons and food.

"But they didn't really make the raids to capture guns and meat. No, they went to free their enslaved families, and friends too. They went to the plantations looking for their parents and sisters and wives and cousins. They could have taken jewelry and silver from the big houses of the masters, but instead they carried off the other slaves, and set them free. But during the first three years no one captured in a raid was allowed to leave those secret villages hidden in the mountains.

"First each one had to prove his loyalty to the cause of freedom. Because even among slaves there would always be a few who couldn't stand the hard life of the wilderness and would try to go back to the plantation with information about the secret villages, and these ones were dangerous. Nothing is more dangerous than information when you are trying to hide."

Of all the grandchildren, the only one who always seemed captivated by Gabriel's repetitions of Daniel's tales was the boy Gabriel called Taíno, because he was timid and serious. His face had the mahogany skin and black eyes of an Indian.

"Tell me about the Lottery," Taíno demanded, and Gabriel took him onto his knee, and told him once again how in Cuba the servants came from many different countries, not just Africa but China also, and all the African slaves and indentured Chinese and all their Cuban-born offspring, all might be allowed, on certain plantations, to work overtime on Sundays instead of resting, in order to save up a little money of their own to try to buy themselves free.

"Only it took so long to earn enough to buy oneself free," Gabriel told the boy, "that by the time you were free you were also very old, too old to work. It was a trick of the masters, really, because by the time a slave was old enough to buy himself free, he would just be a burden anyway and, then, as a weak and useless old man, he could be set free to go off in search of his own place to live and his own food, and the masters wouldn't have to take care of him while he waited for death.

"So the Lottery was the only way out. It was the same Imperial Lottery everyone else played, a game set up by the King of Spain. Slaves were allowed to buy tickets just like anyone else, only the tickets were expensive, so the slaves had to use their little bits of money from working overtime on Sundays, and they had to pool all their money together, and sometimes a group of slaves would win and there would be enough money to free them all. Imagine how they must have felt on that day, walking up to the master's house with their winnings, saying, very respectfully, 'Sir, we've come to buy ourselves free.'

"And for those who never won the Lottery, and could never hope to be free, unless they ran away or lived to be very old, well, there was always King's Day, that one day each year when slaves were allowed to make fun of their masters by dressing up like Spaniards and dancing. What a carnival that must have been, eh? Each group of slaves dressed like Ladies or Lords, priests even, and soldiers too.

"The slaves worked very hard to perfect their costumes for that celebration. And their dances. They invented many dances because during those days dancing was one of very few things that slaves were allowed to do. Practically everything else was forbidden, but dancing was permitted. Slaves invented the rumba, which imitates a rooster fluffing its feathers for the hen, who keeps pecking away at the barnyard, pretending not to notice, but really, of course, she's watching the rooster very closely out of the corner of her eye. And the conga, some say it looks like a line of slaves chained together in the form of a serpent, dancing.

"You know, even today, many people believe that if you dance well enough, a spirit comes into you, and it could be a good spirit or a bad one, there's no way to tell, until it's too late, so you have to be very careful if you call out to the spirits. The slaves could dance until they turned into the spirit of the river, or the spirit of the ocean or the mountains or war or gold, even the spirit of disease, or the devil himself."

Then Gabriel went on to tell Taíno about the Indians for whom he was nicknamed. "They believed that since turtles are shaped like the womb, like the bellies of pregnant women, people must have descended from a turtle-woman, something your uncle calls the primordial turtle-mother. The Taínos knew about the great flood. Everyone on earth knew about it, because it was sent over the whole world, and very few escaped. The Taínos believed that only men survived the great flood. So, after the flood, the men went out and found a turtle-woman and married her. But they never trusted her completely because turtles are very dangerous when they are swimming. If a turtle jumps on your back while you're under water, it can drag you down to the bottom of the sea and it will never let you go. You drown."

Gabriel saw how his wife was looking at him, quizzical and fond, yet disapproving. "Such tales you tell the child," she said, shaking her head. "One would think you had seen these things yourself. As if you've ever been to the bottom of the sea!"

"But that's not all," Gabriel continued, winking at his wife, who picked up his plate and walked with it toward the wash tub, calling out to one of the girls to bring her water from the well because all three of the big ceramic tinajón jars were almost empty.

"Unless it rains," Gabriel's wife called out behind her, "we'll have to fill them up all the way."

"It will rain," Gabriel assured her, interrupting his stories to glance up at the sky, where dark clouds were already beginning to mass. Gabriel liked to imagine that each of the clouds was a horse with its rider, transforming the sky into an entire army of valiant warriors.

"You know what the Taínos believed about guava trees, don't you?" Gabriel asked his grandson.

THE LAST SUPPER*
✠ Roberto G. Fernández ✠

The shots that killed the sniper were drowned out by
the bells calling the faithful to prayer. With the last rounds,
the soldiers finished the operation to flush out the rem-
nants of the rebels that had attacked them from the hillocks
surrounding Xawa during the April Fools offensive. Juan
Benson, Don Andrés' gardener, thought he heard something interspersed with the tolling bells but discounted it
as the buzzing of bees building a new hive to accommodate their queen. Benson was helping the club's gardener
to reshape the shrubs the flying shrapnel had damaged
during the rebels hasty retreat. Inside the kitchen of the
Ladies' Tennis Club, the servants toiled with six crates of
California apples, apricots, and pears that had arrived a
few hours before at the port of Isabella, a gift from Floyd
Conway for the new president's installation festivities.

The inaugural of the Ladies' Tennis Club's new president was Xawa's most exclusive affair. This year the privi-
lege of wearing the presidential sash had fallen to Mrs.
Fanny Fern. Her husband, Mr. Joseph Fern, was Xawa's
most respected sugar baron and the man who had been
instrumental in convincing the government to conduct sat-
uration bombing in the nearby hills. He had ensured his
wife's election by donating a swimming pool to the club
which had helped sway the critical votes. Fanny, who
hailed from New Orleans, had met Joseph during his

From *Holy Radishes!*

school days at Tulane. He had impressed her with his suave manners and his old world charm at the debutante balls during Mardi Gras.

This year's election had been close. Three separate ballots had been required to choose the new leader. Rivalry between Cuquín Valley and Pituca Josende had split the vote, paving the way for Fanny. Her mandate, according to the bylaws, was to last forty-two months and five days.

The dignitaries from outside Xawa had begun to arrive for the occasion. From the port city of Isabella came Mr. Fern's business associate, Benigno "the Basque" Juárez and his elderly mother, Belinda Zubitegüi. Rumor had it the Basque was still bottle-fed at night by the decaying matron. Mayor Sanchez, who was picked up at the marina in Mr. Fern's yacht, came from the capital city. The mayor, who disembarked dressed in blue knickerbockers, came alone, his mistress having registered at the Telegraph Hotel the night before. His wife Claribel, too drunk on a bottle of extra aged dry Bacardi she had started at breakfast, remained at home. She would kill herself exactly two weeks after the party by jumping from the World Line Pier into the shark-infested waters of the bay.

In addition, the poet laureate, Lisander Pérez, arrived with his fiancee, Ana Rey. He was present to delight the exclusive audience with the fruits of his muses. The acclaimed national contralto Aïda Lopez was in attendance, as was Helen Valdes-Curl, wife of the muriatic acid tycoon Peter Frey. She drove the 444 kilometers alone in her red Cadillac convertible, her long scarf floating in the wind.

Father Santos, Xawa's gift to the clergy and the newly-appointed Bishop of St. James in the Orient, arrived for the occasion accompanied by four identical oriental acolytes named Horse, Snake, Monkey and Cat who held the train of his silk and gold-thread embroidered cassock at all times. History would judge Bishop Santos as the man who saved the guerrilla leader, Faithful Chester, thus unwittingly becoming the destroyer of his own class. The neophyte bishop was Nelson Guiristian's godfather.

Joining the outsiders was the cream of Xawa's society. Don Andrés Pardo, his daughter Nellie and her pet Rigoletto. His son-in-law Nelson Guiristian. The President and Vice-President of the Xawa branch of the Royal Bank of Canada, Mr. Floyd Conway and Mr. Howe, respectively. Loly Espino was escorted by her younger brother Cioci; her husband, Senator Zubizarreta was away at a political rally for his reelection campaign. Mrs. Cuquín Valley and Mr. Valley, Maria Rosa, her daughter Macuqui, her husband Dr. Gaston and her mother Mrs. Peña (the emeritus president and founding member of the club), Pituca Josende and her husband Chief Justice Josende, who still limped from the shot he received during the landing at Dunkirk and the only Xawan ever to receive the purple heart arrived in their carriages. Mr. and Mrs. Rudolph Guirstian were driven to the event in their Mercedes.

While the doormen were busy letting the final deliveries in, a number of curious eyes had gathered around the passion-vine-covered chain link fence to get a glimpse of the celebrities. Struggling to climb all the way to the top of the ceiba tree, a pudgy nineteen year old was inching his way to a commanding view of the party. His name was Rulfo. Below the ceiba, the servants, under the direction of Delfina, were busy setting up the banquet table to accommodate the one hundred guests and dignitaries invited to the event. Juan Benson had finished his gardening task and chopped an old avocado tree to feed the club's fireplace.

Fanny had insisted on having the brick fireplace lit, just as she remembered as a child in her mansion in the Crescent City. To counterbalance the effects of the heat radiating from the hearth coupled with Xawa's steamy temperatures, four massive two-ton blocks of ice had been ordered from the ice factory and would flank the fireplace once lit.

The seating arrangements threatened the delicate harmony of the club's membership. After negotiations mediated by Father Santos and Floyd Conway, Pituca Josende finally acceded to be seated at Fanny's left, but with the condition that she was to be absolute programmer for all aquatic events to be held at the new pool and that she would cut the inaugural ribbon. A beaming Cuquin Valley sat at Fanny's right.

"That's not where the forks go," Delfina thundered. "The forks always to the left, the big ones always closer to the plate. No, no, no," she continued, "The napkins must be folded like a butterfly in flight. Please don't make the chairs creak so loudly!" She proceeded to scrutinize the recently delivered oyster sacks and, with contempt, told the delivery man his mollusks weren't fresh enough and to go back and tell his boss his reputation was at stake. Then she turned to her helpers and said, "I wonder what you people would have done if you had to prepare banquet tables for one thousand guests. When Miss Nellie got married that's what I did. That was really something! This is nothing in comparison. The whole Telegraph Hotel was booked solid with wedding guests. The Prince of Spain came personally to present Nellie with a sapphire choker which any of these women would kill just to hold in their hands for a few seconds."

Then Delfina looked up and yelled, "Get out of that tree. This is not for ruffians to see. Out of there or I'll call the rurales."

There was not a word from the arboreal sloth-like figure, but what Delfina couldn't see was the stream of orange piss which fell directly into the punch bowl below.

✖✖

The string of guests began to arrive for the cocktail hour preceding the supper. Fanny Fern, with her plump Teutonic face and the firm stomach that goes with a barren womb, greeted her guests at the club's romanesque entrance. Her hands were already tired and her lips puckered from the numerous greetings and exchanges when Floyd Conway walked in..

"Floyd Conway. Always so punctual," Fanny said sarcastically.

"I know I'm a bit late," said Floyd, attired in a light blue frock coat and breeches the color of clay.

"It doesn't really matter. I was being bad. It's so good to see you. You're one of the first in. You know these people have no sense of time, but don't pick up that nasty habit." Fanny smiled, and her smile was echoed by him.

"I am a trifle late, but I'm rather distressed with the news about the Queen Mother."

"Ah?"

"She was bitten by a pet corgi after she tried to stop a fight among the royal canines at Windsor Castle."

"Was it serious?"

"Her majesty had three stitches on her left hand after the incident. The quarrel involved ten dogs, including two belonging to Princess Margaret. I believe the Lord Chamberlain also was nipped while helping the Princess."

"Well, would you care for some port or sherry to ease your sorrow?"

"I'd rather have some Chivas. It's a mosquito repellent."

"Lazarus, bring Mr. Conway a tall glass of Chibas."

"Yes, ma'am."

"Floyd, I love your kilt! Who made it? Was it Gloria Olivé, the local seamstress or Sarah Bosard, the haute couture?" Fanny seemed genuinely interested in the garment and its maker.

"Oh, no, my dear. They wouldn't know where to start. My sister Vera sent it to me."

"You should come visit. I almost forgot to tell you that we have a Rhodesian Ridgeback. It's a beautiful creature."

"I shall come by tomorrow at tea time. But how did you manage to get such a rare specimen? Was it smuggled?"

"Oh, no. A friend of Joseph's brought it as a gift. Excuse me, Floyd. I see someone at the gate." Fanny walked a few paces toward the main doors, and turning her head around, raised her voice to say, "I do hope the Queen Mother's hand heals in a few days."

"I pray to God it does," added a somewhat solemn Floyd Conway.

Fanny stood under the lintel waiting for Helen Valdes detained at the gate. The incoming guests had a grandiose view of the fifty-two horseshoe arches which delineated the perimeter of the great room, the mozarabic rugs that hung from the marble walls, and above all, the great staircase flooded by the lights of the candelabras and lined with hibiscuses and performing musicians dressed in their terra cotta suits. Helen Valdes was still held back at the entrance, struggling with the uncooperative gate. The latch was somehow stuck and it wouldn't open. It was obvious Helen was getting desperate. The orchestra sounds wafted out across the garden and she could hear a dulcet flute shining over Aragon's Orchestra's rendition of "The Constitutional Cadet," Helen's favorite song. She was about to miss her favorite dancing tune and cried for help. But no one came to her rescue. Juan Benson, still busy dismembering the tree, was too far from the gate to hear her cries or the beeping of the horn. Fed up with the situation, she got out of the car and shook the gates in despair. Finally, the latch gave way and the gates swung open. Helen was in such a rush, she left her car running and scurried as fast as she could, losing one of her high heel shoes in her flight. As she bypassed Franny and entered through one of the side doors, her long Cordoban leather skirt rustled slightly; her tanned, freckled shoulders, glossy hair, and diamonds glittered. Not looking directly at anyone, Helen advanced to the dance floor, ignoring the gentleman that stood silently admiring the beauty of her figure, her full shoulders, her bosom, her back. "What an exquisite woman," the fellows said on seeing her.

"It's marvelous to see you, Nellie." Fanny said with fake eagerness and language. "What a lovely blue gown! Your pet is adorable and I love his teal jacket." Nellie didn't pay any attention to Fanny and settled the folds in her dress. She had never liked Fanny because she was a foreigner and Nellie would have loved to have been one, too.

Fanny's fleshy hands were patting the mascot when she realized Don Andrés and Nelson were standing next to Nellie. "Don Andrés, Nelson! I am so sorry. I didn't see you come in." A look of embarrassment came over Fanny's face. "May I take your cane , Don Andrés?"

"It's quite all right, Fanny. You know how attached Nellie is to Rigo. She made us walk behind in case Rigo spotted a truffle or two."

"Nellie, I hear rumors you're expecting your first? Is it true?" There was a note of sadness in Fanny's voice.

"Yes, it seems that way. Excuse me, I think Rigo has found something interesting in that pot. See how he has straightened his tail and his snout is directly pointing down?"

"Some port, Nellie? Gentlemen, a bit of sherry?"

Nellie didn't answer. She was already next to the potted tamarind. Don Andrés and Nelson, each carrying a glass of sherry, walked inside where a group of men had congregated under the rotunda.

"If it isn't Don Andrés Pardo and Nelson Güirstian," shouted a perk Welshman. "Your father was looking for you, Nelson. He asked if we had seen you. He said you were supposed to meet him here at seven."

Nelson's face turned pale. "Excuse me, Don Andrés, Mr. Conway. I must find Daddy." He walked out with a clumsy pained gesture, holding his stomach in and his forehead beaded with sweat.

Nelson headed for the club's grounds. He was sure he would find his father in the handball courts, practicing his serve. Inside the club, the conversation continued.

"So, Mr. Conway, what's your opinion of the rebel attack?" asked Don Andrés.

"The usual. Nothing to be alarmed about. I've lived through ten of these insurgencies since I settled in Xawa. I don't worry about them anymore. Besides, these things tend to fizzle out like flat seltzer, and if they're ready to face martyrdom, so much the better. I have no respect for martyrs. It's sheer idiocy. Don't lose any sleep over this.

You know very well, Andrés, that with the right amount of money, there's nothing one can't cure. I'm certain last week's bombing has turned the rebels into mashed pôme de terre. Oh, I see Peter Frey coming in our direction."

"Is he coming alone? I saw his wife getting out of a red convertible as we drove in."

"They always travel separately to avoid kidnappers. There are some big concerns, like Gravi Laboratories, that are pressuring Pete to sell them his new formula for muriatic acid with Pirey."

"Hi boys!" Pete Frey greeted the circle, impeccable in the latest Italian style suit, though his hair seemed to have been hastily finger-combed, smooth in the front but sticking out behind like a sea urchin.

"Hello, Pete," the men responded.

"How's business?" Conway hurried to ask.

"Boys, I'm going to make a big request today," he said, gulping his highball. "I drove four hundred kilometers to be away from all that, to have some fun. I don't want to hear about it. So let's ask the poet to recite for us."

"He usually does it during the after-dinner drinks," Benigno the Basque intervened.

"Well, tell him I want to listen to an early recital. Tell him it's Pete Frey who wants to listen to his muse."

"Lazarus," ordered Don Andrés, "tell Mr. Pérez, the man wearing the leaves around his head, that I must tell him something."

"Yes, sir."

A few minutes later, the poet laureate acquiesced to Pete's request, and the circle tightened under the dome.

Lisander cleared his throat and shot a cognac to feed the muse.

> I've seen wings come forth
> from firm women's shoulders
> seen butterflies fly out
> of trash heaps.

The poet made a pause, cracked his bony fingers and continued,

> I come from everywhere
> To everywhere I go;
> I'm art among the arts
> and in the mountains,
> I'm a mountain.

And then, with his eyes focused on the dome, in rapture, with his lips parted, he took a deep breath before his final verse.

> My poems please the strong
> my poems which are sincere and brief
> they're as rugged
> as the steel used
> to forge a sword.

"To forge a sword" was still echoing through the clubhouse when a rather inebriated Pete Frey embraced the poet, impregnating his linen shirt with the stench of minty sweat, and mumbled, "I really love your poems, pal. It's the absolute truth when you say your poems please the strong and that's why I like them. I'm strong! I'm a sword myself and I'll slice like a piece of Swiss cheese any motherfucker who wants to mess with me." Then Pete looked at Lisander straight in the eyes and said, "Buddy, there's something I don't quite understand, that art and mountain stuff."

Lisander, who was obviously pleased, proceeded to explain. "It means that I'm at ease talking to the president of the Royal Bank, for instance, or to my maid."

"No shit, Lisander! I feel just the same." Pete let go of the embrace and, shaking the poet's hand, said, "Next time you're in the capital, give me a call. I'm going to show you the best time in your life. And now I have to take a leak."

The men continued talking about their favorite subjects, women and business, but were careful not to offend Don Andrés with their crude remarks. Don Andrés cleared his throat every so often to signal his displeasure if the boys got carried away. He was regarded as a man of high moral standards, a true gentleman, a man of dignity.

Lisander partook of the conversation for a few minutes and excused himself, promising Pete more poems at the prescribed time. His face still beamed from the adulations as he walked back to his fiancee, Ana, who waved from the bar. Ana was having an intense conversation with her friend Loly and her child prodigy brother, Cioci. The group was discussing Cioci's discovery of a presumed extinct amphibian in a cave near the hamlet of Small Corral. Lisander joined the on-going conversation and took a genuine interest in Cioci's discovery.

"A literary genius," Don Andrés said to Mayor Sanchez, who had joined the group a bit late and had caught the last two lines of the last poem.

"Yes, it's amazing. I've heard him a few times at the Atheneum. I especially enjoyed one called 'Errant Love.'"

"What's the view in the capital of the uprising we experienced in this region a few weeks ago? I read Faithful Chester's manifesto, *History Will Absorb You*, and I must admit it has distressed me a bit." It seemed to be Don

Andrés' opening remark to everyone he spoke with that evening.

"We don't think Faithful Chester, the guerilla leader, has a chance in hell. The minute the armed forces coordinate their efforts, he'll be history, running with his tail between his legs. If you excuse me a minute, Don Andrés, I have to telephone my sugar at the Telegraph. Tell the waiter when he comes by I'm low on my libation. I'll be right back."

Outside, Nelson had looked everywhere for his father. He had checked by the handball courts and the croquet lawn and was about to give up his quest after he passed by the badminton net when he spotted something shining by the pool.

"Daddy, Daddy," Nelson shouted when he saw his father near the pool. "I've been looking for you everywhere. I thought you'd be at the handball courts. Luckily, something was shining that led me here."

"Don't shout! I'm not deaf! Well, it was no star of Bethlehem that brought you here. Probably my gold watch," Rudolph barely glanced at his son, took a final puff from his habano and threw it in the pool. "Where were you? I told you at seven. You have this tendency to muddle and spoil." He sounded angry.

"I know, Daddy, but Nellie wasn't feeling well. You know she's pregnant."

"That's no excuse," he said in a gruff voice. "You're a man and she's a woman. It's her job to be pregnant and yours to come on time when I tell you and carry out in exact detail what I have said. I hate careless people! Did you complete the business consolidations I asked you to do?"

"Yes, sir. Here they are." Nelson took a long piece of paper filled with official seals and stamps. He waited for his father's praise. There was none. The old man read the paper, told him to file it and turned around.

"I'll file it tomorrow, Daddy."

"What do you mean, tomorrow? Go to the office right now and file it. And not a word out of you!"

"But Daddy, the dinner is about to begin and Nellie..."

"I said not a word. You're too fat anyway." At that moment Rudolph Güirstian longed to break something.

"Yes, Daddy!"

❧❧

The club still hummed like a bee hive and a fine mist had started falling outside when there was a sudden stir and all conversation hushed. The crowd rushed sideways and then moved apart to let Fanny walk to the strains of the orchestra, which struck up at once "Pomp and Circumstance." Behind the regal Fanny walked Mrs. Peña, Cuquín Valley and Pituca Josende. The space where Nellie should have walked but refused was filled with Helen Valdes-Curl. Fanny walked slowly, waving to the guests, as though trying to prolong the first moments of her mandate. At Joseph Fern's request, the musicians changed the tune and played "When the Saints Go Marching In," a bit of nostalgia from her native land. When Fanny finally reached the banquet table, her face beaming with bliss, the orchestra switched melodies again to the Club's alma mater, lyrics by Mrs. Rudolph Guirstian set to music by Ernest Lecuona sung with gusto by the invitees and Aïda Lopez, whose deep voice overpowered the rest.

The Little Father, as Father Santos was affectionately called by his friends, stood up and asked the visitors to keep quiet and bow their heads in sign of respect, if not repentance, as he gave the invocation:

In spiritu humilitatis, et in animo contrito suscipiamur a te, Domine: et sic fiat sacrificium nostrum in conspectu tuo hodie, ut placeat tibi, Domine Deus.

The hungry guests sat down at the U-shaped table after a resounding amen but parted with the blessing, which was to produce a soothing effect on their friendly souls.

No sooner had the guests settled down to eat after the Bishop's benediction when Mrs. Peña offered a toast in honor of the newly-elected President Fanny de Fern. The octogenarian raised her glass and, in a thunderous voice that was out of character, said,

"To Fanny, a seed from far away that has rooted deep in the red clay of Xawa."

"To Fanny, To Fanny, Viva Fanny, To Fanny," echoed the walls of the large ballroom.

Only Nellie had remained conspicuously silent and had refused to stand up for the toast.

"What's the fuss about being a seed from far away? I was practically born overseas myself and I don't make a big deal about it," Nellie whispered to Rigo, who was seated at her feet. Nelson hadn't returned from his errand.

The waiters bustled and the room was full of noise and movement following Delfina's orders to bring in the evening's courses. The tiny parchment on which the menu was written in miniature gothic script was rolled up and held with a sterling ring and placed inside the empty crystal glasses engraved with the club's crest. As each guest retrieved the menu, his glass was immediately filled with sparkling Amaro mineral water. If anyone could read lips, it would have been easy to decipher the menu. Helen Valdes was reciting it to herself.

Appetizers:	Oysters Vieux Carre Fanny
	Alligator Tail Fingers
Soups:	Creole Turtle Soup
	Filé Gumbo
Entrees:	Venison Churchill
	with Mulled Wine
	Quail Fricandeau
	with Chiante Classico
	Crawfish Fanny
	with Riscal White
	Bison Tongue in Green Mayonnaise
	with Barolo Red
	Yeux du Pompano aux Fines Herbes
	with Moroccan Bordelaise
Vegetables:	Almond Rice
	Braised Belgium Endive With Walnuts
Desserts:	California Apricots, Pears, Apples
	Fidenze Belforti Parmigiano Reggiano

"The oysters are delicious," remarked Pituca as she finished devouring the last dozen in record time, the empty shells scattered around the plate.

"Yes, they are quite good," answered Floyd, though Pituca's statement was meant for Belinda. "I understand it's one of Fanny's family recipes. And Mrs. Josende, if I may say so, you do have a healthy appetite."

Pituca felt embarrassed as all eyes focused on her debris-filled plate. "I'm afraid I've a weakness for oysters," she said, although she had the reputation of not letting a single dish pass her way without sacking it completely.

"It seems more like a passion," interjected Loly Espino as the waiters were bringing the soup.

There was absolute silence for a few minutes, only the clatter of spoons as the diners touched and emptied the bowls.

"When is Nelson returning?" Don Andrés asked his daughter as he savored the mulled wine.

"I have no idea, Papa! But I don't think Rigo likes this party. I think he wants to go home."

"Nellie, don't make a scene. We will leave as soon as your husband returns."

Don Andrés went back to enjoying the wine and tilted his head to the right to address Rudolph Guistian.

"How much longer until Nelson returns, Rudolph?"

Guirstian, Sr. laughed out loud. "Ha, ha, ha, five minutes, but probably two hours for Nelson, especially after he married into your family." Mrs. Guirstian pinched him under the table.

Don Andrés pretended not to hear him and added, "I hear rumors the communists have infiltrated the guerrilla movement..."

"Such a morbid subject war is. You can talk about it later." Mrs. Guirstian said to be polite, thinking her husband wasn't going to answer Don Andrés.

A tipsy Rudolph with vacant eyes waited a few more seconds to answer him, as if he was ransacking his brains to find the proper words.

"You know what I think of the guerrillas," and without anyone else noticing him but Don Andrés, he grabbed his balls in defiance and shook them for a while, laughing contemptuously.

Don Andrés, taken by surprise, didn't wait for the garçon and poured himself another glass of mulled wine and at a loss for words said, "The venison is particularly tender, Mr. Guirstian."

"I have an important announcement to make," said Helen. "I have convinced my husband, Pete, to donate a new hardwood dancing floor for the club."

There was loud applause.

"On behalf of the Ladies' Tennis Club and in my capacity as President and as my first official act, we thank you and Peter from the bottom of our hearts."

"I also have an announcement," Mrs. Peña said as she washed down the quails with a flood of Chianti. "The Sacred Heart of Jesus Jesuit School will hold its first sixth-grade swimming meet in our new pool facility."

The next round of applause was about to start when Pituca Josende stood up and yelled in anger,

"I am the only one with the power to authorize any aquatic activity. I was promised that if I..."

Floyd Conway didn't let her finish her statement, shouting, "Silence, please. Silence. This is nothing more than a simple misunderstanding, Mrs. Josende. Do you give your permission to hold the Jesuit swimming meet at the Ladies' Tennis Club?"

Once more all eyes were on Pituca and, feeling the pressure, she responded, "I do." Pituca was caught by surprise by Floyd's quick maneuvering. "But all further events must be approved by me one month in advance."

"And now I propose a toast to the new pool." Floyd raised his glass.

"To the new pool," answered the crowd.

ஐஐ

The great cornucopia lay empty and the guests busied themselves by discreetly repositioning their false teeth or chatting with each other with that serenity and good will that only a full belly can induce.

"Isn't it a lovely clock?" said Ana to her poet.

"Yes, indeed. But the beauty of the chronometer cannot match my love for thee." Lisander kissed Ana's hands, leaving a green mayonnaise residue in her palms. She blushed and under Cupid's spell, she kept her eyes fixed inquiringly on Lisander's black pupils. She was moved by the spirit.

"How do I love thee, Lis. Let me count the ways: I love you when you brush your teeth, I love you when you sleep, I love you in the shower, I love you at the tennis courts, I love you when you gargle, but above all I love how you love me!"

"Did you have a nice ride, Mrs. Frey? Ours was a bit bumpy," inquired Benigno the Basque.

"Please don't call me Mrs. Frey. Everybody calls me Helen," she said as she rearranged her bedouin shawl to cover half of her face. "My ride was awful but uneventful! The roads are filled with potholes, but I had some fun running over two roosters and a pig."

"How's your daughter, María Rosa?" asked Cuquín, turning sharply around. "Is she better from her illness?"

"Macuqui is a little better, but she could be much better if she were to listen to Dr. Cabrera and take her medicine properly. I told her not to take her clothes off with the windows open. It was the draft that made her sick."

"I understand perfectly. I know how defiant teenagers can be. I have four myself."

"And your mom, Cuquín, still living at Miramar?"

"Oh no. She lives with us. She lost her mind and doesn't remember anything, not even me. She only remembers the days of the week in French. You know she lived in Blois as a child when my grandfather served as consul in that Gallic city."

"It saddens me to hear it. Loneliness is the only prevention against the outrages of pain."

Cuquín didn't quite understand but, feeling the conversation was getting too personal, quickly excused herself with the pretext she had to introduce the night's performers.

"Ladies and gentlemen. I have the honor of presenting our nation's leading contralto, Aida Lopez. She will delight us this evening with her most famous piece, and immediately after our poet laureate will enchant us with his latest inspirations.

"Music, maestro." Aïda cleared her throat and in her husky voice thanked Cuqui Valley, who had introduced her. Aïda was in the middle of one of her favorite renditions, "Martha, Tiny Rose Bud" at the precise moment when her voice was reaching the crescendo: (Martha, from my garden you're the flower), when a thundering noise was heard and some of the chandeliers came crashing to the floor. Then all the lights went off and the confused screams of the guests rang out.

"The guerrillas! It's another attack. It must be Faithful Chester! My leg. You're sitting on my leg. Rigoletto, Rigo, where are you, baby? Let the rebels know that I'm the only one who can arrange the aquatic bookings. The government will drive them out of here in no time. Be calm. There's no need to worry..."

Aïda kept on singing without the orchestra. She wasn't about to let them spoil her evening. Then she heard a voice ordering her to the floor, and when she ignored it, she was forced down by a blow to her knees. Immediately the guests heard the sounds of someone being dragged along the ballroom towards one of the side doors. There was silence when Rudolph Guirstian gathered enough courage to stand up and, groping through the room, reached the wall and flipped on the emergency lights. Then a scream was heard.

"Pete! They have taken Pete! My Peteeeeeeeeeeeeeee-eeeeeeeeeeeeeeee! I knew it, I knew it," Helen was sobbing deeply and beating her chest.

"Those awful guerrillas. I thought the soldiers had swept them away." Fanny crawled to her side to comfort her.

"It wasn't the guerrillas. I begged him to stay home. They wanted the formula." She sighed in pain. "Oh, Peteeeeeeeeeee!" She cried holding her red shawl in her hands, lifting it from time to time to wipe the mixture of tears and eye liner as it crept down her cheeks.

"Someone bring this woman a glass of sherry! Let the orchestra play. Maestro, please. Nothing has happened here. The party must go on," ordered Floyd. "Carry on, carry on."

INÉS IN THE KITCHEN

✂ Cristina García ✂

Inés Maidique is twelve weeks pregnant and nauseous. Her back hurts, her breasts are swollen, and her feet no longer fit into her dressy shoes. Although she is barely showing, she walks around in sneakers to ease the soreness that has settled in every corner of her body. The eleven pounds she's gained feel like fifty.

When her husband returns home he'll expect her trussed up in a silk dress and pearls and wearing make-up and high heels. It's Friday and Richard likes for her to make a fuss over him at the end of the week. He'll be home in two hours, so Inés busies herself preparing their dinner—a poached loin of lamb with mint chutney, cumin rice, ratatouille, and spiced bananas for dessert.

Richard will question her closely about what she's eaten that day. Inés will avoid telling him about the fudge cookies she devoured that morning in the supermarket parking lot. She hadn't wanted to eat the whole box, but bringing it home was unthinkable. Richard scoured the kitchen cabinets for what he called "illegal foods," and she was in no mood for his usual harangue.

With a long length of string Inés ties together the eye of loin and tenderloin at one-inch intervals, leaving enough string at the ends to suspend the meat from the handles of the kettle. She slits the lamb in several places and inserts slivers of garlic. Then she sets about preparing the stock, skimming the froth as it simmers. Inés thinks about the initial excitement she'd felt when the blood test came back positive. She always knew, or thought she knew, she wanted a child, but now she is less certain.

The mint leaves give off a tart scent that clears her head with each pulse of the food processor. She adds fresh coriander, minced garlic, gingerroot, honey, and a little lemon until the chutney congeals. Then she whisks it together with plain yogurt in a stainless steel bowl. Inés remembers the abortion she'd had the month before her college graduation. She was twenty-one and, like now, twelve weeks pregnant. The baby's father was Cuban, like her, a hematology resident at the hospital where Inés was finishing her practicum. Manolo Espada was not opposed to having the baby, only against getting married. This was unacceptable to Inés. After the abortion, she bled for five days and cramped so hard she passed out. Inés spent the summer working a double shift at an emergency room in Yonkers. Her child would have been eight-years-old by now. Inés thinks of this often.

Shortly before she was to marry Richard, Inés tracked down her old lover to San Francisco, where he'd been doing AIDS research with an eminent name in the field. Over the phone, Manolo told her he was leaving for Africa the following month on a two-year grant from the Department of Health. Inés abruptly forgot everything she had planned to say. Even if she'd wanted him again, it was too late. She'd already sent out her wedding invitations and Richard had put a down payment on the colonial house across from the riding stables. Manolo was going to Africa. It would have never worked out.

❧❦

Ratatouille is one of Inés's favorite dishes. It's easy to prepare and she cooks big batches of it at a time, then freezes it. The red peppers give the ratatouille a slightly sweetish taste. Inés heats the olive oil in a skillet, then tosses in the garlic and chopped onion. She adds the cubed eggplants and stirs in the remaining ingredients one at a time. On another burner she prepares the rice with chicken broth, cumin seed, and fresh parsley. If she times it right, dinner will be ready just as Richard walks through the door.

Her husband doesn't know about Inés's abortion, and only superficially about Manolo Espada. It is better this way. Richard doesn't like it when Inés's attention is diverted from him in any significant way. How, she wonders, will he get used to having a baby around? Richard was the only boy in a family of older sisters, and accustomed to getting his way. His father died when Richard was eight and his three sisters had worked as secretaries to put him through medical school. Richard had been the great hope of the Roth family. When he told them he was marrying a Catholic, his mother and sisters were devastated. Janice, the oldest, told him point-blank that Inés would ruin his life. Perhaps, Inés thinks, his sister was right.

Inés strains the stock through a fine sieve into an enormous ceramic bowl, discarding the bones and scraps. She pours the liquid back into the kettle and turns on the burner to moderately high. Carefully, she lowers the lamb into the stock without letting it touch the sides or the bottom of the kettle, then she ties the string to the handles and sets the timer for twelve minutes.

Other things concern Inés. She's heard about men running off when their wives become pregnant and she's afraid that Richard, who places such a premium on her looks, will be repelled by her bloating body. As it is, Inés feels that Richard scrutinizes her for nascent imperfections.

He abhors cellulite and varicose veins, the corporal trade-
marks of his mother and sisters, and so Inés works hard to
stay fit. She swims, plays tennis, takes aerobics classes and
works out twice a week on the Nautilus machines at her
gym. Her major weakness is a fondness for sweets. Inés
loves chocolate, but Richard glares at her in restaurants if
she so much as asks to see the dessert menu. To him a lack
of self-discipline on such small matters is indicative of
more serious character flaws.

What of her husband's good qualities? Richard takes
her to the Bahamas every winter, although he spends most
of the time scuba-diving, a sport which Inés does not share.
And he is intelligent and well-informed and she believes
he is faithful. Also, he isn't a tightwad like so many of her
friends' husbands, watching every penny, and he doesn't
hang out with the boys or play poker or anything like that.
Richard is an adequate lover, too, although he lacks imagination. He likes what he likes, which does not include
many of the things that Inés likes. Once, in bed, she asked
Richard to pretend he was Henry Kissinger. The request
offended him deeply. If Richard rejected so harmless a
game, what would he say to the darker, more elaborate rit-
uals she'd engaged in with Manolo?

❧❦

The loin of lamb is medium rare, just the way Richard
likes it. Inés lets it cool off on the cutting board for a few
minutes before slicing it diagonally into thick, juicy slabs.
She sets the table with their wedding linen and china and
wedges two white candles into squat crystal holders. Inés
thinks back on the five years she worked as a nurse. She
was good at what she did and was sought after for the
most important cardiology cases. More than one surgeon

had jokingly proposed to her after she'd made a life-saving suggestion in the operating room. But like most men, they assumed she was unavailable. Someone so pretty, so self-contained, they thought, must already be spoken for.

When Richard first started working at the hospital, Inés felt drawn to him. There was something about his manner, about his nervous energy that appealed to her. It certainly wasn't his looks. Richard was skinny and tall with fleecy colorless hair, not at all like the mesomorphic Manolo whose skin seemed more of a pelt. For three months she and Richard worked side by side on coronary bypasses, ventricular aneurysm resections, mitral valve replacements. Their manner was always cordial and efficient, with none of the macabre bantering one often hears in operating rooms. One day, Richard looked up at her from a triple bypass and said, "Marry me, Inés." And so she did.

When Inés was a child, her father had predicted wistfully that she would never marry, while her mother seemed to gear her for little else. Inés remembers the beauty pageants she was forced to enter from an early age, the banana curls that hung from her skull like so many sausages. She'd won the "Little Miss Latin New York" pageant in 1964, when she was seven years old. Her mother still considers this to be Inés's greatest achievement. Inés had sung and played the piano to "Putting on the Ritz," which she'd translated to Spanish herself. Gerardo complained to his wife about sharing Inés with an auditorium full of leering strangers, but Haydée would not budge. "This is better than a dowry, Gerardo." But Gerardo preferred to have his daughter, dolled up in her starched Sunday dress and ruffled anklets, all to himself.

Gerardo expected Inés to drop everything to play the piano for him, and for many years she complied. This became more and more difficult as she got older. Her parents separated and her father would call at all hours on the private phone line he'd installed in Inés' bedroom, pleading with her to come play the white baby grand he had rented just for her. Sometimes he would stroke her hair or tickle her spine as she played, tease her about her tiny new breasts or affectionately pat her behind. Inés remembers how the air seemed different during those times, charged and hard to swallow. Now her father is dead. And what, she asks herself, does she really know about him?

❧❧

Inés turns off all the burners and pours herself a glass of whole milk. She is doing all the right things to keep the life inside her thriving. But she accomplishes this without anticipation, only a sense of obligation. Sometimes she has a terrible urge to pour herself a glass of rum, although she hates the taste, and she knows what it would do to the baby. Or to burn holes in the creamy calfskin upholstery of her husband's sports car. Other times, mostly in the early afternoons, she feels like setting fire to the damask curtains that keep their living room in a perpetual dusk. She dreams about blowing up her herb garden with its fragrant basil leaves, then stealing a thoroughbred from the stable across the street and riding it as fast as she can.

Inés finishes the last of her milk. She rinses the glass and leans against the kitchen sink. There is a jingling of keys at the front door. Richard is home.

CUBA, CUBA, 1954*
✀ Oscar Hijuelos ✀

It was the summertime, and Alejo Santinio had sent Mercedes and Horacio and Hector down to Cuba by airplane. Mercedes had been homesick for Holguín and wanted to see her sisters, and for them and her mother to see the children. And there had been too much fighting in the house, a situation that was forgotten during their visit in Cuba, except that regrets about her life sometimes sent Mercedes to bed at two in the afternoon. Her sisters would comfort her, send the children out to play.

Horacio thought of Cuba as a place of small towns and hick farms. He did not see it with Mercedes's romantic eyes. Romanticism existed in the distant past and died with the conquistadors, gallant caballeros, and señoritas. Almost everyone from the past time was dead, save for the ghost he saw. Most of the people he would have admired were gone, down under the ground with the worms and stone. Teodoro Sorrea, the great artist, was someone he wanted to meet. And why? In his eyes, his grandfather was a first-class hustler. Not the saint Mercedes always made him out to be, but a dude who almost made a fortune off that tax-skimming scheme. But he had stalled for too long and dropped dead too soon. Maybe he would have sent Mercedes off to the university, and she would have become a great poet. Then Horacio would have been born in a beau-

From *Our House in the last World*

tiful house with much sunlight, and his head would not have been knocked around.

Horacio did not see Cuba as a place of romance. He could see under and through things. He saw Luisa's and Rina's nice houses on cobblestone streets. A farm of pigs, sheep, and flea-ridden dogs. Thick, festering bushes full of tiny, red, long-legged spiders, red ants, and thick-shelled beetles that sounded like hurled stones when they flew out and hit the walls. Termites with bodies like embers swarmed in the rotted tree stumps of the farm. And he saw aunts Rina and Luisa and their children: Paco, Rafael, and Delores, who belonged to Aunt Rina; Virginia and Maria, who were so pretty and attentive to their mother, Aunt Luisa, widowed some years before. He saw the ditches, pools of stagnant water, thick clouds of flies and mosquitoes. He saw the clogged-with-shit stone toilets that were made tolerable only by the strong fragrances of the fruit trees and blossoms. Cuba was in the nineteenth century—okay, a nice place, and not anything more. There was a lot of eating going on, some belching, food everywhere, unless you were poor and then worms grew long in your intestines.

He took trips into the country with Rina's husband, Uncle Manny. Trips to the steamy Neptuna, where the Frosty Cool Air Conditioning had broken down. He rode in the truck with Pucho, a mulatto who had been adopted by the family next door, went to Woolworths and came back and found a hacked-up iguana lying in the yard, black balls like fish larva spilling from its torn stomach.

The ghost was the only thing that really impressed Horacio. And Aunt Luisa's kisses. She was all right, good to everyone, especially to him. When they went places, whether to the beach or to the marketplace or to Rina's farm, she put her arm around him and liked to give him kisses. And with no demands! She was thin with a young face and long black hair. She and Aunt Rina had a dress shop, and in the afternoons, she paid Horacio a dollar to watch the store for an hour while she went home to take a nap. Then she would come back, and he could go off and wander around the town with its hot stone roads and square blue, pink, or white houses.

On the weekends they would go either to the beach or out to Rina's farm, about ten miles north of Holguín. This was a real farm with squealing pigs that rolled in the mud and fields of cane and fruit trees. The big event of the day was the cooking of the pig. There were three buildings on the farm: an old cool house from the days when they grew tobacco, a horse stable, and the main house. In front of the stable was a dirt road and a shallow declivity. At its bottom was a chopping block where the family cook would sit, casually hacking the heads of hens with a machete. The hens would run a few feet spurting blood like crazy and then drop, and the blood would settle in a thick pool of feathers and chicken heads that the dogs liked to eat. Then the cook would drop the chickens into a pot of boiling water so that the feathers could be easily pulled off. Flies everywhere. But that day Uncle Manny and the farm hand dragged out an immense pig weighing about ninety pounds, beheaded it, and then cleaved it in half. Horacio was sitting beside Aunt Luisa reading a funny book— *Superman* in Spanish—when Manny, square-shouldered and robust as a bull, called him over to help take the pig away. Horacio went over, and they tied a piece of rope around the pig's hooves and then pulled him toward a barbecue pit. It was hard work. Horacio was rewarded with a Coca-Cola.

The sides of pork were lying next to the pit when an iguana came along and burrowed his way into one of the haunches. Later, when Manny discovered the iguana nestled inside, he tried to pull it loose by its tail. But with its dinosaur teeth clamped into flesh, there was no way of jerking it free. So Manny and the cook dragged the side of pork across the yard and hauled it up onto one of the lower branches of a mango tree, then built a fire of leaves and twigs and newspapers underneath. The idea was to smoke the iguana out.

Everyone waited on the porch for the iguana to run away. There were columns of black smoke, burstings of fruit skins, withering leaves...and soon it let go and fell onto the ground. But suddenly it seemed as though hundreds of black flowers started raining down from the tree. They landed and spun around, creeping like fire in all directions. In fact, they were large, ugly tarantulas. There turned out to be a huge nest of them in the tree. Falling, they scurried in all directions and some went up the porch steps, under the chairs, under the skirts, and between shoes, and into the house. And soon everyone was after them with shovels and brooms and sticks. For an hour this hunt went on, and by then the sides of pork were cooking.

The meal was delicious, too greasy as always, too heavy because of the monstrous portions of black beans and starchy plantains. After dinner it was dull and relaxing to sit out on the porch listening to the "night bells," as the crickets were called, and to watch the stars rise over the field. It was boring but at least it was peaceful.

Before they had left to visit Rina and Luisa, the apartment walls had shaken from things and people smashing into them. Alejo's fist, a chair, a bottle, Alejo pounding the wall and knocking furniture aside, while Mercedes ran in circles inside the circular apartment and visitors tried to come between them but were pushed aside. Kindly visitors, like the three sisters from Oriente, had covered up Horacio's and Hector's eyes and ears with soft delicate hands, while Mercedes fled down the hall. But Horacio had called out, "Stop, you stop, stop, stop, you stop," so much that his voice had grown hoarse. Then for days the apartment had been quiet. No one had spoken, except Alejo, who had swallowed his manly pride trying to apologize for his outbursts. He had sent Horacio and Hector and Mercedes to Cuba because he loved the family and wanted to keep the family afloat.

Besides, Mercedes had promised her mother, Doña Maria, a chance to see the children. Now, during their visit, Doña Maria often sat on the porch in a wicker chair, holding Horacio's hand and smiling at him. She was suffering from heart disease. Her hair had turned white and her hands had begun to shake. Everything she had to say was like this: "You've made an old woman very happy with your visit, Horacio."

Kisses from the aunts, reassurances from Uncle Manny...

The evening ended around nine-thirty when yawning competed with the sounds of night. One by one, the family retired. Horacio and Hector and Luisa stayed in the same room on the second floor. The balcony of this room faced a field. The moon would rise at one side of the field just outside the window. Horacio liked to watch it, amazed that it looked the same as from New York.

They were sleeping the night Teodoro Sorrea's ghost came along. It was well after midnight. Luisa heard a noise and sat up in bed. She woke Horacio. By the balcony was Teodoro, now only a luminescence in the shape of a man,

wavering like light rippling on water. "Dios mío," Luisa
said, making the sign of the cross. Horacio could not
believe his eyes. The ghost seemed to be spreading his
arms open and sadness emanated from him. "Me estoy
quemando," the ghost said. "I am burning." He stood on
the balcony for a few minutes, turned away, and then disappeared. This was really the only thing about Cuba that
made a lasting impression on Horacio.

❧❧

And Hector? For him the journey was like a splintering
film. He was so young, his memory had barely started.
Impressions swooped upon him like the large-winged,
white butterflies in the yard. There were quiet, floating
dragonflies, star blossoms, hanging lianas, and orchids of
sweet smells. The sunlight, *el señor del sol,* a friendly character who came out each day. Nightingales, dirty hens, spar-
rows, doves, chicks, crows in the dark trees.
Orange-bottomed clouds shaped like orange blossoms, sun
up in the sky, big hairy trees: acacia, tamarind, bread-fruit,
banana, mango, cinnamon, mamey. Rainbows arching
between trees, prisms inside puddles... In town there were
old carved church doors, Christ up to heaven, stagnant
wells, a lazy turtle, the sleeping dog...bakery smells, white
laundry sheets, a laundress. Taste of eating Hershey bar,
taste of eating slice of pineapple, taste of eating chicken,
taste of eating trees, taste of eating steak, taste of eating
flowers, taste of eating sugar, taste of eating kisses, taste of
eating fried sweet plantains. "Cuba, Cuba," repeated inces-
santly, "Cuba, Cuba..."

Then something solid happened. He was sitting in the
yard, examining a flower. The flower was purple with
three oval wings and long red and yellow tendrils that

ended in stars. There was a dog, Poochie, licking up his face. Then Poochie rolled over and his pathetic red dick slipped out from his heaving belly. Hector petted the dog's belly, and the dog rolled around on his back. Then Hector heard a noise coming from the bushes. A bird hopped from branch to branch. Poochie, wagging his tail, happily circled the tree and started leaping up and down, anxious to eat the bird. When Hector went to pet Poochie, the dog snarled and Hector began to cry. But in those days things did not bother him for very long. He went and sat on the kitchen steps. A breeze came in across the treetops from the east, and it felt good on his face. He was in his favorite sailor suit but without shoes, so his toes could play with the ants that teemed up under the floor tiles.

"Oh Hector! Hector!"

It was Aunt Luisa. She was in the kitchen, reading the dress-shop ledger book. The light of the afternoon printed a rectangle on the table and over her soft face. "Oh Hector, come and give your auntie a kiss and you'll get a delicious treat."

He kissed her and she laughed, patting his head.

"How affectionate you are," she said and pinched his cheeks. Then he waited for the treat. He loved to eat, so much so that with each day he grew a little chubbier. His legs and belly were fat. His cheeks, so, so plump, were red. In the evenings he was always happy to sit on the floor with his female cousins, eating snacks given by Luisa. Chewing fried toast covered in sugar with his eyes closed, listening to Aunt Luisa's soft, pleasant voice as she answered in the half-light of the room. Chewing sounds and Luisa's voice mingled with the street noises outside: clop, clop, clop of horses, insects' songs, a dog barking, the murmur of spirits in the Cuban ghost land. Taste of sugar and bread. Luisa sighed as she put aside her sewing for the moment and leaned forward to touch Hector's face. "You're such a little blondie," she said.

Aunt Luisa fixed his drink, which he slowly drank down, savoring its taste. It was so good, with nutty, deep-forest flavors, sweet but not too sweet, with just enough bitterness to fill the mouth with a yawning sensation. He asked for more. She kissed him, poured another glass, and he drank that down. It went deep into his belly but shot up again, from time to time, into his sleep, night after night, for years to come. For some reason he would remember that drink, wondering what it could be, so Cuban, so delicious. Then one day, years in the future, Luisa would come to America, and he would find out its name.

He divided his time between the two aunt's houses, eating and drinking everything in sight: caramel sweets, hard candies, plates of fried pork in rice, bananas, sweet papaya ice cream, leaves, twigs, soda, crackers, honey-dripped flour balls, sour Cuban milk, Coca-Cola, and even water from a puddle. At Rina's house he would sit in a chair placed in front of Uncle Manny's workshop and eat his lunch. Uncle Manny was an enormous man with white hair and wire-rimmed glasses. He had a horse face and liked to wear khaki clothing and read newspapers in an enclosure of prickly bushes. He was a bookkeeper but kept this little workshop in the backyard in order to do some silversmithing and watch repair on the side. Luisa and Rina sent him customers from the dress shop. The workshop: a pine shed, boxes of watch gears and tiny screws, coils of soft wire, and a burner used for heating a little pot of coffee. Smell of metal, rubber, silver, talcum, eucalyptus.

Now Hector was watching him melt silver in a tiny ladle over a flame. His demitasse of coffee steamed on the wooden counter. Swirling the silver around, Manny said, "You know what this is, boy? Cuban blood." Hector looked at the steaming coffee, and Manny laughed. "Not the coffee, boy, the silver. You have this in your veins." The silver swirling. "You know what you are, boy? You're Cuban. *Un Cubano*. Say it."

"*Cubano, Cubano*, Cuba, Cuba..."

Hector sat watching Manny for a long time, wondering if the demitasse was full of the exotic, delicious Cuban drink. His eyes would dart between the ladle of Cuban blood and the coffee, and noticing this, Manny let him sip the dark espresso to which he had added sugar and dark rum. Hector spit it out, and Manny laughed again.

"Don't worry, you'll like it when you're older."

But he drank many other beverages: Coca-Cola and orange juice at Aunt Rina's. In town, at the bodega, some kind of crushed ice drink mixed with pieces of fruit and syrup. All so good, but not like what Luisa gave him. And he was always drinking Cuban water, especially on those trips he and Horacio took with Manny out to the countryside. Manny sometimes did the accounting for a pal of his who worked at a pharmaceutical warehouse. His pal used to give him free bottles of medicine and aspirin, which he would give to the poor *guajiros*—"hicks."

"How they can live like that," Manny used to say, shaking his head, "how they can live like that?"

And Manny would take the family up north to Gibara to go swimming. That was where, according to Mercedes, Hector got sick.

The whole family was together: Mercedes, Luisa, and Rina, the cousins, Manny, Horacio, and Hector. All the women sat under a big umbrella, reading fashion and Hollywood magazines with actors like William Holden and

Cary Grant on the cover, while the men ran in and out of the warm ocean. The current whooshed Cuban sand between their toes. There were starfish by Manny's massive feet. His strong hands took Hector aloft onto his shoulders, real high up, the way Alejo used to do, back in New York. He was so high up, he could see all the palms and the Persian-looking cabanas and the weathered boardwalk, the sea all around him, a curly blue mirror.

Breaking the waves, Manny marched out into the ocean, his great chest of white hair foaming. The skies overhead, zooming by. Manny's voice: something about Christopher Columbus and a ship with huge white sails, Indians, skeletons under the water, and the edge of the world... And he was taking Hector out deep into the Cuban sea. Hector held on for his life, his arms around Manny's bull neck, until Manny pried his hands free and let him float off.

But down he went.

"Come on, niño, try, try, try, don't be afraid."

Hector swallowed more water, went up and down.

"Come on, niño."

But Hector went down and tasted salt and his throat burned. He swallowed and coughed, so that Manny finally brought him back to shore, where Luisa cured him with kisses.

When Hector started feeling sick, Luisa gave him more of the delicious Cuban drink, so good in his belly. But sometimes a weariness confused him and he stayed up at night, listening to the Cuban ghosts walking around in the yard. Or he could hear Mercedes speaking in whispers to Luisa. Sometimes his back ached or his penis felt shot with lead, and he could be in a room, drinking his treat, when he would hurt but remain quiet. If he did cry out, Luisa or

Rina cured him with kisses. Mercedes always said, "You were so good, a quiet, quiet boy. If only we knew..."

A Cuban infection of some kind entered him. In any case, that was what Mercedes always said. What had he done? Swim in the ocean? Drink from a puddle? Kiss? Maybe he hadn't said his prayers properly, or he had pissed in his pants one too many times or cried too much. Maybe God had turned the Cuban water against him and allowed the *micróbios*, as Mercedes would call them, to go inside his body. Who knew? But getting sick in Cuba confused him greatly, because he had loved Cuba so much.

❧❧❧

In her way Mercedes made sense of these things. This was what she said about that journey.

"We went there to see my poor mama, bless her soul. She was viejita, viejita, so old and happy to see us. There were other reasons we went, for a vacation, you know. Alejo couldn't take that much time off, three months, so he sent us along.

"When we got to Havana we took the train east to Holguín. That was a long trip, eight hours, but at least we got to see a little of everything: the big sugarcane plantations, the ranches, the mountains, the old colonial towns with their dusty train stations and the poor farmers going everywhere with their caged, dirty, white hens. Horacio was pressed against the window, looking at everything with big eyes, but Hector was too hot for the whole trip, inside a stuffy train. And, Dios mío, it was hot in those days. So believe me, we were happy when we finally came to Holguín.

"My sisters loved both of the boys very much, and they loved my sisters back. The boys were as happy as little mice and everything was pretty: the house, the town, and the flowers that were everywhere. I remember Manny...his children came to America last year on a boat from Mariel Harbor. He was a big man, so good, especially with the poor. He died in 1960, young, like anyone else who's any good in this world, but in those days he took us everywhere. To the movies and out to the farm and to the ocean, where maybe Hector got sick.

"I tried to be good, but it's impossible to watch the children all the time, with all the running around and playing. Horacio was good, quiet and minding his own business, but Hector...he made me go crazy down there. We would leave him in the yard in Luisa's house, saying, Stay put, but he wouldn't do that. Running around, he got into everything. I didn't mind that, but he went around drinking water out of puddles in the yard. There was dirty water down there, filled with little micróbios, which is why he got sick. We didn't know it then. He looked healthy, mi hijito, my little son. He was nice and chubby, and little by little, he put on more weight. Horacio put on some weight, too, all those chorizos and plátanos omelets that he liked so much. So we didn't think anything about it. We went through the days in peace, Horacio having fun and Hector so curious and happy. Who knew that he would be so sick? I didn't.

"Alejo was writing me nice letters, saying nice things in them, saying for us to have a good time. The only thing he asked us to do was to visit his great grandmother, old Concepción. That's where Horacio and Hector got their light hair. From old Concepción. A long time ago, when Concepción was a young girl, maybe seventeen or sixteen years of age, walking in Santiago de Cuba, she met an Irish sailor by the name of O'Connor. He was very light and fair, with blond hair. He had sailed around the world about five or six times and was looking for a place to settle, was swept off his feet by Concepción, and eventually married her. So her name became Concepción O'Connor, and his blood passed down quietly through the generations until my sons were born.

"In any case, we went to see her one day. She was almost one hundred years old. But she was clean and still had all her senses. Her arms were thin, like young branches, and her hair was white, white. But she had young eyes, and was so happy to see us! She always sat in one place on the patio under an umbrella so that the berries dropping from the trees wouldn't hit her in her head. She was something of a celebrity, too, having been written up in the *Sol* and *Diario de la Marina* because she was so old and not yet dead. She was very happy to meet us, and when she saw Hector's little blond head, she got all happy...to think that more of the sailor was around!

"And I took the boys to see my old house. It was just like it used to be, so beautiful, except that now we couldn't go inside. A government man lived there and servants who wouldn't even let us peek around. There it was, a beautiful white house, so nice...the kind of house we could have all lived in if our luck was a little different, and if my poor papa did not die...

"Still we had our fun. We went to the marketplace and saw a bullfight. And then I showed Horacio and Hector where a witch lived when I was a little girl, and we would pass the time watching the farmers going by on the road. Down the way there was a blind negro, un negrito muy bueno, who played the guitar and used to sing for pennies. For hours we would stand beside him or go riding around; every one of us had fun.

"But Hector became very sick and made trouble for me. I don't know what happened. Maybe it was the drinking water there or something in the food, but he got so sick, and Alejo blamed me for it. Maybe I should have known… One day we were at the beach at Gibara and Manny was taking everybody into the water. Hector was having fun on top of Manny's shoulders, going deeper and deeper into the water. You know how sometimes you can think of things, they come to you in a second? I was sitting under the umbrella, because the sun was bad for my skin, when I suddenly felt like a little girl, and as I watched everyone in the water, I had the idea that something was going to get me in trouble: I didn't want it to happen but couldn't tell what it would be. Just a feeling of wanting to stop something before it had started. Like knowing that there are bugs eating up your garden, but you can never find them. That was what it was like. When we left Cuba, Hector was sick but so happy and fat that we didn't know anything. He came back saying *Cuba, Cuba* and spent a lot of time with Alejo. He was a little Cuban, spouting Spanish."

I'M HOLDING HIS HAND...*

✄ Elías Miguel Muñoz ✄

I'm holding his hand. There are crowds and tall buildings, white columns, glass doors. I cling to him, straggling behind, frightened. Why does he push me away? I look up at his moustache, I don't see it. And the woman by his side doesn't have short hair like Mima, but she's pretty and she smiles and she wants to know my name. "Marito," I tell her. She says I must be lost.

People go by. They don't notice my tears. Where's my Pipo? Will I ever hide in his arms again? Will I fall asleep on his pillow, tie his shoe laces, hear his laughter because I make too many knots, open his briefcase where he keeps *chicles* for me, see him smoke his cigars? I long to hear his voice, the love songs he sings in the shower, throw sand on his chest and go fetching sea shells with him, let him carry me on his shoulders so that I can dive into the water from up there. Where? Where is my Pipo?

I see him. I run to him. I hug him hard, as if afraid that he might leave again. He tells me that it was all a prank, that I shouldn't cry, "Tears are for sissies." He had been hiding from me to see my reaction.

✄✄

Mima helped me write the letter. I asked for a bicycle, a train, crayons and coloring books, a watercolor set, a life-

From: *The Greatest Performance*

size doll that you could wind up and then it would walk
and eat; better a male doll, because that way I could pretend he was my brother. And I could give him my name,
Marito.

I imagined the Three Wise Men riding their camels and
wearing pointed boots, the type people wore in the movie
Aladdin and the Magic Lamp; cloaks and layered garments of
lights. It made me happy to think about them, Melchior,
Gaspar and Balthasar, to imagine them walking into my
house after having flown through the clouds, traveling
leagues and leagues from a distant country hidden in
Heaven.

I was already wide awake when Pipo and Mima came
to get me.

They hugged me and we went to the living room and
then I couldn't make up my mind where to run first. There
were toys hanging from the walls. The furniture was covered with them, too. And in the middle of the room, on the
floor, there was a train running wildly, surrounded by
mountains and lakes and green grass. And there were
robots and brand new shoes and coloring books of all types
and sizes and boxes of crayons, and pencils, watercolors,
tubes of oil paint that looked just like little stuffed frogs.
And there were baseballs and bats and gloves and trucks
and cars and war tanks. There were lions, tigers, monkeys,
zebras, giraffes, horses, dogs, cows, bulls, sheep, kanga-
roos, and doves with their nests and eggs and everything...

"And my toy-brother?"

I hugged my pillow. I took the mosquito net off. I
asked Mima for two more pillows. But I couldn't, I just
couldn't fall asleep. My pacifier was lost and we hadn't

been able to find it. She said she'd buy me a new one, same shape and color. But I wanted my old one, and I started to accuse her of having hidden it from me. Then I accused Pipo, because he always said that I was too big to still be sucking that thing and that one of these days he was going to burn it.

The next morning Mima told me a story. She said that she had seen the hand of an angel moving through my mosquito net during the night, and the hand had taken my pacifier away. Then a beautiful white face with blonde ringlets had told her that I should now grow up and become a man.

I had a vision, too, of that same blonde angel, that night. And I smacked it so hard that it swirled around the room several times. I cussed it out, ordering it to give me back my pacifier. But the angel didn't obey me. And the second time I smacked it, it swooned, vanishing forever.

Zenaida cried a lot the day of the quarrel, when the stick fell on her head. It was one of those long, varnished pieces of wood that was used to prop up the mosquito net.

Zenaida was kind to me. She would rock me in a huge chair that had a wicker back with tiny holes in it. She'd close her eyes and start rocking me by my bedroom door, and then she'd open her eyes and there we were, in the living room! "How did this happen, Marito!?" She'd pretend to be surprised, having moved the chair herself, gradually, over the slippery wood floor. "How did we end up over here?!" I couldn't stop laughing.

In the midst of the quarrel—Mima weeping in the kitchen, Pipo pushing and shoving and throwing every object that came into his field of vision—I made an attempt to attack him, grabbing the shiny stick and hitting him with it. Up there, close to the ceiling, rose his double chin, his thin moustache, his *guayabera*, his enormous hairy arms.

I saw Zenaida crying. And then I saw Pipo dropping the stick on her head. I went for his legs, biting them. He dragged me by the arm all the way to my room, "Sit down and don't move!"

That afternoon he took me to the park and told me that he was going to buy me any toy I wanted. Which he did. Lots of toys.

But after the day of that quarrel, Zenaida never came back.

Mima would wake me up and then I'd run to the kitchen, where I would stand watching the bags full of goodies for our weekend trip to Guantánamo Beach.

Pipo would rent a cabin on the sand, by the water. I loved the beach but I hated the fact that those cabins didn't have a restroom; you had to go to the public baths to clean yourself. That was embarrassing. Pipo insisted on both of us using the same shower stall, so he could scrub me hard, the way little boys needed to be scrubbed. Men with long things and boys with tiny ones would pass by and stare, pointing at the father-and-son shower spectacle.

After going through that ordeal we were usually greeted by Mima, who waited for us with a feast, under a pine tree, on one of those tables made of freshly-cut wood, where you could count every single ring. Mima explained to me that each one of those rings was a year in the life of the tree. Once we counted ten rings. The tree had died, I was sad to find out, when it was the same age as me.

The floor had red tiles and the table was long. The chairs were upholstered in goatskins. The hair seemed so real that whenever you sat down, you had the impression you were sitting on a live beast.

Pipo did business with some shop that made belts and he'd had that back room built to store his merchandise. I'd take my coloring books and my crayons and spend hours there, sitting on the boxes that were piled up on the floor. But I never closed the door. Pipo had forbidden me to do that.

He told me the story of a boy who liked to scare his poor parents by shutting himself up inside a little room like this one. "Save me!," the boy would call for help, "I'm being eaten by a spider!" And his parents ran to help him. Then the kid would stick his tongue out at them and laugh in their faces. Until one time when the kid started to scream, sounding more anguished and desperate than ever before, and his parents didn't run to his rescue. The boy stopped crying eventually. And his parents found him, much later, in the stomach of a boa constrictor. The animal seemed inflated and stuffed. You could discern the shape of the boy's body in its belly.

❦❦

It's raining hard. Loud thunder. My window has been bolted; the bolt we use for storms. I pull aside the curtain and I can see the patio through the window. The evil wind is bending the trunk of the tamarind tree. Its leaves are gone, its fruits flying in Heaven.

Knocking. The sounds of the storm? There it is again, so close, in here, in my own room. "Who is it? Who wants in? Get away! Whoever you are, get away!" His face outside, I see it. His dripping face, freezing. I struggle with the heavy bolt. I can't, I can't get it to open! But I must keep on trying. His imploring eyes are telling me, "Help me. I am cold. Let me in."

And I do, I let him in. The bolt finally gives. He stumbles as he jumps into my bedroom. "What's your name?" I ask him. "You don't need to know my name," he murmurs, cuddling up next to me. He seems to be my age, but he doesn't have my ash-brown hair and light complexion. He's dark, skinny, taller than me. He has dark curly hair and dimples when he smiles. And he's smiling now. "I was very cold," he says. I hug him, "You won't be cold anymore."

Music from the radio in the living room. Or is it Pipo singing in the shower? Beautiful melody. A distant echo that transports me, that takes me up among the clouds, that drops me into this bed of sponge where my new friend sleeps, safe from the storm.

I can't do it. What if he finds us. He'll kill me. He won't? You promise? I shouldn't be afraid. You will protect me. Give me your hand, don't let me slip and fall. Wait for me! I'm getting soaked to the skin. Here I go! I'm jumping out!

The raindrops are thick and sweet, like coconut water; they splash against my forehead. Under the tamarind tree. Dark clouds, a body of leaves. Dense mist through which I see his thin, fine fingers like the legs of a spider, the white palms of his hands. Puddles and mud. Tadpoles. Garments that smell of cilantro. I'm free.

◒◒

Three policemen broke into Pipo's back room and made a mess. And they took Pipo away, handcuffed. When he came back, he was skinny and smelled bad, his clothes were wrinkled. That day he started to make plans for us to move. He bought an empty lot on the outskirts of town, and sent for magazines from Miami so we could select the perfect American model for our house.

We were having dinner in our brand new chalet, months later, when he told us that things were getting bad in the country, that he couldn't do his work anymore. The new government had appropriated the shop and now he couldn't sell his belts. And not only that. Now we'd have to explain and justify every one of our moves and thoughts to some black scum family that had moved to our neighborhood, claiming to be the Committee for the Defense of the Revolution.

We had to get the hell out of Cuba, he said. His friends in Miami would help us. We'd be better off in the North.

Kids from the neighborhood came to watch TV in our house. Pipo had warned me the day he brought home the set; and so had Mima, that I shouldn't invite anyone, that I shouldn't tell any of the neighbors that we had a brand new TV. But I told everybody.

The kids marveled at the porcelain vases and glass figurines and all the expensive furniture that crowded our home. I guess they couldn't understand how a wealthy family like us had ended up building a mansion in this part of town, where mostly poor people lived. Come to think of it, I didn't understand either.

One of the women who came to watch TV with her children said, once, that she'd be happy with only half of the things we owned. Just then it dawned on me: we were rich.

The serial starts at seven. *Zorro! Avenging and Righteous Zorro!* And it is fifteen to seven. I have shut the living room door and windows. I hear their knocks and cries; the show is about to start, "Open up, Marito! Let us in!"

She had begun to suspect that Diego is the righteous and valiant Zorro, even if he continues to act like a sissy.

Because she just found him at the mouth of the cave that runs under the mansion, the one that leads to the library. He speaks to her in a deep, virile voice, and cracks his whip; his horse neighs.

No show.

She tells him, "Thank you, Diego," calling him by his real name, "Thank you for helping us."

"Now that you know the truth," he says, "nothing will stop me."

"Watch out for yourself, Diego!"

"I will come back for you."

"Don't leave."

"I have to. But not for long."

"I love you, Diego!"

"Tonight this town will witness the last appearance of Zorro!"

There will be no show tonight, not with this swollen face.

No show.

The bean soup burns my tongue, I blow on it. Pipo tells me yo stop and eat it. "It's not that hot," he says. I soak the bread in the broth. Trying to get comfortable, I straddle the chair as if I were on a horse. He's staring at me. He pulls the tablecloth and my soup spills. He throws a piece of bread at me. He pinches the insides of my thighs, hits my chest. He grabs me by the hair and pokes my stomach with his fingers. "Men don't sit that way, shit!" he yells. "Only broads sit that way, so they can air out their pussies!"

In my room, he tears up my drawings and pushes my face into the watercolor set, forcing me to eat my greens, my reds and blues and grays, my pinks and my browns, the spots of colored water, the fine hair of my brushes.

"Eat it all. Eat it!"

✄✄

But you were the one, Pipo, the one who took me to Hernando's farm. You asked me to go with you. Because Hernando had a plantain field and he was selling his stuff on the black market. And you could buy a lot of plantains and I could help you carry them home.

After our trip to Hernando's farm, Hernando would ride his bike in front of our house every day; sometimes he stopped in. And he would stay for a while watching TV with me and Mima. She would always make coffee for him. He seemed like a kind man.

He showed up one afternoon looking disturbed. The government was going to appropriate his farm, he said, and he wouldn't be able to sell his merchandise to us anymore. If we wanted to buy a last couple of bunches, this was the time to do it. Now. But one of us would have to go with him to fetch the stuff.

Mima said her husband wasn't home, and that it wasn't right for her to go to the farm. Unfortunately, we'd have to pass up the opportunity. So Hernando suggested that I be the one to make the purchase. I was strong enough to help him cut the bunches and bring them back, he told Mima. He'd give me a ride on his bike. And Mima thought that was an excellent idea. I should get ready, she ordered

me, put on my tennis shoes and accompany Hernando. My
Pipo, she added, my Pipo would be very proud of me.

When I go out to the porch, Hernando is already waiting for me on his bike. His pants are large and baggy; he
rolls them up. He says I must hold on tight to his stomach,
otherwise I'd fall. Hold on tight to his waist. Soft, rubbery
stomach just like yours, Pipo.

Hold on tight.

His nervous tic and his relentless coughing. Straight
black hair, thin eyebrows. Aquiline nose and lipless mouth.
Not as tall as you, Pipo. But hairy arms just like yours.

Another boy comes to see him, he says. And they do
things. From a long time ago, he tells me, they've been
doing little things. I remind him of that boy. He knew I was
a *pájaro*, a queer, from the very moment he laid eyes on me,
the day I came to his farm with my father and I acted like a
sissy, refusing to get my feet dirty with mud and complaining about the weight of the plantain bunches. Those plantains were heavy for a kid like me, they sure were.

He says he knows I am in need of a man. Kids like me
need special protection, we're delicate and fragile like girls,
weaker even, and only someone like him, Hernando, can
provide that special attention we require. I will always be a
baby, he tells me, that's my role in life. Even when I grow
up, I will always see myself that way, as an obedient child.

And he's willing to be a protector.

Have I ever had sex with a real man, he wants to know.
Not other kids like me or older boys, that's just playing. He
means a real man with big balls and a huge dick, *un pingón*,
a man who fucks women. No, I have never done anything
with anybody. Well, he's happy to hear that, because he
knows just how to do it. And he wants to teach me. He's a

man of his word; he promises me he'll never tell on me. He'll never say, Yeah, look at him, he's a faggot and he gives me his ass. Never. I can trust him.

Most of all, I shouldn't be afraid.

I hobble over the puddle in front of the door and dirty my shoes. A small and cluttered room. No windows. Clothes everywhere and an unmade cot. Next to the cot a large scale where he places me, grabbing me by surprise and lifting me. He wants to know how much I weigh. Not much, but I have tender full flesh; I eat well, he can tell. He touches my legs, my back, my arms.

"And if you let me," he says, "stick my hand under your shirt, just a little bit, like this, you see. If you let me, I swear I'll do anything for you, Marito. What a good boy you are, letting me touch you under your shirt. Now you must let me touch you down here, unbuckle your belt, nice belt, yes, back here, your little round cheeks, so soft and warm. And now if you touch me just a little, give me your hand, put it here, see? If you touch me just a little, I swear I'll do anything for you, boy. Leave your hand there for a while, yes, like that. Now you can move it inside. The fly is open, try it. Put your hand inside, that's good. It's hard, isn't it? Let's bring it out, I'm going to take a pee. You want to see me doing it? I can pee far, into the puddle, watch me. Look at this, how red the head is getting under the sun. I'll pull the skin all the way back, look how it moves, and then the head gets bigger; it swells up. You lick it with your tongue, like you're tasting *mercocha*, like this, watch my mouth when I lick my arm. Got it? You do it like that. Yeah, that's my boy. What a nice little tongue you have. Smooth and pink. I swear I'll do anything for you, Marito. Anything…"

I want to wash my hands and he points to the makeshift washbasin outside, full of soiled water. I want soap; he doesn't have any.

I ask him why he doesn't have a bathroom in his room; he says that he'll have one made for me. Because I'm going to come back to see him, right? He will give me a bike for my trips and I will come back as many times as he wants me to. We made a pact, he reminds me. I need him and he's going to help me.

I tell him I never want to see him again, and he warns me not to contradict him; he could get mad and smack me, he tells me. Do I like getting smacked? He should've split my ass in half, he shouts, instead of being kind and gentle. He should've made me bleed. But no, he likes me, he doesn't want to hurt me. All I have to do is return once in a while so I can suck his thing.

"One day, we're going to have a real fuck and you're going to love it, kid. Like having all of your insides caressed, that's how it feels. As simple and delicious as that," he says.

❧❧

The stench of beer served in paper cups. Reflectors and streamers, fake palm trees, papier-mâché flowers. Behind the floats, the Guantánamo people. One massive masked body moving to the rhythm. *Guapachá*. And I swing and sway, letting myself be carried by the movement, *Guapachá!* sweating, singing, dancing.

"I know who you are!" I hear his voice. "I know who you are behind that mask!" His carnival face, drenched in sweat. "Who am I?" He takes my hand and drags me to a clear spot on the sidewalk, in front of a shop window. The white palms of his hands rest on the glass; he observes the reflection of my masked face. "Who am I? Tell me."

I can't recognize him because he's older now, he says, just like I'm older, too. But beautiful memories don't die when you grow old. He tells me of a storm and a tamarind tree. He still loves me.

He's become a dancer. Did I see him moving like a demon on top of the float with a mountain? The tallest of all floats, with a perfect replica of Turquino Peak. He helped build it and it took all year. Did I see him? His rumba steps. A personal show for me, I deserve it. I shared my bed with him when he was down and out and soaking wet. He will never forget me.

The asphalt street ends and now we skip over dents and puddles. We turn right to find a narrow street, then a narrower one, an alleyway. We march along the huts, smelling the fried pork and the garbanzo soup.

We turn right again when we get to a kiosk. There, that's where he lives, behind the kiosk. "Not bad for a poor dancer," he says. He unbolts the lock and invites me in. We enter a small room vaguely illuminated by a kerosene lamp, crowded with a table that's too large for it and some chairs.

His face in *chiaroscuro* as he stands next to the window: "Yes, I remember you now." A beautiful melody. A distant echo taking me up to the clouds. His playful silhouette emerging from the darkness and the silence. I can sense him again, next to me, safe from the storm and the cold. His furtive steps, his body writhing through my sheets as if they were a warm coconut-water stream.

There's a kind man who helps him out now and then. "He gave me a brand new bike… and he feeds me." Do I want to meet him? No, I already have a bike and plenty to eat. "What's his name?" I ask him. "Hernando," he answers.

⚨⚨

The alarm clock in her bedroom; damned buzzer. Her feet will slide into the rubber sandals. Her bulging body will slip into a flower robe. Her hand on my forehead, "Wake up, Marito." She'll be waiting for me in the kitchen, at the table, with breakfast ready.

I get into the bathtub and a frog jumps out, the usual morning frog hiding in the shower curtain. I will sing a mushy *bolero*, like Pipo, while I scrub hard... *Lover, if only I had a heart...* Later, I'll dip the buttered bread in the coffee with milk, and Mima will tell me about the things she'll do today. Some sewing, maybe. Or maybe nothing at all.

In line. Your hand to your temple, the right side. And the blue-and-white-striped flag, *La Bandera*, hoisted on top of the world, *To the frontline, Guantánamo men. Your motherland is proud of you, Guantánamo men...*

My desk, the third one in the row closest to the wall. Who will they pick on today? On one of the fat guys, always the fat guys. Carlos the hick, *El Guajiro*, nine-months belly: "Who's the macho father who managed to break through the pig's lard?" Or Heriberto, *El Gordo*, who ended up throwing up on the teacher's feet one day, after taking weeks of abuse: "Evacuate! Evacuate!"

And then the class clowns trying to decipher the fatso's vomit: "Rice with chicken," they notice tiny white grains. "Avocado, too," they stare at the greenish black chunks. "A bull frog!" they point to a blob with beady eyes, amphibian legs and bulging tummy. Heriberto El Gordo being carried by ten guys to the infirmary: "Moby Dick on board!" Then the poor teacher, Señorita Ramírez, having to clean up the mess.

Pieces of chalk shattering against the blackboard; a pencil breaks in half over somebody's head. Señorita Ramírez approaching! "Did you read the *Versos sencillos,* class?" Her watery, blood-shot eyes; her greasy black hair parted in the middle. "Very well, then. You, Mario, recite one for us, if you'll be so kind."

I am an honest man from where the palm tree grows. And before I die, I want to share these verses of my soul… Guantanamera! Guajira Guantanamera…

Her ever present dress, her orthopedic shoes, perfectly tied laces; the thick vein that popped up on her neck, on the verge of explosion, when she talked about our school. A lump in her throat, half-uttered words when she talked about our school born to this holy Revolution.. Free and sovereign, our school, like its students and its teachers, like the citizens of this exemplary land. Our revolutionary school.

She's waving a sheet of paper in the air: "El Che is gone, my young comrades, but he has left us this letter." She will read it to us, "This is his legacy." She'll make an effort to refrain from crying, "*The faith that you inculcated in me, Fidel…* His work is done in Cuba. El Che must now go and wage other much-needed battles and free other people from their yoke… He planted his seed in our soil, my young comrades. He'll always be the valiant spirit of our Revolution…

"*Until victory, always…*"

I could stay at school for lunch, go to the kiosk around the corner and have a mamey shake. Or buy cookies from the fat lady who doesn't wear bloomers and has a deep belly button like a crater that shows through the fabric of her dress; the woman who stations herself with her metal cookie box by the principal's door, sprawled over a makeshift stool like a big white octopus. "Ten for a nickel! Ten for a nickel!" Her cookies are sweet and they dissolve in your mouth.

I could stay at school, instead of taking the bus and going home for lunch, and talk to Antonio. Lately the guys have been teasing me a lot about Antonio. They say he's got the hots for me, that he's after my buns, my *nalguitas*. But I don't think so.

I like Antonio's hair, dense and tangled, his brown face, his green eyes, his Adam's apple. I like his hairless arms and the way he walks, self-assured. Antonio is smart, the only one of us who really knows English. The only one who speaks, confident, fluent, with the teacher. I call him Mister Anthony. But he doesn't like that name. He tells me to shut up whenever I say it.

We're walking home; he doesn't live far from school. Lucky me, walking with Mister Anthony. "Why don't you let your hair grow long?" I ask him. "Let the bangs cover your forehead, the way the Beatles wear it, the way I wear it?" Because, he says, men are not supposed to have bangs. Bangs are for queers and for crazy rock singers, not for him.

I have been collecting song lyrics, all the Manzanero songs, I have them. Does he want to see them? Wouldn't he like to sing those songs with me sometime? They're so romantic… No, he wouldn't. I'll make him a drawing of whatever he wants; his most favorite thing in the world, I'll draw it for him. But no, he wants nothing from me. "Leave me alone," he demands.

Why? I don't have a plan, a secret scheme. I don't want his protection or his brown dick or his hairy balls. I don't want him to do to me what Hernando has been doing to me for months. I swear I don't. Maybe touching his hair, running my fingers through it; maybe touching his neck, his Adam's apple, maybe holding his hand. His friendship.

He hits my face and kicks me. He pushes me against a wall. Will he talk? Will he say anything? Or will he just go on kicking my legs, driving his feet into my stomach?

"I told you leave me alone!," he says finally. "I told you to get out of my way. Go find yourself another macho to fuck you. You faggot!"

꣑꣑

Chalet painted in light flamingo. The porch: slanted columns of sharp edges; a patio and a back yard; a rose garden; an orchard; a careless garage. The most modern house in the neighborhood, right out of the American pictures.

The radio serial: A prince and a princess and an evil witch. Impossible love. After the hour-long fairy tale there will come a show called *Sorpresa Musical*. From the patio, a penetrating smell of boiled clothes; the laundry woman and her daughters, cackling. In the kitchen the pressure cooker squeaks. Garbanzo stew, I loathe the smell. On my desk drawings of male models copied from *Bohemia* and *Vanidades*. And a masculine voice from the radio, deep and resonant, promising a musical surprise. *We are sweethearts,* he whispers, *because we feel this love, sublime and profound.* He sings, he whispers. *This love that makes us proud.* He cries, *This love so weary of goodbyes.* He pleads, *Come hear,* he hums, *Come hear my sweetheart's lullaby.*

Young militia man, *El Miliciano*: "These papers say that you folks want to leave this country. Is that correct?"

"Yes, that's correct."

"In that case, I'll have to inventory your belongings."

"Yes. We know."

"I'll have to make a list of everything you own, even the watercolor set and the boy's drawings."

"We know."

The Miliciano will order the man of the house to go to the fields, to cut sugar cane. The man of the house will live there, in Las Barracas, until the time comes for him and his family to leave. The time when the family receives the exit telegram. Sunday at six in the morning, Guantánamo Park: "You must cut a lot of sugar cane, comrade."

Pipo's willing to pay the price. The sacrifice is worth it if he can get the fuck out of here. He'll work for these bastards, break his back for these bastards. He'll live in filth if he has to, surrounded by hicks and niggers. He'll put up with it all so that one day Fidel grants us exit and sends us the telegram. He'll do whatever he has to.

Now we're the Worms, *Gusanos*. That's what they call us. And we're willing to kiss the Gringo asses. Sell ourselves. Turn ourselves into whores.

I'll have to do my share of labor when my school goes to the country for forty days. The Revolutionary Law: Students and teachers must contribute to the process, offer their hands and their time; they must experience the *campesino* life. *Campesinos*, the peasants, sustain us; they are the blood of our history. We must help them. We owe them this much.

But what about Pipo? They took him to Las Barracas, where all the traitors are being taken to receive their punishment. Faggots are taken there, too, because the Revolution says they're sick and need reforming, treatment. Pipo may have to sleep next to a *pájaro*. Pipo may be doing it to him. Could he? No. Pipo has no prick, nothing to do it with. The Pipo I love has no sex; like the blond angel who stole my pacifier, he has nothing to put inside a boy's ass. So he's safe.

Am I safe? Hernando says they'll never catch me, that I don't look that effeminate. And besides, I'm too young. But I know my youth is no guarantee; the young ones are being picked up, too. The ones with long hair and bangs, the ones who wear makeup, the ones who sing Beatles songs, the ones with tight pants. Even the women, the ones people call *Tortilleras*, they are being taken to Las Barracas. A magical site where sick men and women turn normal and the deserters pay their dues, Las Barracas.

My Pipo has no chance for survival there, he's too weak. The Pipo I know has never hit anybody, much less his own son, and he has never flaunted his huge dick; he has a tiny one. The Pipo I know sings love songs in the shower. He doesn't boast about his strength, doesn't test it out on a little boy's face. He's weak. Right?

His blood will rot in Las Barracas; his skin will dry up and crumble like a cornhusk. He will turn invisible, or green like the underbrush, red like the earth underneath his feet. Bitten by infected mosquitoes. Or butchered by an angry communist machete; pushed down a cliff by envious hands; strangled by a venomous snake; shot in the heart by a demented lover of innocent boys. Alone. And lonely.

Right?

Sunset of bleeding reds and shadows on the crystal-blue surface. The ceiling pulls me, propels me and pulls me. My neck cracks against the ceiling beams. Under my feet, a bridge of rotting logs, sharks down below. A sewer of dead children. Where I fall...

Your arms used to embrace me. There, in front of a window that covered half the wall, next to me, in my bed, you used to kiss me. In my white and always burning bed, your head on my clean pillow, your smell on my smell. Who am I? Who am I now but you, Pipo. And you are me.

I just heard you come in. You're tiptoeing your way to my tiny plump arms. Please come, rest by my side, lie down. Cuddle up to me. Let me caress your peaceful eyelids, watch you sleep. Oh let me love you again, Pipo.

THE HOMECOMING*

❦ Andrea O'Reilly Herrera ❦

The air was cool and silent, except for an occasional cry that sounded from deep within the jungle and caught on the breeze. The old woman opened her eyes and turned them toward the sea to the place on the horizon where the violet light had slowly begun to gather into a dome. With her eyes fixed on the horizon, she broke into a low, quivering chant that seemed to quicken the dusk. Separated from the world below she sat, upright and motionless, rooted into the mountain with her legs spread and folded beneath her and the flattened palms of her hands resting on her knees. Her silvery hair and plum-colored skin seemed to drink in the colors of the earth and the sky and the sea that spread out around her. From a distance she appeared to be part of the landscape.

Cupping the palm of her hand over her brow, the old woman scanned the horizon for fishing boats, but a gauzy mist clung like a net to the surface of the water. As though she were caressing a familiar face, her gaze swept across the tourmaline sea until it ran up against the pink and white sand—ribbed and scalloped sand which bled into the raw, red earth and the deep green foliage that surrounded the little town at the base of the mountain where she sat. She always positioned herself in the same place— beneath an acacia tree—knowing that there the view was widest. From this place she could look down the side of the

From: *The Pearl of the Antilles*

mountain, beyond its jutting precipices, into the town below.

Looking down from her height, the old woman visually traced the irregular shapes of the palm trees and the ceibas that surrounded the convent school, the terra cotta roofs of the white houses, and the tall spires of the cathedral which lay at the heart of the town. She cocked her head sideways, blocking out the cathedral with the palm of her hand, and turned her eyes away from the sea toward the interior of the island. Before her spread a great expanse—acres of white lilies that stretched into cane fields, then groves of wild fruit trees and masses of thickly tangled vegetation that formed a skirt around the amphitheater of purple mountains that rose up in the distance.

Bending her eyes downward once again, the old woman could see that all of the streets in the town spilled into the large rectangular plaza across from the cathedral, just as the interwoven branches of a river empty into the sea. A steady flow of people, coming from all directions, were making their way toward the plaza. Those who had already arrived formed a kind of living wall around a great wooden cart placed at the center of the plaza. The tall palm leaves that they held in their hands fanned the air above them like feathery plumes. Sitting motionless on the mountain, the old woman became conscious of her own heartbeat, pounding in swift rhythm with the movement of the crowd as it shifted impatiently from side to side. Though the townspeople appeared to be indistinct shapes in the distance, the old woman knew that they had gathered together to draw the wooden cart, which would bear the carved and gilded image of *la Virgen*, through the streets toward the sea. Each year on the same day they gathered in the plaza to escort her to the water's edge.

The old woman watched as the cathedral doors swung open and the statue of *la Virgen*, which was resting on a dais, was carried down the steep marble steps. The statue was lifted into the air, high above the crowd, and then placed upon the cart. Then the priests emerged from the cathedral like black birds, cutting a path through the crowd that formed a barrier around the statue. They were followed by a ragged band of old women veiled in black.

"*Las viejas y los curas*," the old woman said aloud, though no one could hear her. The strain of their voices could not reach her, but the old woman knew that the townspeople were reciting prayers, together with the priests, composed especially for *la Virgen*'s feast day. Her lips began to move in unconscious rhythm with theirs, and the soft sounds that she whispered slipped over her tongue like gliding serpents.

"*Prueban y mueren mis nenes*," she said half aloud, "you taste—and though the sweetness may linger on your tongue—you die."

As the bells in the monastery behind the cathedral began to sound, a long procession formed behind the bishop, who had traveled to the town for this special occasion and had taken his place at the front of the cart. A child lingering at his side led a small animal by a rope that was fastened around its neck. The sight of the procession slowly threading its way through the streets of the town recalled to the old woman's mind the vision she often saw just prior to the dawn:

As though conjured out of air, a procession of twelve—robed and hooded in white like orishas with telling beads hung loosely around their necks like nooses and brooms in their hands—

sprung up before her like some unremembered dream. They followed close behind a man with a crooked staff and wings on his boots. His face was partially concealed beneath a flowing beard, and a rosary with a large amulet hung from his neck. He looked like some ancient priest dressed in a dark green habit.

Up the side of the mountain they rose, stepping to the beat of batá drums that sounded beneath the heels of their hands. From the distance came the soft pounding of other drums, issuing from all directions and echoing in the mouths of the mountain caves. When they reached the top of the mountain, the twelve formed a circle around a group of gaily dressed people. As the air began to thicken and swell with the sound of the drums, the twelve began to dance around the crowd. Soon, the people were swept up in the swirling motion of the dance, like leaves gathered up in the wind, pulled into the circle as though by some unseen current. Stripping themselves to their waists, the women slowly swung their hips from side to side. With parted lips and parted legs, they rolled their eyes in their heads and moaned aloud. The men shouted and leapt into the air all around them, bending their supple bodies into a thousand fantastic shapes. Losing themselves in the motion of the dance, it was as though their feet had been given voice.

For a brief moment the people moved together in perfect rhythm, while the initiated danced in pulsing circles around them. Then seven claps of thunder sounded and the sky rolled back, emptying itself of hail the size of pebbles. As though given a command, the cloaked figures threw off their white garments, exposing their bearded faces and the bayonets that hung over their shoulders. The people seemed to recognize them at once, although no one dared to call out their names. One by one, they fell to their knees and together they beat their fists and their foreheads against the ground, crying out in anger and surprise all the while as the soldiers continued to dance in a wild frenzy around them. And then with one voice the women pleaded for the lives of the children they'd concealed in the folds of their skirts, and the men begged the soldiers in olive-colored fatigues to spare their honor.

Without a word, the bearded priest pointed toward the sea, and the women began gathering up their children in their arms. They wrapped them, cocoon-like, in layers of tender green leaves and pushed them off the edge of the mountain. Then they watched as a warm, tropical breeze carried them across the ocean to a land that had two walls. Many followed in their wake, throwing themselves into the water like insects. Those who remained behind called after their children in a foreign tongue. At that moment the earth began to tremble, and the mountain island upon which the people stood began to uproot and split apart. A small piece broke loose and sailed across the ocean toward the place on the horizon where the children had suddenly vanished from sight.

Who will bear the blame? the priest cried out. His voice echoed like a trumpet through the canyons of the mountain. And then the words became a swarm of black birds that swooped down upon the helpless crowd, pecking at the men's genitals in search of seed and plucking the jewelry from the arms and the necks and the fingers of the women. When they had finished stripping the people, they perched on the shoulders of the bearded priest with gold rings and strings of pearls and silver crosses in their beaks. The priest nodded his head in approval, and a wall of fire rose up and fenced in the crowd. Twice the circle of fire that hemmed them in began to contract, shrinking the plot of land beneath their feet.

By that time the mountain valley had become a crucible of seared vegetation that filled the air with the smell of burnt sugar and flesh. As the false dawn broke all around them, a great uproar arose from the crowd. The distant hills took up the sound and carried their hollow cries to the seven seas until their children rose up on a distant shore, barking out harsh sounding words in a response that took flight from their lips like a cloud of doves.

The old woman tried to remember the first time she had seen the vision. Perhaps it was the day that Havana had burned to the ground or the signing of the treaty in Versailles. Over the years, from her place on the mountain she had seen many visions. This was not the only one. With a heavy sigh she recalled the times that she had tried, in vain, to warn her people about the horrors to come. Shaking her head in sorrow she thought of the words that every generation had scrawled in wiry letters across the peeling paint of yellow walls: Never again. Even now, they refused to listen. Like Cassandra, she had been cursed.

The snake-like movement of the procession, as it wound its way toward the ocean, caught the old woman's attention and drew her back to the drama taking place in the little town below her. Although she had witnessed the ritual many times before, it occurred to her for the first time that from such a great distance the townspeople looked small and insignificant, like the painted figures in a diorama.

By that time, the sun had begun to descend. As the procession arrived at the water's edge, a group of men lifted the statue from her dais and placed her in one of the larger fishing boats. An armada of small skiffs escorted her to a floating platform anchored just off of a thin strip of land that jutted out of the mouth of the bay into the ocean. The fishermen and devoted townspeople followed in her wake and scattered flower petals into the water from aft of their boats.

The old woman watched in silent detachment as the bobbing knot of fishing boats launched across the bay. With her eyes she traced the haphazard pattern of the crowd, spread out unevenly across the shore. Some waved their straw hats and bandanas over their heads; others waded through the water after the fishing boats, as the flower petals undulated around them like colorful wreaths. Once having lost sight of the statue, the crowd gradually began to break off into smaller groups, making their way toward the deserted town. The old woman knew that most would return to their homes—the women, to begin making *pasteles* and *natilla*, and the men, to take refreshment and rest.

❧❧

Just as the last seams of violet light began to thread themselves through the evening sky, those who had accompanied the statue to her floating island returned to the shore. With great effort they dragged their empty boats through the flower petals that had caught on the puckered lips of the sand and abandoned them on the beach. Soon, the sound of laughter and distant music reached the old woman's ears as she sat beneath the acacia tree. She closed her eyes, allowing the day's images to parade through her memory, listening all the while to the strain of guitars and the soft, throbbing rhythm of batá drums—the rhythm that the people had been denied for so many years.

❧❧

The carnival lasted well into the night, ending with song and dance and loud drunken quarrels. And as the town at the base of the mountain slept, the old woman remained upright and motionless, with her legs spread out and folded beneath her and the palms of her hands resting on her knees. But her vigil was interrupted by the sudden knowledge that Rosa had returned. Filled with unexpected joy, she pulled herself to her feet and began making her way, through the darkness, along the steep path that sloped down the side of the mountain toward the town.

Rosa stood on the portico with her daughter in a pale ribbon of moonlight, searching for the large silver key that had sunk like a weight to the bottom of her purse. With the moon at their backs, their shadows intertwined and stretched ahead of them. She turned the key from side to side until the old, rusted lock reluctantly gave way. As the wooden door swung open, Rosa felt as though she had rediscovered a world she had somehow lost long ago.

THE DEFECTOR

❧ Ricardo Pau-Llosa ❧

The once large town, on its way to becoming a small city, was immensely proud of its zoo, less because of the rarity of the animals it sheltered than because of the new and distinguished visitors it drew to the town—from all over the world, it seemed to the citizens. Had the citizens of the town ever traveled they would have known that their simple zoo was simply that. They would have nodded self-assuredly but politely at the myriad enthusiastic remarks the visitors made to flatter the Keeper, a man whose generosity was always hostage to the adulation he would receive as the zoo's custodian.

The Keeper was the tallest man in the town. He sported a graying beard and had fiery black eyes. He was given to long speeches and histrionic hand and facial gestures. If contemplated coldly, he would seem the object of pity, fear, or loathing, but hardly anyone could ponder the extravagant Keeper coldly. His charming hunger for praise was never correctly assessed as a cry for the obedience of others.

Not even the animals saw the Keeper in this way, although in their case the blindness was understandable. "One's keeper always has virtues that will make the keeping more enjoyable," was how the zebra liked to think about it. One of the curious things about this zoo was that there was but one example of every beast.

"Is *enjoyable* the best word for it?" would ask the snake. "After all, we are each alone here in our own space, without a mate or a friend of our own kind."

The zebra would despair at the snake's meticulous pondering of every *mot*.

It must be noted that the animals could only communicate to beasts in adjacent cages or containers and that communications between the snake and the zebra, who lived at opposite ends of the zoo, had to be conducted through relay. The snake would pose a question which was picked up by the iguana, who passed it along to the monkey, who repeated it to the elephant, who re-uttered it to the parrot, and so on for another ten or so beasts until it reached the zebra's ears.

There was no danger of distortion because all the animals were utterly bored. Their only job was to be on display, so they had all the time in the world to repeat to each other every word and nuance of a statement being passed among distant interlocutors. Any distortion would disqualify that animal from participating in the only diversion the beasts knew, so everyone took marvelous care to remain within the circuit. All the repetition and confirmation meant that every denizen of the zoo knew every thought being thought by the other beasts. It is true, however, that they sometimes got confused as to the originator and the destination of each message.

Of course, the Keeper disapproved of such communications; that was one of the reasons, if not the only reason, why he kept but one member of each species. To visitors and townsfolk alike the Keeper announced that the zoo, to be the best in the world, could only house the champion of each kind. By definition, the Keeper argued, there could only be *one* best creature.

"Nature never divides its titles," the Keeper would intone in one of his many speeches to the people passing through his zoo. And some would respond to the Keeper, "Yes, and that is why there can only be *one* Keeper for the *only* zoo worthy of the name anywhere in the world!"

Greedy as he was for such adulation, the Keeper knew enough to blush on such occasions and kindly reject such gestures. The Keeper's hatred of other's communications among themselves was proportional to his love of communicating his feelings and desires to others.

While at first it was the townsfolk who showered the Keeper with praise, more and more it was the visitors from outside the town who could be heard chanting phrases of this type. An out-of-town connoisseur and admirer of the Keeper noticed that the praise he most savored, that which triggered in him the grandest generosity toward his guests, were those remarks in which some fragment of his long speeches about the glory of the zoo was used as the premise of a comment about its Keeper. So it was with the transference of logic—the connoisseur's term for this procedure—that connected the solitary excellence of each of the zoo's creatures with the singular majesty of its Keeper.

The nature of the townfolk's growing distance from the Keeper had yet to be scrutinized by this connoisseur or any other of the learned visitors who came to the zoo. The scholars preferred to witness the cryptic signs, the labyrinth layout, the exotic meals the animals were fed, and the exquisite cages and stalls. In truth, the only inhabitant of the zoo they came to see was the Keeper himself, but to be in the legendary Keeper's presence, they had to take to heart the virtues of the zoo as the Keeper understood them.

It was an elaborate but healthy exercise in reflection and identification. The zoo became the Keeper and the Keeper became the zoo. The visitors, too, became the zoo—allowing the zoo's alleged virtues to govern their own perceptions of everything else in the world. As a result, another transference of logic occurred deep in the visitors' unspoken minds. By admiring the zoo, they became Keepers as well—unique, powerful and generous beings who could command the wise fascination of the world.

That is why the visitors liked to ignore the growing disgust the once fanatical townsfolk felt toward their zoo and their Keeper. Everyone knew that the zoo's initial success warranted expansion, and more expansion. In a short span of time the zoo enveloped the town and, indeed, became the town.

The townsfolk learned to huddle between the sumptuous cages. They abandoned their old professions and crafts and all their old customs and habits to live entirely for the zoo, its upkeep, and the attendance of its visitors. They were, of course, proud of the zoo, but they secretly yearned to have a life outside it. The more they yearned for this, the more secret it had to be kept, for the man who was once only the Keeper of the zoo had now become, logically, the Keeper of the town.

Foreign visitors were filled with awe that a town and a zoo could be so perfectly woven together, that a town could dedicate itself so selflessly to the guardianship of such excellent if solitary beasts. "How lucky you are," they would tell the townsfolk, "to have a Keeper and to be a part of this glorious adventure. You are the envy of the world. Why, everyone would love to live as you do, in constant touch with excellence and in a world governed by a

Keeper of boundless intelligence and generosity." The townsfolk usually stared back in silence.

The beasts were not silent because they spoke in a language no one else, not even the townsfolk who lived all around them and took care of them, could understand. This inability made the people seem stupid in the animal's eyes. The Keeper couldn't understand the beasts either, but he suspected what they must be saying. The Keeper would quote himself repeatedly: "For a great man, suspicion is knowledge."

Although the beasts felt contempt for the townsfolk, they knew that without them their cages would be dirty, they would not be fed, and consequently no one—not the Keeper and certainly not the foreign connoisseurs—would visit them. The beasts were alone, it is true (and painfully so), but they were the stars of this zoo which, it would seem, was the most glorious circumstance on earth.

But even the beasts had to deal with the less than glorious conditions which the Keeper and his management style imposed on the zoo and all who lived in it. To put it bluntly, there were shortages of everything. It was not easy to say this, for how does one reconcile glory with pettiness, grandeur with ruin, excellence with meagerness?

I suppose it is time I should say who I am and how I have come to know so much about this zoo, the townsfolk, the visitors, and above all the Keeper. I was the zoo's capybara. And I can write all this and what is to come precisely because I escaped the zoo some nine months ago and nothing in my life has ever been the same.

I do not know if I was born in the zoo or was captured as an infant in the wild. I once thought this detail mattered. I recognized I was a rodent, but clearly I was a far superior and larger one than the pathetic rats, hamsters, and rabbits

I could glimpse from my cage. Yes, once I thought of it as a throne. The Keeper had ordered that my space—I preferred then, and now, this more neutral word (there's a bit of zebra in all of us at the zoo, I suppose, and very little snake)—be lined with bananas, soybeans, and salami. In my natural state, the state I had been taught to abhor, these were not my foods. But the Keeper who had freed us from nature, on the basis of our excellence, prescribed our diet. We also ate eggs. Lots of eggs. We all ate eggs.

The food regimen would change abruptly. Just when I finally got used to salami and soybeans, they vanished. Peaches in syrup took their place, then a foul smelling canned meat, then hamburgers made from ground pigs' ears and snouts. Although we were told by the Keeper that these changes had to do with his design for our happiness, with time we came to realize that the diets were determined by availability. Even in the worst times, the bars of our spaces were covered with these delicacies and, in the name of our excellence and the Keeper, we consumed them dutifully.

It was difficult to leave. I don't mean the actual escape only, though that, too, was no minor feat. It was difficult to give up the thrill of being the world's greatest capybara, the standard by which all capybaras were measured. I remember one time I was just waking up from a nap and, as I always do when I rise, I shook my legs a bit. Just give them a little jolt to get the blood moving through them.

I heard a collection of sighs all around when I did this, so I opened my eyes and beheld myself surrounded by foreign scholars who were heaving their chests and swaying their hands in admiration for the esthetics of my little leg jolts. "So much irony in that gesture," said a woman with thick black glasses, a clipboard and silver gray hair.

"Yes," said one of the Keeper's closest aides who was guiding the group through the zoo, "we consider irony the principal reason for the zoo's glory."

Another of the guests on the tour, a slender man with shaven head and a loud shirt commented, stroking his chin the way the Keeper often strokes his own pensive beard: "But we must be careful not to read our own sense of irony into the zoo's manipulation of this device. After all, this is a revolutionary zoo, so it stands to reason that our own failed, exhausted definition and practice of irony does not apply in this glorious place. If it is irony, and let's say for the moment that it is, it is zoo-irony, if you will, which only the zoo inhabitants can fully appreciate and, hopefully, someday define for us." The others, some twelve or so, all nodded in admiration of these subtleties. So did the guide. They proceeded out of our pavilion and headed for the zebra's stall.

I was still flat on my belly as all this happened. Of course, out of embarrassment, I had stopped jolting my legs as they conversed and I stayed perfectly motionless except for rolling my eyes this way and that to glimpse my visitors as they continued their tour. I was flattered, too, even though I had never heard the word "irony" before. What could it mean and how could this complex term apply to my little leg jolts? Does it have a connection to *iron*? Could it mean that I jolt my legs because I am not getting enough minerals in my diet?

If that were the case, the guide certainly would not have agreed with the observation for fear of offending the Keeper who thought of himself as an expert on everything, and on diets most of all. After I got fully up and munched on some dried codfish—the food of the month which, actually, I had been eating for almost a year now—I went over to the space next to mine.

I noticed one of the townsfolk reaching into my cage to grab a slab of codfish I had not eaten. Usually I would raise a stir, have the creature punished, but when I am overtaken by curiosity, I also become generous and understanding. The connection between these traits I learned, I suppose, from my neighbor to whom I now turned for illumination.

How fortunate I was to have such an erudite zoo mate, the Pekingese. She would sit up motionless or lie on her belly with her head erect and her eyes pinned on an imagined horizon for hours. She would lie on a lavender silk cushion a visitor some years ago threw into her space as a gift. She munched on codfish or salami, which she abhorred, with the same delicacy with which she would slurp a raw egg, which she once liked but also learned to hate after having to eat so many.

"Pekingese, the visitors that were just here were talking about…"

She interrupted me: "Irony. Irony and your legs."

I was relieved she had heard the whole conversation because, being asleep, I hadn't. I asked her to fill me in with the hope that, in her recounting of the event, I would learn what *irony* was without having to ask her directly. I was the capybara—generally considered an intelligent zoo dweller—and, if my legs exhibited irony, I should know what that meant. Pekingese wouldn't embarrass me, but on the other side of my space was Peccary, a lazy, indiscreet, and often irascible creature who, nonetheless, had a good heart. He was fully awake and overheard our conversation.

"My dear Capybara," said Pekingese, "there wasn't much to the visit or the conversation. Nothing we hadn't heard a million times before. You were the luckiest of the three. Peccary and I had had our naps and sat through their entire gabble with straight faces."

"Peccary with a straight face? Really, Pekingese."

At this provocation Peccary entered the conversation, as we knew he would. "If your quivering legs are ironic, then my ass is made of gold," he said scornfully.

"I knew it," I said. "There is something missing in my diet and it's robbing me of iron."

They both laughed uncontrollably, which Peccary was given to do but never Pekingese who, practically choking on a slice of salami, chortled, "And I must be a king, though my name should then be Pequeenese."

"And I fat sinner," said Peccary, rolling in his mud and throwing his legs up into the air and shaking them to caricature me. "And you, Capybara, a castrated bara, whatever that is."

Obviously I had made a blunder, but could I recover, pretend I was kidding? I began to laugh as well, riotously, even more than they.

"My dear and learned Capybara," said Pekingese, "irony is our condition, or rather what contains us. We are the artists of this place."

"Because we are the most excellent creatures."

"No, fool. Because we must create space out of cages, thrones out of tombs. Only imagination could do that. The rest must feed us and starve, think themselves us as everyone once dreamt themselves as the Keeper."

"But, Pekingese, that is Peccary talk. No one can understand us, but still, you are taking quite a risk."

"Impossible," interrupted Peccary. He often threw single words into conversations like that, like dirty bones into someone else's nice clean soup. We had learned to ask for an explanation by simply staring at him in silence and saving ourselves the interrogative utterances.

"Impossible," he repeated, and said nothing more. That was unusual. Peccary would, after our interrogative silence, go into a speech, full of bitterness and humor, about the meaninglessness of his life. Of course, he called it Life, but we all knew he only meant his.

"Impossible." And once again, nothing else. He had not gotten up from his tumble in the mud, although he was now perfectly still. His legs had stopped quivering, which I was thankful for. His upturned face stared at the wall opposite my space, so all I could see was his rear end and his stiff legs.

"Peccary," I called out gently, "are you all right?"

"Impossible."

I turned to Pekingese and shrugged my shoulders in complete bafflement.

"Is it you who are impossible, Peccary?" asked Pekingese. "Is this a confession? No need for it, you know. You are among friends who know you are impossible."

Nothing came out of him. Taking a closer stare, Pekingese saw from her cage that Peccary was dead and she signaled to one of the townsfolk who tended his cage to deal with the situation. After the citizens came in and ate up all Peccary's food, they put his body on a wheeled stretcher and carried him away. Some of them checked out his hide. It was evident they were thinking of butchering him and, judging from the shapes they were drawing on his skin with their fingers, they were designing shoes and wallets from his pelt. It struck me that the only person I had ever seen wearing shoes and using wallets were foreign visitors, the aides of the Keeper and, of course, the Keeper himself.

And that was going to be my future as well—raw material for commercial items. That was the reason I was here, or at the very least the inevitable outcome of my presence here. The most excellent peccary in the world was being kept in a cage until his natural death, only to be turned into luxury items and a sumptuous meal for tourists. But then one of the townsfolk who had come in to carry Peccary away began to choke and sway, and he finally fell dead to the ground. He had eaten Peccary's food. Peccary had been poisoned.

I had never seen death before. Add to this that Peccary, for all his faults, among them that he was a bitter rebel to the end, was a good friend. I always felt it was good for someone to be a rebel. The rest of us talked about rebellion but had never experienced it. "A concept is everyone's legitimate child," Peccary used to say, "but action is always an orphan."

The problem was, perhaps, that for us solitary beasts in the zoo, "child" and "orphan" were also concepts. Our very lives were concepts, I would say, and Peccary would correct me.

"A life cannot be a concept. It's hard enough to bring concepts into line with life. Death is a concept, but never life," he would say.

Pekingese and I began to miss Peccary the moment he died, but while I got sentimental she became hostile. Her insults became unbearable until one day I asked her why she had given up her eternally serene pose.

"Rebellion is a void that demands to be filled," she said, "and you must fill it. Escape," she said.

I noticed something that I had never noticed before, that the bars on Pekingese cage were far enough apart for her to pass through. I pointed that out to her. And she pointed with her snout to Peccary's still empty cage. His bars were wide enough, too. That's when I noticed my bars were also wide enough. All I had to do was pass through the spaces and keep walking.

She wouldn't join me, however. "I must stand guard over myself here," she said. "I have escaped into myself and must cover my retreat, lest they give chase to bring me back." Thinking I did not understand what she was talking about, she said I would someday, long after I had left the zoo behind me. I understood, but I thought she was masking her fear with a pose, and a bad one. I, not Pekingese, would inherit Peccary's role as the rebel.

That night I climbed out of my cage, careful not to wake any of the townsfolk sleeping on the floor, and walked past Snake, Zebra, Horse, Giraffe, Alligator, Hawk, Tortoise, Sparrow, Spider, Eel, and finally Hummingbird. I ambled through the gate and deep, deeper into the great forest which I had heard, from Peccary, had once been and would always be my natural home.

I will not bore you with stories about my first experience in the wild, but I will tell you how shocking it was at first to be among my own kind. Three days after I had left the zoo I saw a group of twenty or so capybaras swimming in a stream, chomping on grasses and small fish. As I approached them I imagined how they might receive the most excellent capybara in the world, and I sincerely hoped they would not make too inordinate a fuss.

I was near them, near enough so that they had to notice me, yet they went about their business of wallowing and swimming and eating. I joined them and felt a little sorry for them, for none had the luster of my hair, the cared-for sharpness of my teeth, or the brilliance of my eye. They were, as Keeper had always said, lost in their own appetites. Lacking excellence, they were unable to recognize it in others.

That was the moment I first realized how right the Keeper had been, at least on the difference between his beasts and the rest of their kind. But I knew I could never go back to the zoo precisely because I am the finest capybara. I deserve the whole world as a cage and not a cage as the world. So, confident in my superiority, I mixed in with the other capybaras, sure that soon they would realize what kind of splendor had drifted into their thin lives.

I was alone among them as I had been at the zoo, except the distance was marked by different bars. These conditions, I began to fear, might not be so easily abandoned as ones which are taken, in the final analysis, for cages. Still, I had to try to escape them, for I could not bring myself to sustain a learned curiosity toward these river-dwelling capybaras. They lived entirely in and for themselves, even if in groups. I had maintained more communication with a lap dog and a large pig at the zoo than they had with each other.

One day, a young capybara drifted toward the main river where hordes of piranha abounded. I noticed the child was being pulled by the current and told one of the others, who misunderstood me and said to yet another capybara that I was cold, who misunderstood that as something else. The others simply watched as the youth swam foolishly downstream. It could have been me, for until that moment no one had told me about the piranha downstream. When the rapid spectacle of his devouring occurred, I was stunned. In no time, the clean bones sank to the bottom of the river while his fellow creatures continued their living chores in the safety of the tributary.

I felt naked among my own and decided to look for others with which to live. The experiments were varied and all disastrous. Regardless of species, everyone in the wild centered their lives around their own well-being. I realized, with time, that it was no different in the wild than in the zoo. And yet everything was different. It all depended on how we define our conditions. If the stubborn chores of getting to the next sunset were different in the zoo and in the wild, the stubbornness wasn't nor the fact that survival entailed chores.

Humbled, I returned to the tributary after a month's absence, and my capybaras were still there. The piranhas were also there, downstream, and the small jaguar, and the blade-broken path of an anaconda was there. And in the trees a bird for which no champion could be found for the zoo. It was the vulture. Another capybara explained, in the first conversation I finally managed with a fellow of my kind, that all vultures were champions.

"A kind of beast in which all are champions," I said, "that is a splendid kind. But maybe vultures are the champions of all kinds."

"Kinds?" he asked, loath to my idea.

"Kinds. We are capybara. He is a vulture. Downstream another kind lives, piranha. And somewhere there are panthers, and peccaries and dogs."

"I see. You have not left the zoo yet," he pronounced with distinct disenchantment and returned to his imbecile chewing.

I was annoyed, down right insulted. "There are many, many kinds of creatures, sir. Ever heard of zebras, of townsfolk? Of foreign visitors and scholars? Ever heard of the Keeper?"

"There is but one kind. The living," he said.

I felt the last tug of yearning for the zoo at that moment, the place where every creature had a cage and a name. If I let go of my life at the zoo, I could go on here forever, in the worried freedom of the forest.

It would be dark soon. If I set my sights on the hills now and never wavered from that direction, even when night blurred the guiding contours of the land and turned everything into an impossible darkness, I would reach the zoo. I knew that each step in the voyage back would be thick with the now, cut away from past and future. The sequentiality of those steps would take me to the zoo, but at no point would I have a sense of direction in the journey. The wild was locked in the timeless exercise of chewing and swimming and mating. It made no sense to rebel there or to flee. So I closed my eyes, as Pekingese did in her furious journey the night I left the zoo, and I began the long dream in which I was going home to my cage.

PALOMA*

❦ Beatriz Rivera ❦

Her land was green and brown, and rolling and grooved by torrents. It rained almost all year long. It rained harder in September, October, November. It was a tropical rain. It gorged the air and the earth. It made the ground swell. Her village was Indian, Mauresque, Spanish, as colorful, as busy, as warm as a Peruvian blanket. There was an old yellow cathedral, a market place, a flower square. There were several parks staked with statues erected in honor of Spanish heroes some of which were now buried in the graveyard adjacent to the church, a tourist attraction. The oldest headstone was from 1518, but the name was impossible to read; the constant rain had made the stone melt. On some of the other headstones Spanish names such as Grijalva, Jaramillo, and Torquemada could be deciphered; names respected and renowned for having imported to the New World the medieval mysticism, the self-punishment, and the humble submission that her people, because of their wise inborn serenity and survival instinct, had accepted from the very beginning. They hardly had enough to eat, but that was God's will; their ancestors too had lived and survived on half-empty stomachs; they even got fat. There was corruption everywhere, but it was so common that it was confused with normality. Those who weren't satisfied with the system escaped to that paradise called the United States instead of complaining or

From *African Passions and Other Stories*

fighting or trying to alter the deeply rooted ways. They'd been taught that any effort here wasn't really worth making. They'd best save their energy and willpower for America. In truth, corruption was so bad that, in terms of money, it took several years of hard labor for those who had no connections to obtain something as simple as a passport. So the luckier ones who held this precious document didn't even travel. They stayed where they were and took good advantage of their passports. But, whether lucky or unlucky, instead of trying to climb mountains, her people did the best they could to make their way around the mountains.

Paloma Sánchez stood five feet two inches on her bare feet. She was a tiny little thing with shoulder-length black hair that was curly because of semi-annual permanent waves. From the time they were twelve or thirteen, the women from her village resorted to this kind of hair treatment; their hair was too straight if left natural, and they didn't seem to like it natural. Paloma's skin was ripe olive. She was lean and muscular. Her teeth were shiny white and perfect. She had black almond-shaped eyes and a little-bird quality to her demeanor. And she was pretty. Extremely so. So pretty that a boy of fifteen had claimed her when she was thirteen, and they were married in haste a month later. But that was normal, about as normal as not being able to obtain a passport without money or connections. Even the homely ones married young. Life was so hard that they did everything quickly, perhaps just to be done with it.

But Paloma wasn't normal. She was among the luckier ones in that at age twenty-five, when she went to the market place with her ten, eleven and twelve-year-old sons, she still made heads turn; men thought these boys were her brothers. She hadn't aged quickly like most of the other women. Rodrigo, her husband, always bragged about having married the most beautiful woman in this land. And Rodrigo was the one who came up with the bad idea of having Paloma's picture taken.

If the sleeping dogs had been left to lie, maybe Paloma wouldn't have gone to prison and hers would have been a normal life.

But to commemorate every special occasion in their lives, Rodrigo insisted on dragging Paloma to a little photo studio in the village. At first Paloma didn't want to; she was scared of x-rays and cameras. And the more she went, the more she was humiliated and terrified now. Rodrigo quickly took to repeating the same exact thing after the flash had gone off and Paloma's image had been gulped by the camera. With a loud sigh of relief he'd say that (at last!) her children and future grandchildren would realize how beautiful she had once been. He'd also add that it'd be different this time, that she'd come out looking as spectacular as she was, technology was advancing, practically every day progress was being made with flashes and cameras. Paloma needn't worry. This time she wouldn't be offended by the developed photograph. She'd have a photo she was proud of! This never happened.

These humiliating photo sessions began when Paloma was eighteen. It was in honor of their fifth wedding anniversary. Paloma had already borne three children then, but she had also managed to graduate from high school thanks to the help and cooperation she got from her parents and immediate family. Rodrigo, too, had graduated from high school and they both had excellent jobs. Paloma stayed in her village and worked as a secretary in the administration. Rodrigo was a customs official in the capital. They only saw each other once a month; but this way of life allowed them luxuries such as photo sessions for Christmas, birthdays and anniversaries, meat or fowl every night on their table, decent clothes, a decent dwelling. The clothes were extremely important for Paloma; she was a gentle, sensitive woman with a little vain streak, it happens even to the gentle and the sensitive—and this is precisely why the photo sessions made her life take a turn that nobody had expected.

Neither Paloma nor Rodrigo were disappointed at first. They laughed and blamed it on the flash. So did they the second time. Then it was the photographer. Then it was the camera. Then it was because she was pregnant for the fourth time. They also tried to blame it on the rain. After that, it was her nerves—everybody gets nervous on special occasions. They tried July, that run-of-the-mill month July, when nothing was happening. Still no good. They finally went to the capital. Photographers in the capital were far more competent; they were sure they wouldn't be disappointed.

But they obtained the same puzzling results and this time Paloma overreacted. She cried and swore that she'd never have her picture taken again. She even wondered if she was as ugly as she appeared on a developed photograph. She sobbed and complained that life wasn't worth living if her—she didn't say "beauty"—if her good looks were to disappear one day without leaving a trace. Her perplexed husband tried to comfort her. It was difficult though, for he himself was disappointed, he just couldn't understand. How was it that he had married the most beautiful woman in this land and that she was so homely on a developed photograph? He always bragged about her to his buddies in the airport and had, time after time,

promised to bring them a photo of her. But he just couldn't
get around to it! How could he show them the image of a
common-looking matron after years of bragging?! They'd
tell him that love was certainly blind! Rodrigo still had to
comfort his wife though, so he put his wounded pride to
one side. It wasn't that she actually looked ugly...it
was...What was it? It was that she looked like anybody else.
Common! Paloma sobbed even harder. Rodrigo's wife,
Paloma. Paloma of all people! Paloma looked common on a
photograph! Even the photographer couldn't understand
what had happened. He argued that he usually made
women look prettier than they really were. He even insisted on taking several other pictures of Paloma who finally
gave in after having chanted and chanted "never again" at
least fifty times. But the same exact results were obtained
again and again. She was as pretty as a bird, but on a photo
she looked like anyone. Like everyone. From that day on,
Paloma and Rodrigo acted as if she were afflicted by some
unknown disease that no doctor could diagnose. For a
while they continued running from doctor to doctor, still
no result.

One day, Paloma finally dried her tears and said with
the resolution of wounded pride, "so be it!" If she was con-
demned to lose her good looks, if in twenty year's time she
wouldn't even be able to produce paper proof of her youth,
well, then, she'd start living. Wasn't she, after all, dissatisfied with her life? She'd married too young and that thrill
was gone. She had children and she was a loving mother,
but the children just couldn't fill the void. What exactly
awaited her? More Christmases. More wedding anniversaries. More birthdays. Her children would grow up and
marry, and she'd most likely be a grandmother before age

thirty, then a great grandmother at forty-five. Then what? She'd wither and die.

Paloma was born strange. She had always wondered about the meaning of life. She was born dissatisfied. Since puberty she had tried to dilute this unpleasantness and swallow it. Like a ghost, it always returned to its haunted house. So if a dull fate was the only thing in store for her, Paloma, who was five feet two inches tall, decided once and for all to walk around it.

She was going to put fine clothes and jewels on her body. She'd have many loves. She'd know the pangs of passion as many times as her spirit could take them without breaking. She'd be married to many, many men. She'd live in sixty different places at the same time. Perhaps she wasn't photogenic. So be it, she'd make the best of it. She knew how to do it. It was a rusty, broken old gift that she'd left behind. At puberty. When she got married and had convinced herself that it was just child's play. Back then it had seemed more important to become an adult, bear children, celebrate Christmas with the family, show your children off, the cute things they say and do, hide behind them, die progressively behind them, give up, be serious. Now she was determined to bring the child Paloma back.

She asked the local photographer to take a small picture of her, the kind you use for passports. A week later, when she went to pick her photo I.D.'s up, the photographer, who knew her well, said, "I think I could sell that exact same photo to any woman who walks in here." Paloma smiled and said, "I know that."

Because she worked in the administration and Rodrigo was a customs official, both she and her husband had certain privileges that the majority of her people wouldn't even dream about. In three months she had her passport.

Rodrigo, who was more than content and even proud of his fate, said, "We're not leaving. We're not going to New York." It was absolutely out of the question. Their people suffered there. "Besides, our whole family's here. And the children need their cousins to play with. And Christmas wouldn't be Christmas..." Paloma interrupted him, she said, "Don't worry, I'm staying right here."

Christmas came and went. It barely gave them enough time to try again at the photo studio, to obtain the same offensive results, and to roast a pig at the routine family reunion. Paloma became distant and aloof. Everything saddened her; the food, the festivities, the gifts, the family. She wanted to cry, she wanted to die. The evil depression was gnawing away at her spirit. She tried to cheer up. It was to no avail. Her black eyes were constantly holding back the tears. What was the use of it? One more Christmas. One more wasted year. She was twenty-six, and she felt old and worn-out. She felt her life slipping by, and her youth. She looked in the mirror and noticed thin lines around her eyes. Nothing to look forward to. Nothing but this. While everyone was merry and sentimental, thanking the Lord that they were together, she felt like dying. She didn't consider herself a part of it. She felt trapped. She suddenly wished her husband would leave her, set her free. Sad heart, dirty hands. For the few days that followed she thought she was insane. Why this grief? Would it ever leave her? Christmas was supposed to be a happy season. But why pretend? So insane she must be. She wanted to die, that was all. Couldn't they just leave her alone?

Then came the feast of Saint Sylvester, the new year. Her resolution was to fly, up in the sky, way up high. Yes! She'd fly! And she'd fly before she became a grandmother. She swore to that!

It so happened that her thirteen-year-old son had gotten a nineteen-year-old spinster pregnant. They'd married in haste like everybody else and the baby was due in March. This didn't leave Paloma that much time to fly.

Three Kings Day she fell into a strange torpor. Sons and daughters and nieces and nephews were happily opening their presents. Children were laughing and playing and running and shouting, but Paloma saw and heard nothing. She still remained a loving mother. She continued being the gentle creature she was. But she was just pretending to be there. In reality, she was dreaming. Dreaming. She dreamt she was flying.

The bird was white. It had swallowed many people. You could see half the earth below you. The bird roared and whistled. It was cold in the bird's stomach. Paloma could see its wings of steel breaking the clouds in two. There was a woman sitting next to her. She was small and thin, and looked just like Paloma did on a developed photograph. And she wasn't the only one. All the women inside the bird looked exactly like Paloma's image on paper. "Are you scared?" the woman sitting next to her suddenly asked. Was there anything to be afraid of? Could this bird fall? She laughed and said, "Oh, you poor thing! The bird falling! That's the last thing in the world to be scared of!" Because the bird will land and you have to walk out of it. Into another world where many, many things are magic. But it remains a hard cruel world, a bit like ours, only different. Different because nothing's really obvious. Not even corruption. The truth is masked. Act normal though. Like a tourist. Tell them you're only here for two weeks to visit your family. If you don't convince them, they'll catch you! Don't worry about getting slapped around. They only do that in our land. At least that's what

I've been told so far. What they do is catch you and send you back! That's when they hit you, when you get back. And they take you by the elbow. Push you around. You lose the freedom you never had. Have to start over a year later when you finally get out of jail. All those years of hard work to get papers and money to climb into the bird...lost! Lost forever! Have to start all over again. Aren't you scared? Of starting all over again? Yes.

The next day was a Sunday. Paloma woke up early. Her hands were shaking. Word got to her unexpectedly. And she knew where she had to go. She was ready. Rodrigo asked, "Aren't we going to Mass?" Paloma didn't answer. He then wanted her to get back into bed. That same afternoon he was returning to the capital, they wouldn't see each other for a month, shouldn't she get back into bed? Paloma said she never ever wanted to be pregnant again. She slipped her passport into her handbag and walked out of the house. She had nothing to hide.

The bus stopped near the market place. Her destination was an hour away. She went down, down; the hills got higher, greener, browner, the torrents became streams. After having stepped off the bus, she had to walk a while. The earth was soft and the mud ankle-high. There was a woman washing clothes in the river and crying. Her husband had had an accident. His legs were broken. He couldn't leave on Wednesday. The money was wasted. They'd have to start all over again. For years he'd planned this trip to New York. He was to work there and send money home. It was terrible because they'd begun building their house when they were newlyweds fifteen years ago. With cement blocks. Then they ran out of cement blocks. The next door neighbors offered to share one of their walls, but that only gave them a house with three walls. Their house was missing a wall. A plastic canvas had been nailed to that empty side. It worked fine when it didn't rain. The problem was that it rained almost every day and the canvas didn't keep the rain out.

Paloma walked downhill with her, and her house was indeed missing a wall. The house had a door though. They used the door. It was even locked. As if the house had four walls. They'd saved a lot of money. It didn't take long to convince the woman's husband. They gave the money to Paloma and Paloma gave them instructions.

She didn't go to work on Monday. With the intention of spending the newly earned money on herself, she went shopping, but ended up buying clothes and toys for her children instead. She also bought a layette for her grandchild that was due in March. By mid-afternoon the money was gone.

On Wednesday she dreamt she was flying. The bird was going down, down. Underneath her was the American city of Miami. Flat and full of lights, it looked like a gigantic amusement park. There was that same woman sitting beside her. She was afraid they'd catch her, and Paloma, too, was afraid they'd catch her. Those people in uniforms. That was their job. To catch you. They ask all kinds of questions. Even if you're telling the truth it makes you nervous. The bird landed. The stairs moved. The rubber rug moved. The suitcases moved like a serpent in the grass; you had to hurry up and catch them. Imagine your immobile suitcase passing in front of you! You wait, that's all. Then there was a line. The most dangerous part. All her people were nervous. What if they were sent back? English was a strange language. You can't understand it. But you could also hear Spanish. With a different accent. The man in the uniform wanted her passport and the yellow card that she had filled out before the bird put its feet on the ground. The woman sitting next to her had had problems filling it out. She could barely read and write. The man looked at her, then at her passport, then back at her. "What's your name?" he asked. So he repeated it in Spanish. Why did he speak English if he spoke Spanish? Paloma Sánchez. Your name? Paloma Sánchez. Your name? Date of birth? March 26, 1962. Learned all that by heart. Your name? Date of birth? First time you've been here? Open your suitcase! Final destination? New York. Where? Why? Where are you coming from? How long? Why? To visit my family. How long? How much money have you got? By the way, what's your birthdate? Step to the side; some women are coming to search you and ask you your name. And ask you to sign your name several times. Paloma had never been as terrified in her life. She felt the blood gushing up to her head. She thought it would burst. How long would this last? Was it worthwhile? What's your name? Paloma Sánchez. What if they caught her? What if they sent her back? Very well. You may go. Have a nice flight. Was that it?

There were corridors and it was cold. Somebody said it was the air conditioning; nobody could live here without it. And the stairs that went up by themselves. And the rubber mat that went exactly where you were going and took you there. Gate fourteen. Was she free? When the bird landed in New York, would they ask her more questions? That woman again! Waiting to get on the other bird. Maybe she'd know. She seemed to know everything. They were both glad they didn't get caught. Then they started talking about the others. The ones who weren't waiting here with them. That meant they had gotten caught, the woman said. She loved talking about terrible things, and pitying the others.

Queens, New York. So many clothes to buy. Beautiful, beautiful stores. The people from this village of Queens are so friendly and helpful. And it's a pretty village. They sell food everywhere. Cheap. The prices don't change, apparently. When it rains, your feet don't get stuck in the mud. Queens is clean. And everybody in Queens seems to own a refrigerator. They put their clothes in machines, wait a while, then their clothes come out clean. Here you don't wash your clothes in the river. A distant cousin of hers who's been here for two years laughed when she asked where the river was. He said that the river here is much dirtier than the clothes will ever get. It's called the East River. Anyway, you can't kneel and wash your clothes in it.

A week later she had a job. They called this town Manhattan. And she kept wondering where New York City was. She wanted to visit New York City. Everybody said it was fabulous. New York City, where was it? And until she learned the truth, she regretted having to work in Manhattan.

One hundred and fifty dollars a week. She was to cook, clean, take care of the children, speak Spanish to the children. Their mother wanted them to be bilingual. What was bilingual? Vacuum? She preferred to sweep. But the mistress was adamant. She had to push that scary machine around. What if it swallowed her? The mistress said you have to vacuum. You have to keep everything very clean. They don't want germs in their apartment. The mistress spoke some Spanish. She said she learned it in Mexico. Every morning, rain or shine, she and her husband would put sport shoes on and go running. Why do people run away from nothing? They said it was to stay in shape. Thin. So that's why the mistress looked like a skeleton. And in spite of all the money they seemed to have, they never put meat or fowl on their table. They said chicken was very, very bad for you. Imagine that! Pork was a bad word. Imagine that! Pork was supposed to be a feast. Now it's bad. Must be the pork here. They ate like rabbits. Maybe they didn't have that much money after all.... No sugar allowed either. The mistress said that sugar gave you cancer. What's cancer? Like rabbits, they ate lettuce and raw vegetables. One day they found out that she was giving their children fried food and they got very angry.

She had decided to save every penny she earned and send it home. But the girls wrote to her and said they wanted American clothes. Could she send them some? Reebok sport shoes, stretch jeans, thick socks... So one Saturday when she was in Queens visiting her distant relatives, she asked them to take her shopping. At first she was cautious. She only spent two hundred dollars. But the following weekend she thought that what she'd bought wasn't enough. Might as well buy more and send one big package home. It wasn't long before that was all she could think about. At night when she was lying in bed, she'd think of everything she had to buy on Saturday. The lists got longer and longer. She began needing things she never needed before. Suddenly twenty pairs of underwear weren't enough. She always needed more. And there was always that extra sweater she couldn't live without. And every time she got a new sweater she needed new pants. And the shoes to go with each new outfit. Every Saturday she ended up buying herself a new pair of shoes. There were so many shoes to buy! Then one hundred and fifty dollars weren't enough. She needed more; she needed to buy more. For the first time in her life she wanted, wanted, and suffered for wanting. Her heart ached when her eyes explored that last store window, and her arms were heavy with packages. She'd already spent all her salary. And that last pair of pants there, she wanted them! She began living for Saturday afternoon. That was all she could think about.

Paloma quit her job in the administration. She said she was too tired. With a sarcastic grin on their lips, her brothers, sisters, cousins, aunts, uncles, and even mother and father wondered why in the world she was so tired. After all, she hardly ever did anything in the house. Her daughter-in-law took care of that. The young girl cooked, cleaned, washed dishes, laundered, took care of the children, and gossiped about how Paloma spent her days either staring into blank space, or talking to herself, or telling the youngest children the weirdest stories, supposedly her adventures in America. Lies, all lies! One day her daughter-in-law asked her why she lied like that. Why tell the children stories of stairs that go upstairs by themselves? Why in the world make up stories when there were so many other things to do in life? Paloma replied that she'd already done all the other things in life.

A peaceful harmony, however, reigned in Paloma's house. Although her daughter-in-law loved to gossip about her and to complain about how she had to take care of all the household chores because Paloma wouldn't lift a finger, it so happened that Paloma's psychic retreat and Rodrigo's absence allowed this nineteen-year-old to be the head of the household. All the orders came from her. She ran the place. She took over. There was no clash between the two women; Paloma gave her daughter-in-law total power, and her daughter-in-law enjoyed that. In little or no time she stopped being a passionate pregnant teenager and became a bossy matron.

Word got to Rodrigo that Paloma was acting strange, that she was always tired, and that his daughter-in-law was now the mistress of the house. So Rodrigo decided to check this out and returned home for a four-day visit at the beginning of February. Instead of running to him with outstretched arms and at least ten contained hugs and kisses, Paloma hardly seemed to notice him. She was too busy getting ready to go out. She said she had an errand to run, that it was very important, and that she'd be back in a little while.

She walked in the direction of the market place and took the same bus she had taken before. This time she didn't have to travel as far. In a little village in the plains, two sisters were fighting. They both had long sharp nails and seemed to want to scratch each other's eyes out. They were also screeching like cats. The fight had begun over a lot of land six square feet big on which one of them had planted alfalfa for the pigs and watched the alfalfa grow until her sister had come to claim this portion of earth a bit bigger than a postage stamp. When Paloma arrived, they stopped screeching and fighting. "Which one of you is single?" Paloma asked. One of the she-cats raised her long-nailed hand and said, "I am." Paloma then followed her to her house, took the money, gave her the passport and instructions of what to do once she got to New York; send the passport back and fifty additional dollars a week for the next six months. They shook hands and said good-bye.

Three days later Rodrigo still hadn't left and Paloma dreamt she was flying. But Rodrigo was angry. He wanted his wife. He said he worked hard. He said he deserved what he wanted. He even threatened to abandon Paloma if her attitude didn't change. Paloma, in turn, gently replied that she was too nervous and too tired. The next day she could barely keep track of the time. She wondered whether it was two hours earlier or two hours later and kept asking her sex-starved husband what time it was. She said she was confused. She said she hadn't slept all night. Rodrigo left that day, threatening to return in a month, and that her attitude had better be different by then, or else.

She was in The Bronx. In a small factory. Four rows of sewing machines, side by side, and benches where four could fit but had to take turns lifting their elbows. There were women from every single country she had ever heard of. Bolivia, Colombia, Paraguay. They worked and talked all day, and each had their own transistor radio. They talked about clothes, makeup, men, husbands, and they also talked about themselves. The ones who had children brought their children to work. They ran up and down the narrow aisles between the benches. The men were on the other side of the wall. Everyone got fifteen cents per garment. They talked about birth control and how you had to pray to the moon if you didn't want a baby. They talked about the men on the other side of the wall. Some were worth marrying, others were going to succeed in this country, and like everywhere else there was one particular man that everyone was in love with and wanted. He was ambitious and handsome. He dressed well and smelled fine and even got a manicure every Saturday. His nails were clean and shiny. The women who didn't hate him called him an Adonis. The others hated him and called him the worst son of a whore that ever lived. Adalberto, that's what his name was, had broken some hearts in this factory. Those hearts were angry now. He'd even gotten five women on this side of the wall pregnant and obviously refused to marry each and every one of them. Two of his children often ran up and down the factory aisles.

At break time, one of her new friends pointed to Adalberto and said that that was him, and she fell madly in love the minute she set eyes on him. Besides, she'd heard so much about him that it was as if she'd already known him for two weeks. Suddenly she no longer felt as lonely in this new country. For two weeks it had appeared empty, but now he was here. She started loving every single corner of The Bronx because The Bronx was where he worked and lived.

She in turn lived with three couples and four women in a gloomy, windowless apartment near the factory. Her rent was thirty dollars a week. The rest she began to spend on tight sweaters, high-heeled shoes, tight stretch jeans, fancy dresses, makeup, love witchcraft, anything to attract him. She wondered how she had managed to live without his presence, without him being around. How boring life appeared up to now. So this was love. She hardly ate. She was determined to look like those girls on the covers of magazines. Every day she had to punch in at the factory at six a.m. She woke at four a.m. with a pounding, passionate heart. She was going to see him! Another day of trying to make him notice her! Life was worth living. Not even paradise could have competed with that factory. Without hesitating, she would have turned paradise down. Adalberto. She wanted to be wherever Adalberto was.

Every morning it took her forty-five minutes to get her hair just right and another forty-five minutes to make her face up. Deep green eye shadow and lots of mascara. Her eyes looked mysterious and big and wonderful. She also put lots of foundation and powder on. The last touch was the blush, from her cheekbone all the way up to her eyebrow. At five forty-five a.m., she was ready to go to the factory.

The rest of the day was spent trying to get a glimpse of Adalberto, as well as his attention. At break time, she'd

look for him in the crowd, discreetly sneak over to where
he was, call a girl friend over, begin a loud show-off conversation about her past and her adventures, and finally
burst out laughing, for example, so he'd turn his head
toward the laughter, certainly wondering what that laughing was all about. She'd then catch a glimpse of him in the
corner of her eye, and look away, or look down, feigning
both indifference and difference at the same time. One
evening when she was punching out, he walked up to her
and said that she had really caught his eye the day she
started working here, but that he hadn't dared ask her out
before. She was so pretty that she most probably belonged
to another man. So if she was engaged or anything, it'd be
O.K., he'd understand. He'd always like her though, he
even thought he was in love with her. Would she like to go
out with him? Of course she would! No, she meant that,
yes, she would. She meant it'd be nice.

   They went out on Saturday. While they were dancing,
he whispered in her ear that she should try being a model
or an actress. She was way too pretty to be at the factory.
She was the most beautiful woman in the factory. While
they were sitting at the bar he said that he loved her dress.
It was really sexy on her. He caressed her knee and told her
she had spectacular legs. They ordered more beers. He
caressed her thigh and told her that he'd noticed men looking at her while they were dancing and that he felt like
walking up to them and punching them because he just
couldn't stand to have a man setting eyes on her. In the car
he continued talking about how jealous he was. He fondled
her breasts and drew her closer to him, whispering I'm so
jealous, I'm so jealous. I'm so scared that another man will
take you away from me. I'll kill him, I swear. She thought
she was in heaven. He lifted her skirt. He said the factory

was just a stepping stone for him. He had many ideas. He said he was going to start his own business. He slipped her panty hose off, said he wanted to feel her skin, that was all. He said that his business was going to make him rich. In a month. He was going to begin in a month. The factory was just a stepping stone. In this country you have to be intelligent. If you don't have money you're nothing. He took her panties off. He said he had millions of ideas. He said he'd never been in love in his life until he first laid eyes on her. Then he laid down on top of her. There was barely enough room in the car, but there was enough room anyway. While they were making love, he kept begging her to marry him, to be his wife, forever. He said that if she didn't become his wife, he'd either kill himself or die.

The next day she announced her engagement at the factory and also talked about how horribly jealous he was. She loved it! The other women agreed that when you make a man jealous you've got him. She giggled and proudly continued talking about him. One of the jilted women slapped her and she slapped her back.

They spent Sunday together. A friend of Adalberto's lent him a dirty, stinky bachelor's apartment. Adalberto bought imitation champagne and wondered where they should spend their honeymoon. On Monday at the factory she talked about wedding dresses. On Monday night, once again, they made love in Adalberto's car. On Tuesday there was a new girl in the factory. Perhaps she had tighter jeans, higher heels, and tighter sweaters. Perhaps she was seventeen. But the important thing was that she was new. She'd also laugh out loud and pretend Adalberto wasn't around. On Tuesday night in the car, Adalberto told her that the new girl wasn't half as pretty as she was. He then proceeded to slip off her panty hose and panties. On Wednesday she caught him talking to the new girl at break time. She screeched and tried to scratch her face. Adalberto had to separate them. When they were alone, he repeated that she was indeed the love of his life, but they simply had to wait a while before they got married, a man like him needed more room, he had millions of ideas and was going to start a new business next month. Since she didn't get the point, he said he didn't deserve her. He almost cried. Then he cried. She tried to comfort him. Everything would be all right. Adalberto didn't think so. He complained about being too jealous. They made love. Then Adalberto got angry. He accused her of flirting with some other man in the factory. She swore it wasn't true, but he hit her and pushed her around. She cried. On Thursday morning she announced that they'd quarreled. All her co-workers were interested and wanted to hear more about it. She cried and she cried. He started ignoring her. Maybe this was just a lovers' quarrel. He was so jealous! She waited. Then she slowly became friends with the other jilted ones. Two weeks later the new girl was also a jilted girl. She cried. Adalberto had promised to marry her! He'd talked about how jealous he was! Said he'd never had this passionate feeling for a woman in his whole life! He even threatened to commit suicide! She joined the club. They hated all the new girls that came to the factory. At least they hated them until the engagement was called off. They also hated Adalberto. But they continued aching for him. He'd been working there for two years, but the factory was just a stepping stone. Next month he'd start his own business. He said he was intelligent and had millions of ideas.

Paloma told Rodrigo that she never wanted to be with a man again. Men were liars and traitors. Rodrigo pushed her around and hit her and tried to force her. Nothing

would do. She said she hated men. He finally left the next
day and threatened to return in a month and that her attitude had better be different by then, or else.

Word started getting to Paloma unexpectedly. She even
had to turn down some of the women who came to her
with their requests. But whenever she had dreamt she was
flying, she usually accepted their money. Only cash. Mean-
while, in the capital, Rodrigo was surprised to encounter
so many traveling women named Paloma Sánchez. At first
it had only happened once a month, then twice a month,
now once a week some common-looking Paloma Sánchez
would be traveling to New York. And they never returned.
Nobody expected them to anyway. They left and disappeared into the American woodwork. So far he had counted fifteen women by the name of Paloma Sánchez. This,
combined with the hard time he was having at home, most
likely gave him the idea that Paloma Sánchez, his Paloma
Sánchez, was probably not the only fish in the sea. There
even seemed to be a surplus of her namesakes!

So, Rodrigo ended up taking a mistress by the name of
Gladys. Perhaps Gladys wasn't as pretty as his Paloma
Sánchez, but she was sweet and available and always eager
to see him. He had grown weary of his distant wife. Not
only that, but Gladys was photogenic. She looked beautiful
on a developed photograph, which allowed Rodrigo to sat-
isfy his lifelong dream: everlasting proof of what a woman
of his had once been. He even wanted to have children
with Gladys. Just so the hypothetical children and grandchildren could admire her photos in the future.

Back home, Paloma could barely keep up. At least the
flying didn't make her as nervous anymore. It was even
beginning to bore her. The taking off, the landing, those
people in uniform with their questions, ready to send you

back if you make the slightest mistake, she felt like an expert. She was more than used to landing in New York and disappearing into the woodwork, as they say. At four a.m. she was putting blue eye shadow on her eyelids, at five a.m. she was sleeping in a little bed in a little room, either on Park Avenue, or on Fifth Avenue, or on Central Park South or West, at six a.m. she was mowing lawns in Montauk, Long Island, at seven a.m. she was painting a house in Poughkeepsie, New York, an hour later she was madly in love, rushing to have a cup of coffee with a new love, or she was missing her husband, or she was missing the love she'd left behind to come here and make lots of money. It's terrible to miss someone. The whole country seems empty if that one person isn't around. She'd then be hating her lover and saying terrible things about him and wishing he were sick, old, in a wheelchair, paralyzed. She made friends with all the women who'd loved him and together they'd wonder if he'd ever really marry. By mid-morning she'd be reading letters from her children; she had forty children now and six at her breast, seven on her lap. She was carrying three or four different children in her womb, but she went to a clinic and got rid of one because she had been forced in Brooklyn. This kind of thing never happened in her land, to get rid of a child. Before this she'd never even heard of it. At lunchtime she was either having a meat-less, salt-less, sugar-less, sodium-less, and choles-terol-free meal for her figure, or trying on tight jeans in the stores of Queens, or gossiping about the people who stayed back home, the ones who tried coming to New York and had failed, the ones who had made it and already had a car and a refrigerator, the ones who hadn't made it and had gone to jail, either here or there. Or she was aching for some new man and she was convinced that it was really love this time. Or she was still aching for that same one, who was now engaged for the fifteenth time since she'd arrived. Why was he so handsome? She loved him so and wished he were dead right now. Or perhaps he'd catch that dreadful disease that the buses and the subway and the radio talked about all the time. On Wednesday evening, she was unfaithful to her husband then she missed him terribly because he was such a good man. Then, after having finished painting the house in Poughkeepsie, she started taking the paint off her hair with turpentine. The next day she lost her index finger to a lawnmower. The needle from one of the sewing machines went right through her thumb. On Friday she had a date and she was passionately in love. She bought a party dress and high heels and fancy stockings. And she cleaned offices until twelve midnight. Now she was flying again. Her husband was waiting for her in New York and she hadn't seen him in three years. She was only twenty years old. Then she died. It happened suddenly. After having cleaned the lawyer's office, she was waiting for the train. It happened in the subway. Four men killed her. It hurt. They named her Jane Doe and it was cold in the morgue. Nobody to claim her body. Then she became an alcoholic. Then she was a drug addict. Then she met that horrible man who promised her the world. All she had to do was carry a suitcase from New York to Miami. One day they caught her. The suitcase was full of flour. They put her in prison. Oh, she was so happy the day her husband got his green card! That meant they could lead normal lives. No more fear of getting caught by immigration and sent back. Out of the woodwork. No more hiding.

Paloma's husband left her for Gladys. She hardly noticed he was going. As a matter of fact she was a bit relieved; a peaceful harmony reigned in the house when he was absent. But she didn't even have time to wonder how she felt now that she was an abandoned woman. It was Tuesday. On Tuesdays she rushed to the post office. Her passport always came back on Tuesday.

She asked Rodrigo if she could leave for New York. She said she wanted to start a new life there. Her daughter-in-law had turned out to be an excellent matron, so they didn't need her at home. Paloma even spoke English now. Rodrigo didn't seem to mind, he was too busy admiring and showing everyone the latest photographs of Gladys.

They said good-bye at the airport. Not that he accompanied her there, but that's where he worked. His last words were, "I'll probably never see you again." Paloma boarded an Eastern Airlines flight to Miami. She was thirty years old, three times a grandmother, and as beautiful as ever. She had money, she spoke English, she dressed well. And she knew customs and immigration by heart for having gone through there so so many times. She also knew what the questions would be and how to answer them. They'd ask her to sign her name several times, but that was her signature. Anyway, she had nothing to fear, she had a passport, quite a bit of money, and a visa.

Passport. Your name? How long do you plan to stay? Why? Where? How much money are you bringing? He opened her passport and looked at her photo then looked at her then back at the photo then back at her and smiled. He asked, "Amiga, do you think we're blind?" He called a co-worker of his and exclaimed, "Hey, Joe, look at this! Our amiga here must think we're blind. What do you think?" Joe thought out loud, "I think we've got one here." They both asked her if she really thought they'd fall for that. They had thousands of her kind leaking in through here and they had, what they called, the professional eye. "I can spot them from a mile away," Joe said. "Amiga, it's not that easy to sneak into the United States," the other one added. "Did you really think we'd fall for this?" he asked and slapped the passport. "You're way too pretty."

They showed her to a small waiting area, offered her coffee, then dinner. She waited hours. Some of her people were also in there. Waiting. Waiting for the plane that would take them back. It was hard getting into the United States, they agreed. You couldn't just slip by the customs officials like that. They had the "eye." Even the men cried. They'd be put in jail the minute they got back. But Paloma's eyes remained dry. "Aren't you upset?" someone asked her. "No. There are sixty-seven of me here already," she replied.

HEADSHOTS

✘ Virgil Suárez ✘

Payne's instructions sounded simple enough. I placed the yellowish, diamond-shaped piece of paper in my mouth and chewed on it, just like gum. "Just like gum," that's what Payne kept saying while we sat in the parked car. He repeated it to Cuervo, who looked at his own reflection on Payne's sunglasses, smiled and began to chew, then to Mason. But Mason declined. It induced guilt and paranoia. Having once tried pot way back in high school, he did not want to chance it with acid.

"Com'on, Mace," Payne said, "I bought four hits. One is yours."

Again Mason refused.

"Very well," Payne continued, "I'll just have to save it for another time, another place." Carefully, he folded the extra hit in the wax paper and put it in his hand-tooled leather wallet—a Christmas gift from his adoptive parents who lived in Pennsylvania.

"When does it start to take effect?" Cuervo wanted to know, anxious to get to the French Quarter.

"Give it twenty to thirty minutes," Payne said and, after combing his red hair, scratched his beard with his thin, long fingers. "You'll know when it happens. All you do then is spit out the paper."

"What happens when *it* happens?" Mason said. He looked at the rear view mirror.

"Hey, hey," Payne said to him, "don't ask. Haven't you ever heard of first-hand experience?"

"Leave him alone," I said. Mason was my roommate, had been so since our freshman year. Because he was small and extremely thin, I often couldn't help but feel brotherly toward him. We were all seniors at LSU and had come down to New Orleans just to break the routine. "Besides," I added, "it's a good idea one of us doesn't drop this shit, you know. Mason'll keep us straight, right Mace?"

"Yeah," said Cuervo, his jaws working fast, "for all we know we might start freaking out or something and…"

"Nobody's going to freak," Payne said. Of the group, he knew the most about drugs. His was a sort of socio-anthropological-hip interest. From pot to peyote. He often mentioned Castañeda's book, *The Teachings of Don Juan*, as a source of reference.

"It's getting too fucking hot inside this car," Mason spoke up, rolled up his window, removed his keys from the ignition, and opened the door. Payne followed him out.

Cuervo, who was from Grass Valley, California, smiled at me and said, "Shit…and to think that the closest I've ever been to doing drugs was this one time I lit up my ex-girlfriend's pubic hairs and inhaled the smoke."

I got out of the car, wondering if the stuff had already reached my blood stream and was on its way up. If acid was anything like alcohol, which it wasn't, then any sudden movements might trigger the first effects.

As we started to walk up Chartres Street, where Mason had parked the Toyota, past the mortuary at the corner, I thought about dying, but I snapped out of it when Cuervo finished telling Mason about burning his girlfriend's pubic hair this one time he took her camping. "Christ, it was so dark inside the tent. I found my handy Bic lighter, flicked it, and swoosh!"

"What did you need light for?" said Mason, who deserved credit for having come up with a nickname like Cuervo. Cuervo's real name was Alex, and he had a reputation for providing tequila chasers during progressive beer parties at the dorms.

Payne laughed, perhaps because he was as familiar with Mason's way of reasoning as I was. Sometimes late at night Payne came to our room, wired out on God only knew what, to write his anthro papers on Mason's computer.

"Have you ever tried to put on a condom in the dark?" Cuervo asked Mason.

Payne said he always carried his on him, just like his American Express. "Never know when I'll be called on to hide the salami," he said and smiled.

At that exact moment I shuddered. It felt as if somebody had taken an ice cube and run it along my spine, but I didn't mention it. I just kept on walking, hands in my Levis, down Elysian Fields.

We were heading in the general direction of the French Market, which at this time of the afternoon was supposed to be packed with tourists. We had no particular destination in mind; the more aimless, the better, that's what Cuervo had said.

The mud and trash smell of the river hung in the air as we walked. I blamed it on the heat and the rain, the fact that the humidity level rose so high. Overcast sky overhead, which meant more rain in the evening. We weren't planning to stay overnight. Mason had to return to Baton Rouge to write a computer program.

Cutting across a huge, empty parking lot that had all kinds of weeds growing between cracks and potholes, it hit me again. This time it lasted longer, a fleeting sensation of instability and light-headedness accompanied the chill. "I felt something," I said to Payne, who was walking with Mason ahead of me and Cuervo.

"Touch the tip of your nose," Payne said and stopped. "Is it clammy?"

I touched my nose, but didn't feel anything.

"My mouth is dry," Cuervo said, running his tongue over his bloodless lips.

"It's taking effect a lot sooner than I thought. Give it five more minutes," Payne said and once again started to walk.

I heard Mason ask him if he felt anything, to which Payne answered that a reaction for a veteran took a lot longer.

A beat-up, Ford pick-up drove up and parked in front of a rundown oyster warehouse. The black man behind the wheel saluted us. We saluted him back. Oysters, what a way to make a living!

Cuervo and Mason started humming the "Peter Gun" theme. Compared to Cuervo, Mason looked like a crawfish next to a lobster—he was that small. But under the I LOVE N.Y. t-shirt, there was a strong body. Mason had been on the swim team and had run cross-country in high school.

I knew everybody's reasons for coming. Mason wanted to buy a gift for his sister, who was having a baby. Payne came so that he could browse through all the record stores for replacement albums that were stolen from the university's radio station, where he DJed part-time. He wanted to be promoted to music director before graduation.

Cuervo had all the reason in the world for wanting to be there. All week he quarreled with his fiancee over the phone, until Thursday night when she called at the dorms

and told him the ring was in the mail. Since then he had
been staying up late and drinking up a storm, but in the
morning, after taking four Tylenols, he managed to survive
the hangovers.

New Orleans, I figured, seemed like the best place for
somebody like Cuervo to visit and forget about things for a
while. It wasn't the first time the four of us had driven
down from Baton Rouge. What I liked most about the
Quarter was that everywhere you stood and looked, there
was fast-paced action and bumper-to-bumper fun. I
remembered the first time I drove down with Mason: on
Bourbon Street we saw this guy go into a strip joint and,
just as fast as he walked in, a bouncer threw him out for
shouting an ugly remark at one of the female imperson-
ators.

This time, Payne convinced me to come down; he
knew that if I didn't, Mason might change his mind, and
then they would have been without a ride down.

"Wait a minute!" Mason said. "Jesus, I just thought of
something!"

"What?" Cuervo said, squinting.

"Xavier, my god, my god!" Mason said to me. "Man,
what have you done? What if they test you for this shit
before a game or something?"

"It's too late now," Payne said. "He can't throw up the
stuff, he can't drink anything for it, can't have his stomach
flushed. Nothing, once it gets in the system..."

"Fucking A," Cuervo said, then softly, "fine thing
we've done here."

"And it's going to last for roughly eight hours," said
Payne and continued walking.

Mason got my attention. I knew our goalkeeper had
been tested for steroids. If they tested me and found a trace

of acid, they would take away my scholarship and kick me off of the soccer team, which meant my chances of ever making it into the pros were shot. Playing soccer was one of the few things I did right.

"I can always dig for bones, right, Payne?" I said.

"You make anthropology sound like dog's work," Cuervo said.

The French Market, when we got there, wasn't as crowded as I expected. Sure, there were tourists, mostly people trying to work up an appetite by walking around the fruit and jewelry stands. Behind us rose the sound of hooves clicking against the asphalt—horse drawn carriages, one of the very few traditions left in that city.

Cuervo slowed down and pointed to a blond woman who was wearing a very small tank top rolled up in a strange way to look like a bra. She was with this older man who was trying on a pair of space-age sunglasses.

"Probably somebody he called up," Payne said. "Who would want to fuck that old geezer?"

"An escort," Mason said.

"Keep it down, guys," I said.

It looked like Payne was right, though. A lot of businessmen came to New Orleans for conventions and ended up being escorted by beautiful women.

We approached the stand for a better look at the blond. She flirted with the Oriental salesman. What did she want, I thought, a bargain? Cuervo tried on a couple of pairs of shades. One of them looked like the round kind John Lennon wore, except these were mirrored.

Finally, to the salesman's dismay, the man and the blond walked away empty-handed. So the salesman turned to us and asked if we needed help.

"How much for these?" Cuervo asked, taking off the shades.

"Three dollars," said the salesman.

"Give him two bucks," Payne said.

The salesman nodded and smiled. A large, golden medallion hung from his neck. "Cheap already," he said, "can't sell cheaper."

Cuervo returned the shades to their place on the plastic display and we moved on.

As I walked I realized that the people going by were glowing. This took me by surprise. It wasn't so much that they were glowing, but that a brilliant prism, or aura, moved with them. A florescense. I looked at my hands, but what I saw on the other people was not happening to me. Instead, my fingers trembled. I couldn't stop them, so I stuck my hands way inside my pockets. Then the shakes started to happen in shorter intervals.

I caught up with Payne and asked him real quietly if people were likely to notice any strange behavior. "I mean," I said, "can they tell I'm under the influence?"

"No," Payne said, "just relax, man. Nobody knows, not unless you tell them."

"I'm not telling anybody," I said, "but, Jesus, I feel weird. My hands are shaking."

"Make them stop," he said, "you can, you know."

I brought my hands out of my pockets, stared at my fingers and chewed up nails and thought about making them stop. The tiny wrinkles over my knuckles criss-crossed, making deep patterns on my flesh. The more I stared, the more intense the sight became. Coming out of my pores, the black hairs grew out of proportion. There was a rough texture to them.

"See," Payne said, "they're no longer shaking."

Cuervo walked over and said to look up at the sky.
Payne, Cuervo and I stood by a parking meter looking up
at the clouds. Mason watched too. "Wow!" Payne said.
"Check it out."

The clouds formed right before our very eyes. From
see-through air to swirls to white plumes, they evolved.

"Ah, guys," Mason said, tapping us on the shoulder, "I
think we better move along, huh? There are people going
by and looking up."

"Don't you see it, Mace?" I said, still looking up at the
sky.

"What I see is three loonies," he said and egged us to
move on.

We were his responsibility now, I thought. My heart
beat fast—I could hear it thumping, or was a horse
approaching?

"I'm hungry," Payne said, "let's stop at Frank's and get
a muffuletta."

"Can we eat?" Cuervo asked.

Mason said, "I think we should stay out of public
places."

"Be serious," Payne told Mason, then to Cuervo he
said, "We can eat and drink."

So now we were on our way to Frank's. At the next
corner we spotted a young woman trying to break into a
white Chrysler convertible which had its top up. The coat
hanger she was using to open the door with kept turning
in the wrong direction. Her cheeks, I noticed, were flushed
as though she had been crying. Every time she missed the
tip of the lock, she pulled and yanked the wire out, cursing,
bent its tip into a smaller hook and stuck it back in again.

She was great-looking. Short, feathered hair pushed
over her ears, which earrings the size of an M&M accentu-

ated. Though her eyes were wet, they looked intense and lusciously green. Pissed, she removed her bracelets, put them on the hood, and tried one more time.

Cuervo crossed the street and approached her. Then we followed but stopped on this side of the car. He apparently said something that made her stop.

"You guys should pay me for baby-sitting," Mason said and walked over to rescue Cuervo from embarrassing himself.

Without asking any questions as to why the girl was trying to break inside the car, Cuervo proceeded to help her. Mason stood by and watched. Payne and I joined him.

"This is my boyfriend's car," she explained, "so it's not like I'm breaking in."

"What happened?" Payne asked. "I don't see the keys in the ignition."

"No," she said, "*he's* got the keys. I just want to open the car and wait for him inside."

Payne looked at me as if to say, Yeah, sure, and she just won the Miss America beauty pageant.

"I can help you hot-wire the bastard," Cuervo said, his hands holding the wire steady.

"Whoa!" I said, fully aware that Cuervo was quite capable of doing so. "She doesn't want to take the car, right?"

"No, I want to sit in it," she said, then, "Look, thanks for the help, but..."

"No trouble," Cuervo said and let go of the coat hanger. Again, she took over.

All four of us stood back and watched her work. She was dressed in going-out clothes: gray, tight-fitting slacks, black pumps and a pinkish, long-sleeved shirt with the cuffs rolled up.

"So you just want to break in and sit inside," Payne said in a mocking tone.

She sighed and stopped, leaving the wire sticking out between the window and top. Her eyes watered as she leaned against the door and explained what was happening.

Her boyfriend, the asshole, had brought her to the Cavalier for a couple of drinks, but then for no reason at all he ignored her and started to play machine poker with this other woman in the place. Her boyfriend was an alcoholic with a terrible habit of spoiling a good time after several drinks.

"Sounds like a real jerk," Cuervo said.

Throughout all this I noticed Mason acting real jittery, not knowing what to do with his hands. Payne just stood there with an ugly smirk on his pale lips.

I knew that if I stared too hard, she might tell me to fuck off or something, but I couldn't stop looking at her eyes, her pupils dilated according to the way her head moved.

"Forget the car," Cuervo said. "Why don't you join us? We are on our way to lunch."

I checked the time on my watch. It was sixteen past two.

"Yeah," Payne said, "it might give your boyfriend something to think about."

She looked at each of us, then grabbed her bracelets and put them on one by one. "This is not the first time this has happened," she said, "the bastard likes attention..."

I sensed she was trying to make up her mind, so I told her that she'd have a good time if she came with us.

"Where are you guys from?" she asked.

"We're students at LSU," Mason said.

Payne looked at him as if Mason had said the wrong thing, then he introduced us.

"I'm May," she said, shaking hands.

Cuervo held her hand the longest. For a minute I thought he was going to put his arm around her. Her hand, when she took mine, felt as smooth as a flower. Hers were the types of hands oblivious to hardships.

"Well, May," Payne said, "gonna join us or what?"

"Sure," she said, then looking at the car, "why not? He probably won't even miss me."

Next thing I knew, May was walking with us, between Payne and Cuervo. Mason and I fell back to have a good look at her ass.

On the way to Frank's, our conversation sounded trivial, mostly stuff about school. She revealed a couple of interesting things about herself. One, she had been married to a rich guy in Lafayette; two, she divorced him after a year—she mentioned boredom as the reason; and three, she worked as manager of a shoe store on Canal Street.

Having been born and raised in Jackson, Mississippi, she spoke with a heavy accent. Her voice, though, was suave, and for some reason it reminded me of shaving cream.

She was talking about her new boyfriend when we arrived at Frank's. At first glance the place looked too crowded, but Payne spoke to a waiter, who took us all the way to the back. We watched him clear the table, then after he wiped it clean, we sat down and he brought us menus. I already knew what I wanted, so I didn't even bother to open the menu. When the waiter returned to take our order, I told him I didn't want anything. The last thing I needed was an upset stomach. I felt jumpy enough as it was.

"Nothing to drink?" the waiter said.

"Come on, X," Cuervo said, "at least have a beer."

I looked at Payne for approval, but he was scraping something that wasn't there off his hand. That's when I began to worry. "All right," I said, "bring me a Dixie."

"Creature of habit," Payne said.

The waiter repeated the orders, then walked away and brought us the drinks. May, too, ordered a beer. When it came, she immediately put her lips to the bottle, tilted her long neck back and drank. I sat staring at the way the foam rose and how the individual suds popped on the surface.

For a while nobody spoke, then Mason brought up the cultural scene in New York: poetry readings, summer park concerts, Off-off-Broadway plays, and the abundance of art galleries. Not that she didn't seem interested, but May looked like she had started to wonder what she was doing there with us. You could tell by the aloof gleam in her pretty eyes.

"Ever been on a Kawasaki?" Cuervo asked May.

"I can't say I have," May said, peeling the label off the bottle with her unpolished fingernails.

"Alex here likes fast bikes," Payne jumped in. "He races them in California."

"Quake City, U.S.A.," Cuervo added.

Mason kept an eye on all of us; he probably expected a whole avalanche of strange actions and reactions.

I drank and while drinking my hand touched the tip of my nose, which felt cold, just like a dog's. But the truth was I felt all right, more nervous from knowing what I had done than from the actual effect of the acid.

"Where are you from?" May asked, looking at me.

"Florida," I told her, "I'm from Miami."

"I stopped there once," she said, "on my way to honeymoon in Jamaica."

The sandwiches arrived and the waiter asked if we wanted more beer. Payne ordered another round.

What happened next could not be prevented. Bits and pieces of the other conversations going on around our table became audible, too loud and clear. A whole collage of words. My lack of concentration unnerved me. "...on the plane," the voices went, "...stewardess spilled some coffee on this baby...mother didn't complain...she covered... nothing like a fast bike...stewardess got worried...lean forward...full throttle...baby didn't cry...eighty miles per hour... How come you never eat all your food, Mace?..."

I shook my head several times to make the voices stop, but it was no use. I got scared. "...it turned out the co-pilot came over...nothing like speed, you know...the man with the woman got nervous...at night I used to take this curve in my BMW...the baby was dead...Jesus... You know what, May?... What Payne? ...they took him away from the woman... If we're acting a little strange it's because... No, Payne, don't tell her...you could see the little stitch marks on the baby's stomach...go around the curve as close to the inside as possible...the motherfuckers stuffed the child with cocaine...."

"Christ!" I said, and the voices stopped. Everybody looked over at me. Mason covered his face with his hands.

"What's the matter, X?" Payne asked.

"Nothing, nothing," I said, "I gotta go to the bathroom."

I stood up and hurried away from our table down this corridor to the bathroom. In front of the mirror over the sink, I looked at my face. My eyes were open real wide, like a horse's. Sweat drops ran from my hairline down my forehead and temples. Quickly, I twisted open the faucet and splashed water on my face. The surface of the sink warped and undulated and the faucet started to melt. "Shit," I said over and over.

Somebody knocked on the door. It was Mason. "Xavier, are you all right?" he said, then, "Open the door."

I let him in and told him what was happening. He put his hands on my arms and held me steady. "Take it easy," he said, "they're just hallucinations. Nothing that you are seeing is real, okay. Just…just keep that in mind."

"I'll be fine," I said, opening my eyes. Mason's face looked like Mason's face. There was a slight resemblance to Griffin Dunne, the actor, except Mason had brown hair and a mustache.

"We're getting out of here," he said. "Payne just gave May the extra hit."

"Why'd you let him do it?"

"She insisted. She's done it before."

"Oh, shit," I said, "we need to go somewhere until this is over."

Mason led me out of the bathroom. When we got to the table, all the food was gone. It was as if we had just walked in and the whole thing was going to repeat itself.

Payne collected the money to pay for the bill. How could he do it, I thought: concentrate on minimal shit like adding up the bill? May looked at me and smiled. Her jaws were already moving, but that wasn't gum she was chewing. She put her hands on my arm and said, "We're going to have fun."

"Let's walk around," Cuervo said.

"Are you up to it, X?" Payne asked.

"Let's go to my apartment," May said and told us she lived off St. Charles in the garden district.

Mason agreed that that would be the best thing to do—he wanted us off the streets. I pulled Payne aside and told him I didn't think I was having too good a trip.

"It happens sometimes the first time," Payne said, looking at the money in his hands.

"I don't like what's going on."

"Okay then," Payne said, approaching the cash register, "let's go to her place."

We walked out of Frank's and headed back to the car. Being out again helped, but before we reached the car it started to rain. We had to run the rest of the way, not Cuervo though. He walked. By the time he arrived, Mason had already put a plastic bag over the seat so that the water wouldn't seep through when Cuervo sat down.

Payne tried to make a move on May. He told her about how he planned to buy a motorcycle and travel all over the country this summer. He was going to stop at the University of Arizona in Tucson and apply for graduate studies in anthro.

Tuning out, I sat upfront with Mason and watched the patterns the raindrops formed on the windshield. I saw the faces of animals, things, and places. My father's face appeared. I heard him arguing with somebody, probably my mother from whom he was divorced. My father was the president of a bank in Miami. He used to take me and my brother, who is five years younger than I, fishing in the Everglades. One time we saw this water moccasin cutting across a canal, then all of a sudden an alligator surfaced and bit the snake in two. My mother thought he was a failure, but then she thought everybody was a failure. She wasn't too excited when I received the soccer scholarship. As far as she was concerned, college was for an education, not sports.

Again, I shook my head to stop thinking. It throbbed. When I looked at my watch and saw that only two hours had passed, I panicked. Things were bound to escalate.

❧❧

As much as I remembered, May's apartment looked impressive. It was an upstairs apartment with high ceilings from which chandeliers and wicker fans hung. The floor had an incredible lustre to it, as though it had just been waxed and buffed. The most striking feature was this aquarium over the fireplace, which reached the ceiling. In it were anemones and clown fish, angel fish, starfish, and a lion fish which moved slowly all alone in one corner of the aquarium.

Mardi Gras porcelain and feather masks adorned the walls behind the plush furniture. On the glass coffee table sat several *Cosmopolitans* and *Vogues*, a mother-of-pearl vial, and an ashtray made out of seashells and sand dollars.

"Is this your place?" Payne asked her.

"No, it's my boyfriend's," she said and excused herself to go to another room.

Alone in the fairly large living room, we tried not to look at each other. Cuervo approached the fireplace and stood in front of the aquarium looking at the fish.

"Check this out," Payne said, pointing to a black stereo system. He started to finger through the record collection. "What the fuck!" he said. "The Bee Gees. Tsk-tsk!"

"I think we should get out of here," Mason said.

"Relax man," Payne said, "maybe if I find a Barry Manilow album I'll put it on."

"This guy," Cuervo said, "has a strange taste in fish."

May returned with a porcelain box and sat on the sofa. "I've been saving this Columbian, but I might as well share it," she said, opening the box.

"Dig in," Payne said.

On the coffee table she opened two pieces of Zip rolling paper, pinched some of the pot out of the box, and made two lines on the paper. Payne helped her roll the joints. Once ready, she lit one and Payne the other.

"Come on, guys," she said, inhaling, "this is great stuff."

Cuervo and I moved closer to the coffee table—I thought the pot might help to slow the acid down. Mason stood by the wall, a feathery mask in his hand.

"Mason, you want some?" May said.

"Let's not waste it," Payne said.

Mason put the mask on and said, "Sure, why not? I'm not going to be a party pooper."

"Atta boy, Mace," Cuervo said and patted him on the back.

Payne handed Mason the joint and let him inhale a couple of drags before taking the joint back. Payne's greed upset me, but it really wasn't so much the greed as the fact that what he wanted was control. Always, he wanted to be the lead man.

So. We all sat around the coffee table, May being the center of attention, and got high. I had my share of hallucinations. I saw insects crawling over May's face. I saw the feathers on the mask on Mason's face turn into a black crow which fluttered around the room and picked up a tornado of dust and fashion magazine pages. I saw another bird fly over the aquarium and dive for the lion fish. The fish, their multicolors blended like paint on a canvas.

After tuning in to a jazz and blues station on the radio, Payne took the liberty of rolling up a couple more joints, one of which Mason smoked all to himself as he stretched out on the couch. His free hand rested on May's hair.

May sat still, smiling foolishly like the rest of us, the absent-minded way people smile when they get high. The more I looked at her the more in love I fell, but, I thought, I would not bother to make a move when Payne and Cuervo were trying so hard. They were flanking her.

She was saying something about the guy she was married to. Remembering how she lived when she lived with maids, fancy cars, a house big enough for people to sleep over when they partied, she began to cry. Neither Payne nor Cuervo reacted, but I moved closer to her and hugged her. She hugged me back hard, her warm breath hitting the side of my neck.

"You know," she said, "you grow up and the older you get, the more you realize that fucked-up people don't change."

I told her I knew what she was talking about. My own parents were as fucked up as people can get, and neither one made the effort to change, to improve their lives. I remembered the night my father left the house for good: very little was said by him or my mother. They just looked at each other, and you knew by the glow in their eyes they hated each other, not because of what they had become, but because of what each had depleted in the other. I tried to spare my little brother the sight of my father ranting about the house, kicking and throwing things, but he saw, he knew what was happening.

When May kissed me, she did it so quickly that nobody saw. Payne and Cuervo were talking about the aquarium. They were tripping. Mason had fallen asleep on the couch. I took advantage and slipped my hand inside her shirt. Her nipples got hard.

She was unzipping my fly when we heard somebody trying to unlock the door. She didn't even try to move away, so I pushed her away and stood up. The quick motion gave me a headrush.

The door opened and May's boyfriend walked in. He was tall and robust, but having had too much to drink, he was clumsy. His first words were: "You fucking bitch!"

"These are my friends," May said.

"I don't give a fuck who they are," he said and threw the keys at her. The keys landed on the coffee table, but the glass didn't break. The noise startled Mason, who sprung from the sofa and, before you knew it, he was standing up.

"I'm moving out," May told him, starting to roll another joint.

Payne and Cuervo moved to the door as soon as May's boyfriend got out of the way.

"Moving out," he said, "you are moving out, eh?"

"You're drunk, so shut up," she said.

Mason headed for the door.

"Ah, come on pals," May's boyfriend said, "not leaving so soon, are you?"

"Look," I told him, "I think you've had a lot to drink."

"Oh yeah," he said, "you believe…no, you think. You think I've had too much to drink."

"Let's get out of here," Payne said.

"What's the rush?" the man said. "Don't you guys want to stay? Maybe she'll let one of you bang her."

"Fuck you!" May said as calmly as possible without destroying all the work she was putting into rolling the joint.

"There's no need to talk to her like that," Mason said.

"Perhaps it is you whom Lady Death here wants," he said to Mason.

"Come on, guys," Mason said, "let's get out…"

The man stopped him by the door. He held Mason's arm in a tight grip. You could tell because Mason's flesh turned white.

"Let go," Mason said.

"Let him go, stupid," May said.

"Let's all drink and get high," he said.

That was when Mason lost his cool and let the man have it right on the jaw. We heard the snap when Mason's fist landed. Something cracked and I thought every bone in Mason's hand was broken.

The man fell against a chair. Quickly, he got up and went for Mason, but Payne and Cuervo stopped him. The man was drunk, but not drunk enough to stay pinned. He broke loose and this time attacked May. He grabbed her hair and slapped her a couple of times.

"Stop killing me, fucking bitch!" he said and slapped her again.

May got on her knees, unbuckled his pants, and unzipped his fly. I couldn't stand the sight, so I left, the guys following. As we hurried down the stairs, we heard the man asking us to stay.

We were speechless. We climbed inside the car and took off. Mason drove back to the Market, found a parking space, parked the car, and got out. I was sure his hand was hurting by the way he let it hang by his side.

"Hey, Mace," said Cuervo, "where are you going?"

Mason didn't say anything, just kept on walking. We got out of the car and followed him to this river landing between Café du Monde and the old Dixie brewery. We crossed the railroad tracks and went down the steps of the landing to the edge of the water. Mason sat down and leaned against the piling.

The sun was setting and a light drizzle started to fall. We sat next to Mason and looked at the murky water making ripples against the rocks. This was as good a place as any to sober up, I thought. We kept looking at each other as if one of us could offer an explanation to what had happened, but we didn't speak. Payne closed his eyes. Cuervo took out his pocket knife and carved something on the side of the piling. Mason kept opening and closing his hand, rubbing it.

I opted for the sound of the water lapping against the rocks when the boats passed, their bullhorns echoing in the distance.

◆◆

After Mason sobered up, he drove us back to Baton Rouge while the rest of us slept. It wasn't until several days later that we got together in Cuervo's dorm room and started to talk about what had happened in New Orleans. Payne discarded the whole situation as a bad trip. "That guy was fucked-up, all right," Cuervo said. But Mason, Mason was superstitious. He said it was a bad sign, an omen of bad luck. What he thought May stood for he didn't want to say, but whatever it was, was bad. Payne asked me what I thought. I told him we should forget about the whole thing, forget anything happened. "Payne's right," Cuervo added, "we were all tripping anyway." We promised ourselves never to talk about it, although I was sure that if they were asked, their versions would be as different as fall and spring.

During the last game before spring break, I injured my knee. Nothing the ten-day vacation wouldn't fix. I came home and found out from my mother that my little brother was arrested for possession. He and a friend were caught with a whole rock of crack in the high school bathroom, just enough to be arrested and booked.

My father and I went to see my brother at the juvenile center today. On the way, my father complained that it was all my mother's fault for my brother's upbringing. "That kid's a troublemaker," my father said, both hands on the wheel. He said he didn't understand what had gone wrong. I didn't know if he was referring to his marriage to my mother or to the problem with my brother.

Then he told me how much like him I was, and that he was so proud of me. He just knew that what had happened to my brother could never happen to me.

"You're no fuck-up, you're straight, you know what I mean?" he said and smiled without looking at me.

That was what got me thinking about that crazy day in New Orleans.

LIBERATION IN LITTLE HAVANA

✂ Marisella Veiga ✂

More than an hour had passed since Nelson Jr. had left for the job interview, yet Marta had not started sewing the stack of collars that was due in two days. Instead, she had wandered through the rooms of her small house considering what might happen if her son was hired as a full-time assistant librarian downtown. Her meditation ended in the dining room, next to a mahogany table.

She adjusted her cotton dress so the seams laid properly on her hip bones. The sewing could wait. She would make *arroz con pollo* to celebrate a victory this afternoon. Marta took the two plastic breakfast mats off the kitchen table and shook the pale crumbs of Cuban bread into the garbage can. With a damp sponge in hand, she returned to wipe the table.

Marta loved her table and all the things in her house, despite much of the furnishings being second hand. Her husband Nelson, mother Elena and she had rented the little wood and concrete house on Southwest Sixth Avenue right after coming into exile almost thirty years ago. The family's fine linens and dishes and furniture had been left behind in Cuba. They set up housekeeping in the new land with mismatched dishes and three old kitchen chairs that had been donated by the church. As soon as they found jobs, Marta began buying other necessary items at the Salvation Army store downtown.

Five years later, Nelson Sr. started feeling cramped. He made room for Nelson Jr. by moving to New Jersey shortly after Marta announced her pregnancy. As a result, the boy was raised by two women who sought advice on masculinity every now and again from a Spanish parish priest. Though he never wrote a word to his son, Nelson Sr. was not a bad father, Marta always said. He mailed regular child support payments from Union City. The checks continued while Nelson was in college. The month he graduated, they stopped.

Then, after Elena's death four years ago, the house seemed a little lonely. Soon Marta learned to sleep alone in the bedroom they had shared. She liked having full run of the place, at least during the day. Some days she refused to dress at all. At the industrial sewing machine between the twin beds in her bedroom, she worked happily in her nightgown. Evenings she waited for a bored and silent Nelson to arrive from one temporary job or another. She adjusted to his odd moods and eating schedule, although she was tired of having to cook dinner every night, as if her son were a husband. She often stared at the colorful packages of frozen dinners through the glass doors of the freezers at the grocery store. Their convenience tempted her, but she would not buy them. Only Americans served their families those, she told herself as she walked away proudly.

Marta recognized that Nelson's indecision about a career, a woman, might become a problem. It was already a bother, like the quarter-size cyst on her back. She reached under the collar of her dress to touch it. So far it caused only slight discomfort. One day she would have it drained at the clinic.

She turned into the hallway and stood at the threshold of Nelson's bedroom. The door was open. Through the years, even during his university days, she noted, he had kept it simple. He slept on a single bed. A scholarship student did not buy expensive electronic equipment. Instead, Nelson bought books. The standing bookshelves he built along one wall were full.

Marta went to the window and pulled aside the black and white gingham curtain she had sewn. When Nelson married and moved out, she would put her sewing machine directly under the window. She passed the damp sponge over the closed venetian blinds. When she finished, she lifted them to let the sun into the room.

On the window sill was a piece of paper folded to the size of an ice cube. A note. A secret. She picked up the paper and unfolded it. "To Gabriela," Nelson had written in Spanish, "for sharing your incredible vision."

Beneath the dedication in pencil were several lines of what appeared to be verses of poetry, in English. A dark line crossed through one of them. Marta did not read English; there was no telling what he had written. She frowned.

She folded the paper along its original lines, returning it to where she had found it. What mattered to Marta was that there was someone in Nelson's life. Gabriela!

Marta started to make the bed, then decided against it. He would know she had been lingering in his room too long. She turned to her son's dresser to rummage through the drawers, having done that often through the years. She decided she had enough information and stopped herself. More would come, she thought, a little at a time.

It was hard keeping the discovery to herself. She wished her mother were alive. She would look for Elena in the back yard, where more than likely she'd be hanging the wash on the clothesline, even though they owned a dryer, or fussing with the gardenia bushes. She would have shared the secret. For a moment, Marta was stilled by a longing for her mother.

After it passed, small waves of doubt began to overcome Marta about Gabriela. How would she encourage Nelson to pursue a relationship with someone like her? What kind of woman was Gabriela that she had given him a vision? She needed to consult someone. Concha was the best bet.

Marta returned to the window. "Concha, Concha!"

"Coming!"

"How are things this morning?" Marta greeted the neighbor, despite her desire to blurt out the news.

"Fine. Everybody's out who has to be out, so now I can get some things done." Concha's in-laws were home, permanently home, like hermit crabs. Marta didn't know how her neighbor could stand it.

"Nelson's at a job interview. I have a feeling he'll get it."

"Where?"

"The downtown library."

"Come over. I'll make coffee."

"I'm coming," Marta said, leaving the window. She stopped to look at her reflection in the large mirror in the dining room. For the past few months her shoulder-length hair had been dark brown; she kept it back in a pretty barrette while she sewed. She came closer to the mirror to inspect the roots. She also checked her face for new lines.

At forty-seven, she neither dated nor wanted to. Marta refused to remarry, although she liked being attractive to men. She made sure her good dresses, worn regularly to Mass and to occasional get-togethers with relatives, were in good shape and fit nicely. On the days she ran errands, to the bank or market, especially the fish market, she wore the

more faded ones. They were years old, but made well and
of good fabric. When she was out alone she went without
lipstick, so men would not get any ideas about her. She
took an umbrella to protect her skin from the sun.

She found the house key on the nail next to the front
door. The mid-morning sun was hot on her arms and face.
It was a quick walk into the shade of Concha's porch. She
knocked twice on the silver frame of the screen door to
alert the family and opened it. Concha yelled she was in
the kitchen.

"It's on," Concha said. "Tell me."

Marta looked around to see if anyone was within hearing distance. "I've been worried about Nelson. He hasn't
had a girlfriend since Sandra." She pulled out a chair.

"What about the job?" Concha asked.

"This is more important. Nelson is in love," Marta
said.

"In love! How do you know?" Concha gathered the
bags into a pile and flattened them a final time with both
hands.

Marta told her about the note.

"We'll see if it works," Concha said.

"He was in love with Sandra for so long. Maybe he's
still in love with her, not Gabriela, whoever she is. I hope
she's Cuban."

"Love is life's biggest motivating factor," Concha said.
"With love, anything is possible. Even a job. Everyone
knows it."

"I hope Gabriela will be the one. He is twenty-five
years-old."

"A home of one's own is important for a man. For a
woman too. God knows I would have liked some time

alone, especially with my husband when we were first married. But we moved right in with Mima and Pipo."

"Why wouldn't she be the one? After all, Nelson is educated, good-looking, healthy," Marta said. She pictured her lanky, black-haired son at his most handsome on Saturday nights when he emerged from the bedroom immaculately dressed and smelling of good cologne.

"I'm going out," he'd say.

"Where?" his mother would inquire.

"Anywhere," Nelson would respond.

Although she never told him, she was pleased that he showed some rebellion toward her inquiry. She worried when he began to socialize less and less. She wanted him to have a girlfriend again. He should marry. It was time.

Marta waited to see if Concha would bring up the fact that Nelson never went to church. Or mention her unfortunate divorce. The two women had discussed it often. They believed it had disillusioned him about marriage. But Nelson knew it had been his father who had broken the commitment. Nelson also knew she had remained faithful to the marriage even after it was over. Marta had never had a man friend again.

"You say he doesn't use drugs," Concha said, tucking the paper bags under the sink.

"I'm certain." Marta said tersely. She smelled the coffee coming up.

Concha quickly took the *cafetera* off the burner and poured a little coffee into a glass with the right amount of sugar. With a spoon she beat the mixture until it was a consistent caramel color. She poured the remaining coffee in, stirred and distributed it into four porcelain cups.

"Mima, Pipo, coffee!" Concha's mother and father-in-law were in the Florida room listening to Spanish talk radio above the shaking metal sounds of a square window fan.

"What are you making for lunch?" asked Concha.

"*Arroz con pollo.* The chicken's been marinating for two days. Should be good. Why don't you come over about one, to celebrate?"

"Thanks. I'll be there. You know, he's a man, Marta. He'll do what he has to do."

"I was married six years at his age."

"Things are different here."

"It's been more than two years since he graduated. I don't know what's wrong with him."

"Only God knows," Concha said, handing her friend the cup and saucer. "And Elena, in heaven. I miss her so often."

"So do I. Thank you, Concha."

The women were right about Nelson. He was undecided and uncertain. Those feelings were with him in the library as he waited for the interview on a sofa covered with clear plastic. His legs were stretched out and crossed at the ankles. He admired his well-polished leather shoes, then smoothed his only silk tie. He checked his watch. Fifteen minutes left until the interview. A smiling head librarian wearing a short sleeved suit would open a white door to welcome him.

The cover of a travel magazine attracted him: a photograph of a big mountain capped with snow promised adventure. But the article about the place, somewhere in that huge tract of land called Alaska, was boring, he decided. He laid it aside.

Nelson spotted a reference librarian, a small, balding pink man wearing a wild print shirt and dark knit pants. He had completed the outfit with a blue polyester tie. Nelson watched him come from behind a counter to attend to a patron in a business suit. Apparently the job required one to move quickly for information, as the librarian wore running shoes. He noticed they were dirty.

Perhaps his mother was right, he thought. It was a good place to work. He could be around books, with professional people, even though the tie was the only thing that distinguished the librarian as one. Not too many people. That suited him. The mandatory silence was attractive.

Suddenly, the patron's papers ruffled loudly. He gathered them together scowling and shaking his head in disgust. Behind the patron's back, the librarian threw his arms into the air. Then he turned to his desk to sit before a computer.

The library is for cowards, Nelson thought. He sat up and put both feet on the floor. He looked again at his watch. At five minutes to the interview Nelson walked out of the building to find his old Datsun. He would not work there. If the option was to work there or nowhere, he would not work at all. He would stay home, listening to the stops and starts of his mother's industrial sewing machine on the piecework for the factory.

"That's fine for the morning," a voice said. It belonged to his grandmother Elena. "But what about the rest of the day? The rest of your life?"

"I'll play basketball at the university. After dinner I can hang out with the old men at Domino Park."

"Is that what you want?"

"Maybe I'll go down to the river and watch the boats."

"The boats, Nelson?"

As a child he loved boats. Fishing boats, tugboats, speedboats, rowboats, the big ships that dared to take up so much space on the banks of the narrow Miami River.

Even before he could read, he would walk a few short blocks there with his grandmother. She pointed out the vessels with Spanish names and read them to him: *Miranda, Sebastián, Bonita*. Once Nelson went to school and learned to read and speak English, he returned the favor. He read the English names to her, pronouncing them over and over until she said them correctly. Nelson would tell her their meanings. *Bahamas Daybreak, Getaway with Me, New Moon, Afternoon Delight*. Elena marveled at these names because they suggested adventure.

His dark eyebrows drew together when he remembered one boat with which he was quite familiar. It belonged to his friend Carlos' uncle. The houseboat was docked on the river behind a mechanic's garage.

He remembered the first time Carlos and he, both honor students at Belen Jesuit Prep, went there. Carlos tried to quiet the two leaping Dobermans while fumbling with a padlock that closed the tall chain-link gate topped with spiraling barbed wire. When they walked in, the dogs backed up but kept their paws on the ground. They seemed on the verge of jumping. Nelson had closed his hands into fists and held his breath while the dogs nervously smelled him. Carlos waited. He had been introduced earlier.

After that the dogs knew them. The animals barked and whined with excitement on the Saturday nights when they arrived. In order to insure the dogs' continued acceptance, the youths brought treats for them. The houseboat had been fun. There, Carlos and Nelson had smoked marijuana with public high school girls. At times they had paired off and kissed the girls for hours at opposite ends of the boat. Outside on the deck, one or two had let Nelson feel their breasts.

During their college years the friends brought women to spend the night there. Those American women had come to study in sunny Florida from the northern states. The houseboat was an off-beat sort of draw. It was there where the young people could partake of the flesh freely and fully, without the familiar walls of dormitory rooms reminding them of their obligations as students.

His mother never said a word about how late he stayed out. Marta's unspoken rule was that he would be in bed, alone, before sunrise. He respected the rule, of course, as he was still in his mother's house. The women complained about having to awaken and abandon such a cozy spot to be dropped off in the bright lobby of a dormitory a halfhour before dawn.

The mornings after these get-togethers, Elena brought Nelson breakfast on a tray. Her grey hair combed into a French twist, the grandmother sat on the edge of the bed talking pleasantly while he ate scrambled eggs with tiny pieces of ham, Cuban toast, *café con leche*. When he finished, she would take the tray away. He slept until he awakened naturally after noon.

Nelson opened the car door and sat behind the wheel. He heard the metal click when he fastened his seat belt. There was an hour and a half's worth of time on the meter. He lowered the window. "Now what?" he asked himself. He looked around.

From the west, he heard the regular sound of metal being pounding inside a hull. He closed his eyes to listen to what resembled a welcoming bell. He listened a few moments longer. Then he knew.

"Yes!" he said, pounded the steering wheel with his fist. That sound made sense. He would respond to it. He would join a crew, he would live and work on the water.

Later, he could become a boat captain. Nelson started the car.

As he pushed down the accelerator and turned away from the curb, Nelson remembered the houseboat again. Before leaving for law school in Gainesville, Carlos had offered him keys to the place. Nelson had refused them. Shortly thereafter, he abruptly ended a three-year relationship with a tearful Sandra.

Nelson knew his mother was disappointed, depressed actually, about what had not transpired. He should have married Sandra. Marta would consider this decision more bad news. Today he would be a proud cat bringing its owner a beautiful dead bird. Why, she would ask, and she had every right to inquire, had he gone to such an expensive university to be a boat captain?

Nelson parked the car next to the curb in front of the house. For a moment, he thought Marta might have a heart attack. He had heard of such drastic responses from Cuban mothers before. Carlos' mother, for one, complained of *taquicardia* when he announced he was going away to school.

Nelson opened the door to the house and smelled the cooked garlic, onions and green peppers. The oval table was set for three. Marta and Concha's voices came from the kitchen.

He considered constructing a lie about how the interview had gone, so the two would think he had tried. Then he decided to tell the truths, one right after the other, like a man. The young man knocked once on the table for good luck as he passed it to see them.

"Good afternoon," he said. "What did you make?"

"You look very handsome," Concha said.

"Nelson, son, how did it go?"

"Pretty well," he said, loosening the knot on his tie.

"Good, good."

"Tell us what happened," Concha said. She crossed her arms.

Nelson started with the scene involving the male librarian.

"That's fine," Marta said, impatiently. She was eager for the real news. "How did the interview go then?"

He leaned against the stove. "I walked out. I didn't go. I'm sorry, but I can't work there."

"What do you mean you can't work there? What kind of thing is that, being so selective about a job?" Marta brought one hand to her forehead and tapped it quickly, as if her mind was having trouble understanding the words. She turned into the dining room.

"Mami, wait!" Nelson followed. He was afraid that she'd hyperventilate.

"Do you think when we came to this country we waited for the perfect job? We worked at anything, Nelson, anything. Call the woman and tell her, not me, you are sorry. She may give you another chance."

"I know what I want to do," Nelson said, relaxing a little. His mother would survive.

Concha appeared in the dining room.

"What? What? Just what is that?" the mother asked.

"I'm going to work on a boat."

"*Virgen Santa!*" Marta put a hand down on the table to steady herself.

"Which means I'll be away most of the time."

"Am I hearing you correctly?"

"Yes. I'll be out as soon as I find the right boat. It won't take long. I'm calling Carlos' uncle this afternoon."

"A boat, Nelson? With your education?" Concha asked.

"That's what I've wanted all my life."

"What about Gabriela?" Marta asked.

"Who?"

"Your relationship with Gabriela?"

"I don't know what you're talking about."

"Gabriela, Gabriela." Marta insisted on knowing why the woman he had dedicated verses to did not mean enough for him to comply with a regular job and life. She found the paper and brought it to him.

"This."

Nelson took the paper. What he unfolded was his earlier futile attempt to write a poem in honor of the poet Gabriela Mistral. Her verses had moved him in ways that other poets' had not. He tossed the opened paper on the table.

"It's for a poet, Gabriela Mistral." Nelson wanted to snap at his mother for snooping. But he decided to ignore her invasion of privacy. After all, he remembered, a man picked his battles.

"She's a poet then. What else does she do?"

"She was. A Chilean poet, she was famous. She died in 1957."

Concha let out a sharp laugh, then covered her mouth with a hand.

"This is not funny to me," Marta said quietly.

"I'm sorry, Marta, Nelson," Concha said quickly.

"I'm sorry, Mami."

Marta let disappointment, the unkind laughter, the social embarrassment stemming from naive hope, wash over her body. Finally, the hairs on her arms stood on end. Nelson would be going. The house would be hers alone.

Then she forgave them.

"Let's have our celebration, even if it is for something different than what I expected," she sighed. Nelson kissed her on the cheek and she went to the kitchen.

She brought the *arroz con pollo* to the center of the table. The rice was a beautiful yellow, made even livelier by the contrast of the green peas and neatly placed pimento strips. Concha and Nelson said marvelous things about the way the meal looked and smelled. She returned from the kitchen with a chilled bottle of wine and a corkscrew.

"It's all yours," she said, handing them to Nelson. She sat down at Nelson's usual place at the head of the table. He uncorked and served the wine.

Marta rose to serve. She saw the outline of her head and shoulders on the table. She smiled at her guests, then took the serving spoon in one hand and Concha's plate in the other.

THE GUNS IN THE CLOSET*

❧ Jose Yglesias ❧

Until now, Tony believed he had been liberated by his Venezuelan grandfather's name—freed to be the special person that for years he unthinkingly felt himself to be. Ybarra. "Basque, you know," he would say when the subject came up. He was an editor in a New York publishing house, and author of an occasional essay, and it was understood, especially by European editors visiting his office, that his name set him apart from—well, whatever American foolishness or provinciality or philistinism infected the scene at the moment. He was aware that there was more than a trace of snobbery in this; aware, too, of the defensive residue, for he never forgot the discrimination that his name had subjected him to—mild, he admitted—during his adolescence in New York public schools and even at Harvard, though never in publishing, he liked to believe. Motel desk clerks in New England and the Midwest still took a second look at him when they noticed the name on the charge card, and allowed his appearance and his speech to convince them that he was all right. Those tiny encounters when he stood for inspection kept him, he thought, open to the world of the ghettos—the blacks, Puerto Ricans, and Chicanos—and it pleased him that his son, Bill, who he had made sure learned Spanish fluently, should have lately come alive to the name. It amused him when Bill referred to himself in company—so as not, per-

From *The Guns in the Closet*

haps, to be challenged by his parents—as a Third World person. Today, Tony was uneasy.

Bill had come down from the apartment near Columbia University that he shared with other students—like him, activists who had been suspended after the campus strike—to have Sunday brunch at home. A surprise, for these were not family brunches, and Tony knew that Bill could no longer bear the two or three writers and editors, all West Side liberal neighbors, who would be there. "It's the Third World that's important, not the American moral conscience!" he had yelled one Sunday three months earlier. "Up the NFL!" And he had not been back since. Today, Bill sat out the two pitchers of Bloody Marys, the quiche, the fruit salad, the French loaves and cheeses from Zabar's, and tension grew between him and Tony as suppressed as Bill's opinions were today.

Tony thought about his old friend, Clifford, who would have been here if he were not in Algiers on a writing assignment. "Dear chaps, you're luckier with Bill than others are with their children," he'd said the last time Tony and his wife, Gale, had discussed Bill with him. "*They* deal with their kids as if they were a declining power negotiating with a newly emerged nation. The new diplomacy, right?"

Right. Tony saw that Gale had caught him studying Bill, and he smiled thinly, as if to say *Don't ask me*. And Bill, of course, intercepted all this and, unseen by the guests, winked at his parents, as if he in turn were replying *I'm here, that's all*. But later, when the others had left, he offered to go down with his father to walk the dog, and Gale explained triumphantly, "Aha!" Bill laughed helplessly as in the days when he was a boy and they had uncovered one of his ruses.

"Shall I take money with me?" Tony asked as if asking an audience.

"No money," Gale said.

Bill shook his head and threw up his arms. A routine family charade, and Tony decided that his anxiety was baseless. But when Bill was saying good-bye, Gale took the boy's head between her hands, as she had begun to do during the strike at Columbia, and kissed him. Trouble, Tony thought; she always knows.

Going down in the elevator, both quiet in the presence of other tenants, Tony noticed that Bill wore a J. Press jacket he had not seen in a long time. No army fatigue jacket. His hair was almost short, his pants were not jeans, his shoes were not work boots, and there were no Panther buttons on his chest. He seemed to have abandoned the new lifestyle, and it surprised Tony that his son's appearance did not please him; he looked ordinary.

Ordinary? Then he must not be a Weatherman. Thinking about Bill afflicted Tony with non sequiturs. "Bill, you don't have money to keep your apartment, do you?" he said. "You're not there anymore. We haven't been able to reach you for two weeks."

Bill shook his head. "No," he said, "but I don't want to be up there anymore."

So he was downtown. "Are you in a commune?"

Bill pulled the dog toward Riverside Drive. "Too many people on Broadway," he explained, and crossed the drive to the park. When Tony caught up with him, he was bending down to unleash the dog and let him run.

"Well, are you in a commune?" Tony asked, and smiled to appear casual.

From his bent position, Bill looked up and smiled a mocking smile; he shook his head. Tony was not reassured—not even when Bill straightened, threw out his arms, and took a deep breath, as if that was what he had come out for. Bill began to jog down the path to the esplanade and motioned his father on. "Good for you!" he called, and again he went through the motions of inhaling and exhaling with vigor.

When Tony got to him, he said, "Listen, Dad, I'd like to bring some stuff down tonight from my place. For you to keep for me. Just for a couple of days."

There were people rushing by. "Sure," Tony said, thinking it was books or clothes. "We're not going out. Anyway, you have a key." Bill looked at him so seriously that Tony stopped, suspicious again. "What stuff?"

Bill turned his head away. They were alone on the path now. "Guns," he said quietly.

Later, Tony wished he could have seen his son's face when he said that, but only the back of his neck was in view. There were wet leaves on the ground, and everything was still. Then a burst of laughter from a group of young people who appeared in the path on their way out of the park. They crowded Tony to one side and gave him time to think. I must not show my fear, he thought, especially my fear for him. But the questions burst out of him like exclamations. "They're not yours, are they? Whose are they?"

"No questions like that," Bill said. In a moment, he added, "Of course, they don't belong to *me*."

"I see," Tony said, subdued. They had come onto the esplanade and there were people everywhere, walking their dogs, sitting on the benches, or simply strolling. Tony did not know whether it was their presence that forced him to speak causally, that created a new equality between him and Bill, or the boundaries that Bill had set up. I do not own this part of him, he thought; I can say yes or no, but that is all. He had liked being a father and it shamed him now that he was elated, as he walked alongside him, to find that Bill had his own mysterious corners, his own densities.

Finally, he said, "I shall have to talk to Gale first. It's her decision, too." He had never, with Bill, called Gale anything but "your mother," and he knew he was being mean in his new equality. Both to Bill and to his wife. Bill could walk away from their lives—perhaps even should—but parentage cannot be removed. He reached out and touched Bill's shoulder.

"O.K.," Bill said. "You tell me when I phone you later."

But he had come to me—*me*—and in the wind that blew from the river, Tony's eyes teared. "You said they were at your place," he said. "Is that uptown?"

Bill nodded.

"And your friends living there—do they know?"

Bill exhaled and began his explanations. "They were away last weekend and the FBI broke in. The kids next door told them about it. The agents went through their apartment to get to the fire escape—it's kind of hard to get into ours with the locks I have on the door—and the kids came home while the agents were there. The super had let two of them in, but the kids told them to get out. So the pieces have to be removed right away. They were just lying under the bed in duffel bags—they must have seen them. My friends have been trying to get to me all week."

"And the apartment is in your name!"

Bill did not answer.

"You can bring them," Tony said. "It will be all right with your mother, I'm sure."

"O.K.," Bill said. "I have to go now." He handed his father the leash. "I'll call you tonight." The dog followed

him, and he turned back after a few paces. "Listen, when I
call I'll ask if I can sleep over and tell you how soon I'll be
there. You be down on the street when I arrive."

"All right," Tony said, and the sound of his voice was
so strange to him that he leaned down to hold the dog to
hide his sensation. Bill's legs did not move away, so Tony
looked up and saw him bring a hand up to his waist and
make it into a fist quickly, casually.

"All power to the people," Bill said in a conversational
voice. Then he smiled, in order, as they said in their family,
to take the curse off it. "See you."

Alone, Tony felt cool and lightheaded. He wanted to
run and did, and the dog ran after him. Nothing unusual—
the kind of sprint that men walking dogs in the park will
often break into. During the war, he had reacted this way
when, as pilot on a scout observation plane, he climbed to
the catwalk and into his plane to be catapulted from the
ship: his hands checked the canopy, the stick between his
legs—all concentration while his emotions unreeled without control and unrelated images flitted in and out of his
mind. He knew only that he was being observed and that
he must be true to some unconfessed vision of himself.

He walked back to the apartment slowly. How to tell
Gale. Dinner guests would have to be put off. Last summer,
the caretaker of the Maine estate they rented had asked
him what kind of name his was, and when he replied that
it was Spanish—no use saying Basque—the old man had
said, "Spanish! Now, there's nothing wrong with that, is
there?" The guns must go in the closet in his study—that
was one place their thirteen-year-old daughter, who now
should be back from her friend's apartment, never looked.

In the elevator, he thought, but if *they* didn't come back
to the apartment with warrants, then they must have a rea-

son to wait. Do they hope to catch Bill? Do they have a watch on the place, and if Bill walks out in a few hours with... He could not say this to Gale. She was lying on the living room couch with the Sunday *Times*, and he got a pad and pen and sat next to her and wrote out the conversation—the gist of it—he had had with Bill.

Gale smiled when he handed it to her, but when she had read it she sat up. "But—" she began. Behind her came the wail of a Beatles record from their daughter's room.

Tony put a finger to his lips. "Not here," he said.

The color went out of her face. "I've got to go out for a cup of coffee," she said. "Right now!"

They walked up and down Broadway and sat in a coffee shop and talked. She wanted to be angry at someone. "Couldn't you have brought him back to the apartment?" she said.

Tony felt like putting his head in his hands. "I didn't think..."

She waved a hand defeatedly, in understanding. "And there's no way of getting in touch with him?"

By the time they returned to the apartment, the exhilaration he had first felt was gone. They were no sooner inside than Gale had to take up the pad and write on it a warning about their daughter: *She must now know unless it is absolutely necessary.* He nodded, noticing the misspelling. And the cleaning woman who came three times a week, she wrote. She must be kept out of his study. He nodded again and took the sheet from the pad and went into the small bath off the study and tore it into small pieces and flushed them down the toilet. Thank God, Gale had not thought of the danger to Bill when he removed the guns from the apartment uptown.

Tony sat in the study and knew that Gale was restlessly tidying the apartment. Later, he heard her on the phone calling off the evening's appointment, arguing with their daughter to keep her from having friends in. Then silence. He could not read or write. He kept visualizing the walk-up near Columbia, which he had visited only three or four times. So many of the tenants were young people moving in and out that surely duffel bags would attract no attention. He thought of the solution: a decoy. Someone must first leave with the duffel bags that had been under the bed, but with something else in them. Of course. He got up from his chair to tell Gale. No. It was Bill he should get to. Run up to the apartment? Ten minutes by taxi. Gale wouldn't notice.

He had taken his jacket out of the hall closet when he realized that he dare not be seen up there today. Which of Bill's friends could he call? Which of them had gone this far with him in his politics? He did not know. He told Gale, who was lying on the couch again, that he was going down for cigarettes. She looked blank, then questioning, and Tony smiled and shook his head. From a street booth, he called a friend of Bill's who had been with him in the Columbia strike. The operator came on and asked what number he was calling. He told her—safe enough in a public booth, he thought. In a moment, she came back on to say the number had been disconnected. When he got back to the apartment, Gale did not look up from the couch. As he put his jacket back in the closet, he saw that she would not look up. She had thought of the danger.

He went to his study and tried not to think. There was a manuscript in his briefcase that one of the young editors liked. Another book on Vietnam. They already had one for the winter list. It was foolish not to talk aloud to Gale in the apartment. He could not believe the FBI had time to listen to his phone, to the hours of his daughter's, his wife's, and his own conversations, just because of Bill. He remembered a manuscript on surveillance that his house had turned down. To cover the whole apartment, the sound would have to be transmitted to a nearby station no more than two or three blocks away, to be either recorded or monitored. Thank God, he was not a paranoid left-winger.

Yet when the phone rang at eleven forty-five and he heard Bill say, "Dad?" he gave way to the fear that had made him write on the pad. He had to clear his throat before he could answer.

"Listen, Dad, I'm in the neighborhood." His voice was easy—he was a good actor. "I'm at a party and I don't want to go all the way downtown when I leave, so I'm going to do you and Mom the honor of staying with you overnight. O.K.?"

"O.K.," he said, and knew he was not playing his part well. He tried to ask the question. "Bill…"

"I'll be there in an hour," Bill said with that touch of highhanded misuse of parents that had once been genuinely his. "Thanks," he added, out of character.

"Bill…" Tony began again and then did not risk it.

After a pause Bill said, "See you then," and hung up.

The next hour would tell. Tony went to the bedroom where Gale was watching a talk show and said with the casualness he had not managed on the phone that Bill was coming by in an hour to spend the night. She looked at him with the kind of reproach that women transmit with a glance when they think their men are acting like boys. He shrugged, went to the kitchen, heated some coffee, and drank it in his study. Once *this* was over, he told himself, he would make Bill have a long talk with him. There had been no battles during his adolescence—none of the rows that are usual with fathers and sons—and he did not want Bill's activities now, whatever they were, to be surrogates for them. He had been proud when Bill so suddenly, at Columbia, had become political; he had alerted everyone at the office when Bill was scheduled to appear on a program last year of the show Gale was now watching. He had not used parental concern as an excuse for trying to keep him at school or to deflect him—not even when, after Dean Rusk had spoken at the new Hilton, Bill came home battered from a fight with the cops on Sixth Avenue.

Ten minutes before the hour was up, Tony went downstairs. Between midnight and one, the doorman was always in the basement helping the janitor wheel the garbage cans onto the street by the side entrance. A police car was parked at the corner, its lights on; one cop stood at the back entrance of the bakery two doors down, waiting for the pastry they cadged each night, and the other was at the all-night diner for coffee. Tony lit a cigarette and stood at the door of the building as if he had come out for a breath of air. There were still many people on Broadway, but fewer, and the prostitutes were more visible. The cops went back to their car to drink the coffee and eat the Danish. He raised a hand in greeting when one looked his way, and both of them grinned. Nothing suspicious about me, he thought; I'm a respectable, middle-aged West Sider.

The cops pulled out as soon as they were finished, having lit cigarettes and set their faces into the withdrawn, contemptuous expressions that signified they were back on the job. A Volks station wagon turned into the street, paused, and then parked where the patrol car had been. Bill sat next to the driver; the friend Tony had tried to call earlier was behind the wheel. Tony walked over as Bill got out; his friend stayed inside and did not turn off the engine.

"Everything all right?" Tony asked.

"Great!" Bill said. He walked to the back of the car, opened the window, and beckoned with his head. There were two long leather cases lying in the car; they looked handsome and rich. "Golf clubs," Bill said, and picked up one and handed it to Tony. He took the other, fitted an arm through its strap, and carried it over one shoulder. With his free hand he waved to his friend, and the car drove off.

"Thank God, you didn't bring them in the duffel bags," Tony said, almost gaily. "I wanted to call and tell you that you should first have left the house with the duffel bags and then…"

"That's what we did," he said. "Sent a decoy out first."

Tony put his arm through the strap of the second case and walked alongside Bill to the entrance of the apartment building. We are the perfect picture of the middle-class father and son, he thought. I would say, seeing the two of us, that we belong to a country club in Westchester, play tennis from spring to late fall, swim, golf, of course, and keep a boat at the Seventy-ninth Street Basin. During the winter, we get together at the Athletic Club for handball, followed by a short swim in the heated pool. The son dashes out immediately after, but the father gets a rubdown and later joins two or three others his age for lunch upstairs by the wide, tall windows looking down on Central Park. Ah, yes. His Venezuelan grandfather's name and his childhood in the Spanish section of Chelsea would keep him always on a circular stage slowly revolving to the view: you never cease to act the role that the eyes of others create.

Tony said, "You're going to find your mother very upset."

"About this?" Bill said. "I'll talk to her."

"Well, not inside," Tony advised. "We've been careful to say nothing that we wouldn't want overheard."

Bill looked down, but Tony saw he was amused. "Well, Dad, it's not very likely," he said in the lobby. "Their tapping equipment must be overtaxed these days. Too many groups into heavy stuff, you know." And in the elevator he explained, in such detail that it alarmed Tony that he should know the subject so well, how you can detect with the use of an FM radio whether there is a bug in the apartment.

"We have to talk about you," Tony said. "I don't know what *you* are into, and it worries me."

"Sure, O.K.," Bill said. They were on their floor, about to turn to the door of their apartment. "Look, you know I'm grateful to you that I learned Spanish and something about the culture. I got you to thank for that." He stopped, and Tony thought there must be many things Bill did not thank him for. "But I'm a Third World person, you know, and that's how I'm going to live."

Gale was not at the front of the apartment. Tony led Bill through the dining room and kitchen to the study. They leaned the cases against the back wall of the closet, and when they closed the door on them Bill said, "It'll only be for a couple of days. We'll let you know when."

"Remember, I stay home Tuesdays to read manuscripts," Tony said.

"O.K.," Bill said, nodding, and on the way to the living room turned and added, "It won't be me."

Gale was standing in the living room in her robe. She held one hand up in a fist and shook it at Bill in pretended anger. He laughed. Well, for Christ's sake, Tony thought.

She asked, "Can I make you something to eat?"

"No time, Mom," Bill said. "I've got to go."

"But you said—" Tony began.

Gale completed it: "You were staying overnight!"

Bill's expression reminded them of his old joke that his parents talked like an orchestra. "I can't. My friend is waiting for me."

"But he drove away," Tony said.

"I saw him from my window," Gale added.

"He's two blocks farther down, waiting." Bill walked over to his mother to say good-bye. "I'll be in touch."

Tony watched her hug him but could not hear what she whispered in his ear. When she let him go, she was pale and ready to cry. Tony said, "I'm coming down with you."

In the hall, he tried to tell Bill some of the things he had thought that day. They came out badly. "I have to tell you that I don't agree with what you're doing. They're the wrong tactics. They won't work here. You don't know what real Americans are. You'll bring down the most—"

"Christ, Dad, you're not on the Susskind program." That special hardness was in his voice; Tony did not know where he got it. "You know all the arguments as well as I do. Remember the time you came off his talk show and said there's just no way to make radical change palatable to liberals like that?"

"You're not going to compare me to him!"

"Not unless you force me," Bill said, and stopped because people had gotten on the elevator.

In the lobby, Tony let them go ahead. He said quietly, as if making a new start, "I'm worried about what's going to happen to you."

"Don't worry, I'm learning karate," Bill said seriously. "No pig is going to run me down and twist my arm behind my back. From now on we're doing the Bogarting. Twice a week I go to Connecticut to the rifle range and practice shooting." He laughed. "I need a lot of practice."

"What's that for?"

"I've got a very simple test for radicals," Bill said. "When I read about some radical movement, I ask, did they arm themselves, did they pick up the gun? If they didn't, they aren't serious."

On Broadway, Tony flinched when he saw a middle-aged writer coming toward them with his young wife—his third. They had the giggly look of people who have been turning on. And an after-the-party boredom with one another. Tony introduced them to Bill, and the writer made an effort to focus on him. "Pretty quiet at Columbia this year," he said. "Anything happening?"

"I wouldn't know," Bill said.

Quickly, Tony asked the writer how the new novel was doing. He began to talk about the reviews. Tony saw Bill edge away, and the writer tried to hold him by saying, "Say, you ought to take a look at it. It's a revolutionary book."

"We have to go," Tony said. "I'll call you tomorrow."

Bill was down the block and the writer called, "Read the book, kid. It'll blow your mind!"

Tony was breathless with the need to say something to his son that would somehow get to—what? He didn't know; he simply exhaled when he reached his side.

Bill shook his head. "Don't worry," he said, as if he understood. The Volks station wagon was at the corner waiting, and Bill paused. "You know, I've been down to Fourteenth Street several times, eating at the Spanish restaurants and sitting at the bars. A couple of old Republicans like Fidel, but none speak well about the Puerto Ricans." He shook his head again.

"Well…"

"You say your grandfather was an anarchist—right?" Bill asked. "Did you talk to him much? I got to talk to you about him. Sometime. O.K.?"

"Yes, yes," Tony said. He wondered what that old man—wearing a beret while he fixed the windows and doors in the worn-out apartment and built cages for the pigeons on the roof—had thought of him and his books.

When he got back home, he found Gale lying in bed reading. He felt sure she had been to the closet in his study. She looked up when he took out his robe and began to undress. "I don't want to talk about it until they're gone," she said. "And that had better be soon or I shall go out of my mind." He didn't answer, and after a moment she asked, "When is that going to be?"

"Two days," he said, but he did not really know. He lay next to her, his arms folded over his chest, and went over everything Bill had said. He could not quite remember what was to happen. Someone would get in touch with him. There were the facts of Bill's day-to-day life to piece together. And all that rhetoric. He was going to live like a Third World person. What the hell did that mean? This is the real generation gap, he thought—you can't grab hold of these kids; they sum up your life and their own in a phrase and leave you gasping. They wrench you out of the dense element that is your daily life and there you are—on the shore, on the shore, on the shore.

At breakfast the next morning, Gale announced that she was going to do volunteer work at the pubic school all week. Penance for sending their own to private schools, but also this week, he suspected, to be out of the way.

Tony went to the office late. There had been no call at the apartment, and there was no call here, either. He returned early with three manuscripts to read the next day. Again, no call. Gale was not home and he took the dog and headed for the Drive, as if that would help him recall his talk with Bill. He let the dog loose and stood at the parapet at the esplanade and smoked and stared at the river.

A short, dark man who looked to Tony like a typical Puerto Rican came over with an unlit cigarette, asking for a light. Tony handed him his cigarette and he held it delicately and took a light from it. He looked Tony directly in the eye when he thanked him. He did not walk away but turned to study the river, too, and it was then Tony realized that the man had spoken to him in Spanish. "If you are home tomorrow morning," he said now, still in Spanish, "someone will come to pick up the packages you have been so kind to hold for us."

Tony smiled in a kind of reflex and found that he could not turn on his fake smile. He thought, this is a trap; I must get away. Instead, he replied in Spanish, "For us?"

"Your son did not tell you whose they are?" He had the sweet accent of Puerto Ricans.

Tony shook his head.

The man said, "MIRA. Have you heard of us?"

Tony nodded. The bombings in the Bronx. An underground terrorist group operating in New York. A bad manuscript called "Colonies in the Mother Country" had mentioned them. Crazily, he wondered if he had been right to reject it.

The man seemed to watch all this going on in his head, and as if to help him added, "We are madmen."

"Talk to me," Tony said, and pointed to a bench. "What about my son?"

"Your son?" The man waited for him to sit first, bow-
ing a little and standing to one side. "But you must know
better than we do—if he trusted you with packages. What
can I tell you?"

"We are very worried about his activities," Tony
replied. "I do not want you to divulge anything that is con-
fidential, but if you can tell me something…"

"Oh, there do not have to be any mysteries between
us," the man said, and looked around at a man going by
with a dog. He waited until he had passed. "Your son is
very much of an Hispano. He is closer in feeling to us, he
says, than to any of the others."

"Others?"

"The other revolutionary groups," he explained.
"American ones. We are all in touch. He is a liaison man
with us. There are certain things that a Puerto Rican cannot
do. It looks funny for us to be in certain places or buy certain things. Too conspicuous. You understand?"

Tony nodded and looked at the river, trying to place
Bill in all this. His dog came back to the bench and the man
leaned down and patted him. "What a friendly little dog he
is," he said. "My younger brother was killed in the independence uprising after the war. Just one of the many
killed in Puerto Rican towns all over the island… One of
our problems is getting guns to comrades on the island,"
he said inconsequentially, talking as if this might help Tony.
"What better proof that we are an oppressed colony than
the fact that guns, which are so easy to come by in these
states, are almost impossible for Puerto Ricans to obtain."

"The laws are not the same?" Tony said.

"Jesus Christ himself could not qualify to own a gun
there."

Tony took out a pack of cigarettes and offered it. The Puerto Rican accepted with the grace that only a Latin seems able to put into such a gesture. "I admired your article on the Latin-American revolutionaries very much," he said, and Tony was startled—could this man have read the quarterly in which he had published two essays in the last five years? "The one on their situation after the death of Che. I had not known that wonderful saying of Marti's: 'El arbol que mas crece es el que tiene un muerto por debajo.'" ("The tree that grows tallest has a dead man buried beneath it.")

"That is what I fear," Tony said.

The man squinted and then struck himself on the forehead. "What a fool I am! You ask me about your son. You are worried like a good father, and all I talk about is dying and killing. Forgive me, compañero." They were quiet a moment. The Puerto Rican looked at his cigarette and flicked the ash off it carefully. "It is true that for us it is especially necessary to think about the possibility of death, to get used to it even. But that is not what interests us— that does not interest us one bit."

"Forgive me if I tell you that I do not think you have a chance," Tony said.

"That, too, does not interest us," the Puerto Rican replied very gently, in a tone that seemed solely concerned with Tony's feelings.

Tony got up and, because he was suddenly ashamed at the abruptness with which he was ending their talk, extended his hand.

The man took it in both of his. "I know what it is you are too polite to say," he said. "That your son is not a Puerto Rican. But do you not find that wonderful? Is not that the best guarantee that we will win this time? Look, those

Young Lords in the barrio want to free Puerto Rico, too, but almost none of them can really speak Spanish. Some of the older nationalists cannot believe in them, but I say it is what is here"—he stopped to place a hand on his own heart—"that matters."

"I wish you success," Tony said.

The man nodded slowly, solemnly. Then he smiled. "Perhaps we shall see one another again. If you go to the island to write one of your studies, there are people we would like you to meet. See what Yankees we have become—we know the value of publicity now, even if only among the professors who read the magazines where you publish." He laughed and added, "At ten tomorrow morning then, a girl will ask you one more favor—to help her take the packages to her car."

It was Gale's custom to look at him carefully when she greeted him—her way of asking for news—but today she began a story about a Taiwanese child at school, so pointedly, Tony felt, that it was a rebuff. When she stopped, he said, "Tomorrow."

She stepped over to him and pecked him on the cheek. "How do you know?" she whispered.

He lied. "Bill called."

The phone rang, and Gale picked it up. "Cliff!" she exclaimed.

"Tell him to come over," Tony called. Back from Algiers, thank God—the one person he could talk to about all this.

"He heard you," Gale said, "but he hasn't unpacked."

Tony insisted, as eager as when they had been undergraduates, "Tell him to come over and we'll open cans for dinner—I want to discuss business."

Clifford had spent a month in Algiers talking to Eldridge Cleaver. The last time they had spent an old-fashioned evening together, Tony had come up with the idea of the trip, and he did want to know if Clifford was going to get a book out of it. He wanted to talk about simultaneous hardcover and paperback publication, but it was really the chance to spend the evening with something in mind other than the guns in the closet that attracted him. And the possibility that Clifford could help with Bill.

Clifford had gotten a bottle of Cuban añejo through customs and he held it out in greeting. "Limes and Seven-Up!" he called. "I feel like my comic-strip name—Clifford Moon!"

Gale said, "You don't look it!"

He was wearing a Pierre Cardin vest suit and a flowered silk shirt with wide sleeves. In the month he had been away his sideburns had grown long and bushy; his mustache curved over the corners of his lips. He stretched out on a chair and showed his Moroccan slippers—sheepskin with embroidery.

"In Algiers, everyone is stoned all the time," Clifford said, beginning on his first Mojito—a Cuban drink he had brought back from trips made to cover the Cuban revolution. "You really should have fresh mint for this, but it'll do. They just don't know what the joys of drinking are in Algiers. I think I shall have to take a stand against hash, pot, grass—what inelegant names! It turns everyone into lobotomized types."

"Never mind all that," Tony said. "Have you got a book?"

"Dear chaps, I've scarcely been allowed to turn the experience over in my mind," he replied, and he let his arms droop down the sides of his chair. "I haven't even called my agent."

Tony waved a hand. "Oh, your agent—we've already discussed it."

"Did he say there won't be any minimum royalty on the paperback?" Clifford asked, sitting forward.

"Well..."

"I want more than the five per cent for my share," Clifford said. He laughed. "I'm getting myself a fur coat this winter."

"Well!" Tony said, and he didn't know if it was envy that made him decide then that he could not discuss Bill.

Gale said, "Let's drive down to Washington together for the Kent State demonstration. Or do you have to work?"

"Yes, no—yes!" Clifford said. "Dear me, I mean yes. There'll be beautiful, young people there from all over the country. They're bound to get stoned and disrobe—like Woodstock. And I can work that into the book." He picked up his drink from the floor and looked slyly at Tony over the rim of his glass. "How the revolution sells nowadays. Though I don't know to whom. The young don't read. I daresay it's the anxious middle-aged who want to know what their children are doing. In the fifties they would've gone to their analysts. This is better for us." He looked sly again. "Right, chaps?"

Promptly at ten the next morning, the downstairs buzzer sounded. Alone in the apartment, Tony opened the door, and a few minutes later watched the girl walk from the elevator toward him. She wore a maxi raincoat unbuttoned over a mini skirt. Her legs were stunning. "Is everything all right?" he asked.

"Oh, hi!" she said, delighted. "I'm parked just across from you."

He had thought that if she was alone he would have to make two trips with the cases, but she touched her right biceps and said, "Muscles," and took one of them. Tony watched the doorman study her legs when he held the door open for them. Damn. The writer whose new novel was just out was on the sidewalk—alone this time.

"Hey!" the writer said. "You didn't call."

"Stay right there," Tony said, following the girl. "I'll be right back." She opened the trunk of a Mercedes Benz at the opposite curb, and while he placed his case in it, Tony was aware that the writer watched them.

She brushed her long hair back when she straightened, and said, "Thanks."

"O.K.?" Tony said, wondering if he should shake hands.

"A message from Bill—he won't be in touch for a while," she said with a smile.

"What!" he said.

"Your friend is waiting," she said, and turned away.

He hovered as she got in behind the wheel. "Tell him we want to see him, please," he said, and watched her smile in that nonwavering, idiotic way.

When he got back to the writer, they watched her drive off. Without looking at him, the writer said, "You play golf?"

"Me?" Tony asked. "Oh, no, just helping a neighbor."

"Wow!" he replied. "You got that in your building!"

When Tony walked into the apartment, it felt eerie, like the time they returned from the theater to find that someone had broken in. He went straight to the study and closed the door to the closet. He could not concentrate on the manuscripts he had brought home. He made a cup of coffee and tried to think of what Bill's message meant. He would not tell Gale. On the radio in the study, the news commentators said that the national revulsion against the Kent State killings was escalating. The third time he heard the same news on the hour break, he turned the radio off and remembered Bill's instructions about how to find a tapping bug. He flicked the radio on again and dialed to the low end of the band and slowly moved up. On the third try, he caught a faint beep. He held the dial there; it built in volume. With both hands he picked up the radio and moved in the direction of the wall phone. The beep became steadier and louder: the tap was there. With shaking hands Tony put the radio back on its shelf and turned it off. Something else to keep to himself.

Later in the week, he and Gale went to Washington with Clifford and walked among the young people on the green. He looked for Bill, letting Gale and Clifford sit through the speeches while he roamed. He came back exhausted, and when Gale said, "Aren't they beautiful?" he could only nod, because his eyes were full of tears and his throat was tight. He felt better for being there, but on the way home anxiety returned; and each time a bomb exploded that winter he fought back the desire to call the police and find out, before the *Times* got to the stands, who was involved. He went to all the demonstrations. They were dear to him. He looked at the young people, no longer searching for his son, who had never called, and said inwardly, over and over, without irony, accepting his country at last while he repeated Bill's name in Spanish— Guillermo Ybarra—*I commend my son, fellow Americans, to your care.*

Drama

ONCE UPON A FUTURE*

❧ Matías Montes Huidobro ❧

CHARACTERS

MOTHER
DAUGHTER

SET

A living room with antique furniture: a sofa and a small table facing the sofa; on the opposite side, another small table with a bottle of red wine and a goblet; placed anywhere, a table with a telephone. At the front of the stage, facing the audience, an imaginary window.

TIME AND PLACE

Uncertain

The Daughter *is near the door, as if going toward it.*

MOTHER (*Energetic, domineering.*): You are not going to leave! Don't take another step forward.

DAUGHTER (*Stepping backwards, nervous, overwhelmed.*): I don't want to leave, Mamá. I don't dare. (*Surprised, her hands over her face.*) My God, I'm afraid!

Translated by Doris Waddel. I would like to acknowledge the generous assistance of Heather Kurano and Kurt O. Findeisen in the preparation of the final English version of this play.

MOTHER (*Furious, makes a confused move, unexpected, unreal, twisted.*): Fear! Fear! It's exactly what you need! (*Sinister, and, at the same time, almost euphoric.*) That is good. It's healthy.

DAUGHTER: I remember the nights... The nightmares...

MOTHER (*Strangely caressing her daughter's head, perhaps pulling her hair; a kind of cruel caress.*): My poor child! Poor wretched dear.

DAUGHTER (*Fleeing.*): Trapped. Hemmed in on all four sides.

MOTHER (*Laughing.*): What an exaggeration! What a way you have of changing things around. Maybe... maybe we could do something more constructive.... Find another way to entertain each other. (*Pause.*) I understand that it's hard to find something to do... Inside these four walls! But you can always find some other way to fill up all this time...all this nothingness.

DAUGHTER (*Slowly, reclining.*): I don't know what you mean, Mamá.

MOTHER (*Frivolous, banal.*): What do I mean? The piano classes began at five o'clock and the music was always pleasant. Why don't you think about that and forget about everything else. Don't think about anything bad, dear.

DAUGHTER: I can't agree to all this.

MOTHER: And who can? I have a heart too. (*Another cruel caress.*) Is it hurting you? Or maybe I'm hurting you? Come here! (*Bringing her towards her.*) Sleep. Rest. (*Softly.*) "Once upon a time..."

DAUGHTER: I can't sleep. You've probably noticed it. At night I go to bed and I start moving around. I start sweating as well. The pillows get sticky and my entire body becomes sweaty as well. It makes me sick.

MOTHER: It's summer. Oh, such endless hot summers! We take a bath and in a minute we're sweating.

DAUGHTER: You can't sleep either.

MOTHER: Sometimes, no.

DAUGHTER: It must be my room. There isn't a single window, and the heat fills it up like an oven.

MOTHER: I've told you to leave the door open. That way you can catch the breeze from the living room.

DAUGHTER: I'm tired… I'm tired of these daily conversations, of this constant litany.

MOTHER: And what do you want? After all, life in a small town is like this, slow like an old woman.

DAUGHTER: Something has happened, though…

MOTHER (*Firm.*): Don't fool yourself. Everything stays the same. In the long run, nothing has happened here.

DAUGHTER (*Unexpectedly violent.*): But you were listening! You knew the whole truth… The torturing in the basement!

MOTHER (*Startled, but without losing her temper.*): What do you mean? What are you talking about? The basement? You must mean the wall. I've told you more than once that it was a wall. A wall with no meaning. A wall is a wall. (*Aggressive.*) Do you understand now? Will you understand some day?

DAUGHTER (*Evoking, almost superficial.*): In the winter this house is humid. Then, you can't sleep because of the humidity and the cold. That makes you lose sleep too. I couldn't help waking up.

MOTHER (*Following the* Daughter.): You spied on us. I should have punished you the first time. I didn't do right. Now we know the rule: A timely punishment is a cure forever. But I hesitated. I was too weak and now I am paying the consequences.

DAUGHTER (*Turning around.*): I listened to your conversations… I knew it… After all, you were talking about
him.

MOTHER: The first time that you talked about the basement I should have gotten up, reached out my hand,
and slapped you. (*She gives her a slap.*)

DAUGHTER (*Moving away angrily.*): It won't do you any
good at all. It can't do you any good!

MOTHER: Father Ramos told me so. I spoiled you. He was
right. Everyone in this town knew it. Wasn't I a model
mother?

DAUGHTER (*Frantically.*): The Mayor… The Minister…
The Governor… The Senator… The Chief of Police!

MOTHER (*Haughty.*): Our friends, of course… Another
class of people.

DAUGHTER (*Confused.*): I'm too nervous. The only thing
that I've been good for is clearing off the table.
(*Begging.*) Mamá, please, I can't live by turning my
back to everything!

MOTHER (*Softly, almost tenderly.*): Dear child… My
daughter is trained the old-fashioned way. It's not your
fault. Everything is too complicated, and you're just a
girl educated in a convent… (*Nostalgic.*) Our town…
The church… Saint Mary's Chapel… The nuns that
love you so much… The sweet priest that gave you
confession… Wasn't it nice, dear? We cared so much…
I'll bet you remember… Right? The convent had such a
beautiful cloister! And you… all dressed in white!
There was a delicate scent of jasmine everywhere. No,
how can we forget… True, it's been a long time. Centuries maybe. (*She laughs.*) Do you remember? Or have
you forgotten? Back then life was different.

DAUGHTER: However, the chains were just the same.

MOTHER: Nonsense! (*Pained.*) Why are you saying that?

DAUGHTER: Everything is too far away. Many things happened later...

MOTHER: You were happy, remember?

DAUGHTER: Why are you trying to deceive me?

MOTHER: I did everything possible so that you would be happy. I didn't want you to be hurt. I wanted you to be safe.

DAUGHTER: Lies... Lies!...

MOTHER: I believed it was best. After all, I was surrounding you with security.

DAUGHTER: Security?

MOTHER: A little barrier that would free you from certain things... A kind of alarm system that would protect you from thieves and criminals. You should be grateful, dear.

DAUGHTER: And the basement? What do you have to say about the basement, Mother?

MOTHER: It didn't exist then. Why are you thinking about it?

DAUGHTER (*On her feet, facing the audience.*): Then, it did exist before.

MOTHER (*Laughing, evasive.*): Why do you want to talk about unpleasant things? There are other subjects... The birthday parties... The picnics in the countryside... The weekends at the beach...

DAUGHTER: Then, it's true.

MOTHER: You're wearing me out. You're so boring! Do you think that I don't want to forget? I've almost forgotten, but you're compelled to remember what shouldn't be remembered. That's dead and buried. What an absurd compulsion! What an unusual idea! It no longer exists, child. When you open the door you find a wall. A plain, brick wall. And that's it.

DAUGHTER: However, the door was there... "Once upon a time..."

MOTHER: And who can prove it? It's not there any longer. You can rest now. The two of us can sleep in peace. I myself, at night, put an end to that turbid history that only persisted in ruining me. (*Threatening.*) I'm warning you that you can never do otherwise.

DAUGHTER: You're trying to confuse me, to cover my eyes so that I can't see. But I have to know it all... "Once upon a time..."

MOTHER: I am trying to guide you down the straight path, but that's not what you want. As if you wanted to go astray perhaps... (*Laughs.*) You're a rebellious girl.

DAUGHTER: Once upon a time, Mamá... (*Almost authoritative.*) "Once upon a time..."

First sequence of "Once Upon a Time." Lighting change.

MOTHER: You want me to tell you everything. Okay. Don't tire yourself remembering. We no longer have anything else to entertain ourselves with. (*Pause.*) "Once upon a time a mother, a daughter, a basement and a ferocious wolf..." (*Transition.*) You must remember that morning long ago when they began to bring the bricks... Those dirty, repulsive guys, almost naked, covered with that sour sweat that inundated the house and made me want to vomit. (*Violent.*) But you have to tolerate them! (*Pause.*) They placed the bricks next to the door. And the sacks of cement. I told you that I wanted to make a shelf. It was an absurd idea, I know.

An unbelievable story, don't you think? Those bricks in the living room, in the bedroom, all over the house. A fantasy. I think I was insane, don't you? How could you believe me? Maybe you just didn't want to know the truth. (*Pause.*) In any case, you were in one of those states...sweating...with those turbid nauseating spasms. (*Pause.*) I began my work. I had to do it all by myself. Several nights of exhausting work, I tell you! Was I to expect any help from you? (*Looking at her hands, theatrically.*) Just imagine these small, womanly hands that had never been soiled with mud. (*Transition.*) But I couldn't wait. Day after day the situation became more embarrassing. I wanted to do a good job, perfect, without knowing about it. (*Lightly.*) I walked downstairs with a few bricks and a bucket of cement. It was like a game. Playing cards by myself in the middle of the night! A house of games torn to pieces! You know, I had a good time too! What a strange happiness! It was kind of passionate and crazy. It was...it was as if I were born again... No, it's useless for me to try to explain it to you... You wouldn't understand.

DAUGHTER (*As if suffocating.*): I understand.

MOTHER: Is it possible?

DAUGHTER: You were setting a trap. You were setting traps all over and that fascinated you, it made you crazy. I understand, Mamá, I understand. Your favorite game! I understand your feelings and your game. I seem to understand you. Maybe someday I can learn too.

MOTHER: You're so deluded! What a crazy idea you've got in your head!

DAUGHTER: Continue your story, Mamá. Tell me about your steps on the stairs, the tension in your chest.

MOTHER: You know it. You know it all.

DAUGHTER: No, no. I feel I want to learn. If I remember now, I might discover the truth and see myself the way I was.

MOTHER: Oh God! I bet you're not going to like it.

DAUGHTER: Everything was confused, frozen, sticky...

MOTHER: It's too easy for you.

DAUGHTER: Go on...go on...

Under the effect of a blue light, the Mother *recreates the scene, making the movements suggested by the text.*

MOTHER: The hallway... The stairs... I was afraid of falling down... After all, I'm not young.... The hallway was dark and I was afraid that some neighbor might open the door at any moment. One night I bumped into someone. I can't remember who, exactly. I'm sure he was drunk. His breath was so repulsive! I know it so well! He questioned me hesitatingly. I told him that I was going to plant jasmine in the garden. Naturally, that didn't make sense. But, what's the difference? At times, I start thinking that it was an illusion, a nightmare. We began to laugh at the same time. (*Changing her voice.*) "Jasmine in the garden?" he asked me. "At this hour of the night? Don't you know that you should plant it during the day?" It was difficult for me to explain all that: the bricks, the bucket, the cement. (*Changing her voice.*) "I don't believe in those modern ideas," I answered him. (*Changing her voice.*) Everything was absurd. While I was saying it, I realized that the garden didn't even exist. I had invented it suddenly as if it were really at the foot of the stairs. Do you understand?

End of "Once Upon a Time" sequence. Lighting change.

DAUGHTER (*Laughs, almost childlike manner.*): It's fun, Mother! "Once upon a time..." It's as if you were singing a lullaby to me and I were going to sleep... At times, in the middle of this boredom, I get a feeling that some day similar things will happen to me.MOTHER: You can't imagine my predicament. Fortunately, he was drunk. I told him the first thing that came into my head, and he didn't realize a thing. Sometimes I think that he was...a terrorist... That he might have killed me on the spot. Or maybe a criminal, I don't know. Or just a homeless person. I have seen him many times, in my own nightmares. (*Pause.*) I was alone there to sort things out. I couldn't count on you. You were so delicate! So susceptible! Maybe you made yourself the frail one. As far as you were concerned, I was the only one who had anything to do with it!

DAUGHTER: And me, Mamá? Didn't I have anything to do with it?

MOTHER: In a certain way.

DAUGHTER: In a certain way? I don't understand. I didn't understand a word. Remember I couldn't take two steps on my own, not even to open the door...forced to take the piano lessons...the music class...the evening prayers...

MOTHER (*Sinuously strokes her hair.*): It is so easy to live like that! Then, you don't have to feel guilty about anything. Isn't that the way it goes?

DAUGHTER: You forced me to! I was always repeating: "Mamá doesn't want me to." "Mamá won't allow it."

MOTHER: Okay, I'm not accusing you. But someone had to put his foot down in this house. Those were bad times, you can't deny that. I had to face shortages of food. We had to live, right? I couldn't sleep in peace.

Everything was too risky. For you too. I was afraid someone would open the basement door and suddenly find it. The Police Chief had left it all in such a strange, unexpected state. It was so disgusting! It was really repulsive! You should be happy! After all, repeating "Mamá doesn't want me to," "Mamá won't let me," turns out to be much easier.

DAUGHTER (*Facing her.*): But I wanted to! I wanted to. That's the difference.

MOTHER: You didn't have to face that unbearable stench...clean the blood-stained floor...the remains of the butchery...

DAUGHTER: What else? What else?

MOTHER: It doesn't make sense to talk about a past that is dead and buried.

DAUGHTER: I'm trying to remember. Didn't I speak up at all?

MOTHER: You hushed in such a way that it seemed like you had been silent forever.

DAUGHTER (*Inquiring into her own truth.*): Perhaps, in a whisper... I vaguely remember... At times, while I was stretching out my hand, like this, over the table, and while you and Father Ramos chatted, suddenly...I barely remember it...barely realizing it... I said the word exhaustion...freedom...

MOTHER (*Laughs hysterically.*): You said it? Did you even dare? That must have turned out to be really funny.

DAUGHTER: It was...as if I said it in such a low voice... that not even I myself could hear it.

MOTHER (*Sarcastic.*): Maybe you did. I'm not going to deny your brave gesture, but since not even you your-self heard it, it was as if you had never ever said it.

DAUGHTER: I didn't dare shout it.

MOTHER: I raised my voice a little, only a little... (*Laughs.*) I laughed.

DAUGHTER: Let's say it again.

MOTHER (*Almost on top of her, mistreating her.*): Because you were a coward. We all knew it. You were ridiculous with that fear in your face.

DAUGHTER: "Mamá doesn't want me to. Mamá won't let me." (*Violent.*) It was not my fault! You know full well! The Chief of Police was sitting there, calmly, hours and hours, smoking his cigars and looking at me, waiting. He made me tremble.

MOTHER: But, my dear, he barely said a word.

DAUGHTER: The basement! The basement! That's what he said over and over again!

MOTHER: You were in the know about everything. You knew as much as I did.

DAUGHTER: You made me seem stupid, insignificant, wretched...

MOTHER: You realized and understood the difficult situation that your father had left us in... His gambling debts... The mortgage on the house... You know how he was. I had to get money from somewhere. We had to eat, you know... The basement was empty and they knew it. Those things were done. It was common practice at that time and I couldn't do anything. The ball was in their court.

DAUGHTER (*Dejected.*): A miniature nightmare.

MOTHER (*Caressing her, sinuously.*): What a way to put it! You have always been a sick creature. (*Lifting her head lightly.*) Let me see your face. (*She looks at her.*) You're pale, you're trembling. (*The* Daughter *allows her an embrace, terrorized.*) Are you afraid? Why be afraid? Why don't you forget all about it and decide to live in peace? We're a little bit upset. That's all, but we will stay here. I've told you a thousand times. Everything will turn out fine. Nothing has happened here.

DAUGHTER (*Separating herself.*): And if I told you that I'm listening?

MOTHER: Listening to what? There is nothing to listen to anymore.

DAUGHTER: Where have you locked me up, Mamá? In what prison have I been living for all these years?

MOTHER: In a cell where you were safe and where no one could hurt you. A cell that I built myself for your safety and security. You are so ungrateful. You don't realize the danger that lurks everywhere. Keep this up and you will soon see where that contagious happiness, that enthusiasm, gets you. (*Shaking the* Daughter.) Are you listening? What are you listening to? (*Leaving her.*) No, you're not listening to anything.

DAUGHTER: That man?

MOTHER: Which one?

DAUGHTER: The homeless one at the bottom of the stairs.

MOTHER: How silly you are!

DAUGHTER (*Pointing to the window that, supposedly, faces the audience.*): Do you hear it?

MOTHER (*Moving toward the window.*): Those noises don't let you sleep.

DAUGHTER: I'm listening, Mamá.

MOTHER: No, you're not. Dust and dirt come in from the street. (*Closing the window.*) Let's close it.

DAUGHTER: I need a little sun, a little bit of air.

MOTHER: Forget it. Don't think about it.

DAUGHTER: Remember, Mamá, remember. Sing that lullaby to me again: "Once upon a time... Once upon a time..."

MOTHER: Hush, entertain yourself with something else. Those performances are tiring me. I'm too old to play that role! And that's not going to get us anywhere!

DAUGHTER (*Gripping her mother.*): I want that excitement, Mamá! I haven't lived through anything else. "Mamá doesn't want me. Mamá won't let me." Will I be able to do anything?

MOTHER: You can't do anything.

DAUGHTER: Then give me that poison. "Once upon a time…"

MOTHER: I don't want you to…

Second sequence of "Once Upon a time." Lighting change.

DAUGHTER (*Extends her hand as if creating the magic of a theatrical performance.*): They're entering.

MOTHER: But this can't be…

DAUGHTER: The General… The Mayor… The Governor… The Senator… The Chief of Police… The Old Clique, Mamá.

MOTHER (*Nervous, fixing her hair, entering the stage.*): But they have entered too soon. Do you want me to look ridiculous in front of them? I haven't fixed my hair. You haven't fixed the set. The coffee cups…

DAUGHTER (*Placing some imaginary coffee cups on the coffee table.*): It's ready now.

MOTHER: Doesn't the Police Chief seem like a very nice man to you?

DAUGHTER (*In a low voice.*): But he has a blood-stained shirt.

MOTHER: It isn't blood. It's wine.

DAUGHTER (*Whispering.*): His shirt is stained with blood, Mamá. Can't you see it?

MOTHER (*Irritated.*): That isn't so! You never said that!

DAUGHTER: I told you. I warned you, but you didn't want to listen to me.

MOTHER: You're good for nothing! You're setting the scene all wrong. (*Acting her part.*) "The coffee, honey. We're all waiting for the coffee."

DAUGHTER: It's on the table.

MOTHER: If you would at least arrange things as they were. The coffee wasn't there. You arrived with it on the tray.

DAUGHTER: I'm sorry. (*The* Daughter *simulates picking up the coffee cups, placing them, supposedly, on a tray. Afterward, she moves away toward the door, but she doesn't exit.*)

MOTHER: You were trembling. The mere presence of the Police Chief made you nervous. I, on the other hand, was dying of laughter. (*The* Mother *simulates soundless loud laughter.*)

DAUGHTER: But he was a little bit nervous.

MOTHER: You really didn't know him very well. He never, ever got nervous.

DAUGHTER (*Approaches once again the little table facing the sofa, and places "the cups" on it.*): Suddenly, as I leaned toward you, that unexpected machine-gun fire…(*Under the effect of a blue light, recreates the scene. She repeats her soundless laughter.*) The cups tremble on top of the tray. You didn't stop laughing. I became frightened. Something was happening. They ran across the roof. I remember. How can I forget! They were running, they were trying to escape… The Chief of Police started with his dirty jokes and you didn't stop laughing…. You were trying to drown out the footsteps, the human hunt, the howl of the dogs, the victims' shouts… With your laughter, Mamá, your laughter! Were you ever going to stop laughing? And I was seated between the two of you, prisoner, in my small world of terror that I couldn't escape from.

MOTHER (*Standing up.*): They let them run away. That night four of them escaped.

DAUGHTER: You never told me.

MOTHER: Why should I? I wasn't going to give you the pleasure. I knew that you were on their side. It was an ember of happiness I had to keep under lock and key.

DAUGHTER: Maybe one of them was the man...

MOTHER: What man?

DAUGHTER: The one that you saw later at the bottom of the stairs.

MOTHER: You're not going to scare me, honey.

DAUGHTER: All of a sudden the Police Chief became pale.

MOTHER: He had a keen ear. He recognized the howl of the dogs. Someone was escaping.

DAUGHTER (*Changing her voice as if she were the Police Chief, firm but covering her ears.*): "To the basement."

MOTHER (*Acting out her role.*): "No, leave it for now..."

DAUGHTER (*Changing her voice, covering her ears.*): "And when do you want me to leave it for?"

MOTHER: The devils, spurting blood, joked once more. The blood squirted through the window.

DAUGHTER (*With her back to the audience.*): I had my back turned. I couldn't see it.

MOTHER: It was a river of blood that stretched everywhere. How could you possibly not have seen it?

DAUGHTER (*Herself.*): "Don't go, Mamá. Don't follow him."

MOTHER (*Herself.*): "I'm going."

DAUGHTER (*Herself.*): "I'm afraid."

MOTHER (*Next to the door.*): Then what did you do?

DAUGHTER: What could I do? I stayed behind by myself. I couldn't move. I waited. What was all that about? Did I, perhaps, know something about it? I was confused. It was a nightmare incomprehensible to me. I felt surrounded, closed in from all sides. Why didn't you tell me we were dealing with criminals?

MOTHER: I didn't have anything to tell. Following the gunshots, I ran after the Police Chief. You saw me leave. Couldn't you see that a crime was committed. Stop acting as if you didn't know, and end this mockery once and for all.

DAUGHTER: They came back.

MOTHER: And you were next to the door, lying in ambush.

DAUGHTER (*Acting out her role.*): "Those footsteps..."

MOTHER (*Acting out her role.*): "You're pale. What's the matter with you?"

DAUGHTER (*Acting out her role.*): "Has something happened?"

MOTHER (*Acting out her role.*): "What could possibly have happened?"

DAUGHTER (*Questioning an imaginary person.*): "Has something happened, Governor?"

MOTHER (*Changing her voice like the governor's.*): "Nothing has happened here, my child."

DAUGHTER (*Running toward another side of the set, asking.*): "Has something happened, General?"

MOTHER (*Changing her voice like the General's.*): "Nothing. It's the wind. It's September and the hurricanes..."

DAUGHTER (*Repeats her questions over and over to imaginary characters. She flees, she tries to escape. Her mother tries to pursue her. Changing her voice, playing the roles of various characters*.): "Has something happened? Nothing has happened?"

MOTHER: "Tie her up! Don't let her leave!"

DAUGHTER: "Has something happened? Nothing has happened?"

MOTHER: "Over there! Over there! On the other side!"

DAUGHTER: "Let me go! Help! Get me out of here!"

MOTHER: "To the basement! To the basement! Don't let her leave here alive!"

DAUGHTER: "Help! Help! Get me out of here!"

MOTHER (*Grabbing her* Daughter.): "Hush. Be quiet, right now. Don't you realize what you're doing? Do you want to end up like all of them? If you don't shut up, you won't be able to leave here alive."

DAUGHTER (*Running away*.): "Let me go! Let me go!"

MOTHER (*Ferocious, she changes her voice*.): "To the basement! To the basement! Don't let her leave here alive!"

End of "Once Upon a Time" sequence. Lighting changes.

MOTHER: You are lying! Why are you making me say words that I never said?

DAUGHTER: You said them, Mamá. You said them all.

MOTHER: Do you think that because everything has changed and this house isn't the same as before, that I'm about to put up with anything?

DAUGHTER: Now I know things that I didn't know before.

MOTHER: Too late. I won't allow you to fill in words to the past that were left unsaid.

DAUGHTER: Because you were drowning me. That's why they weren't said.

MOTHER: Now you are stuck with them caught in your throat forever. You never said them and you'll never, ever be able to say them.

DAUGHTER (*Begging.*): You just don't get it, Mamá. Do you? I only wanted a little air... That's not asking for a lot... Sometimes, through the Venetian blinds, I see the streets and I don't understand... The people... The sidewalks... The cars...

MOTHER: And what right do you have to look? You have to live with your memories, but with a memory without words that you never said.

DAUGHTER: But I hear sounds, voices, words. Strange words are in the air and that can't be silenced. They can be heard everywhere, like a murmur that inundates the city and surrounds everything with different sounds, a new melody, a different chord...

MOTHER: What do you mean?

DAUGHTER: New words that I want to understand, because you've never taught me their meaning.

MOTHER (*Threatening.*): One by one, you will repeat those words to the Chief of Police.

DAUGHTER: The Police Chief is dead. He's been gunned down, Mamá.

MOTHER (*Approaching the telephone.*): Are you out of your mind? I'll call him and you'll have to eat those words once and for all.

DAUGHTER: He's been shot, Mamá. You know very well that we are isolated, locked inside these four walls like prisoners of our crimes. You're through with conspiring with anyone. The telephone will no longer serve as a tool for your crimes. Your crimes, Mamá. Those of you and all the others.

MOTHER: You're planning to fence me in, but you're mistaken, because I'll find some other way of escaping.

DAUGHTER: You stopped next to the window and you saw them. You saw the youngster on the corner and you easily recognized the guilty ones. The innocent ones, I mean. The ones guilty of heroism.

MOTHER (*Laughs hysterically.*): Oh, my God! What a speech, what a way to talk! (*Sarcastic.*) Where did you learn those words, honey?

DAUGHTER: And he saw you too at the bottom of the stairs.

MOTHER: That man? He was drunk. He remembers nothing. What can he do?

DAUGHTER: The truth, Mamá.

MOTHER (*Sarcastic.*): The truth? The whole truth and nothing but the truth. Words! Words! Words!

DAUGHTER: I want to live. It's just that only now am I able to find the words.

MOTHER: Lies, you find nothing but lies surrounding you everywhere. What world do you think you live in?

DAUGHTER: How should I know? I'm surrounded by mist. Everything is vague, uncertain, hazy. But maybe… Somewhere else… I don't know… The past is filled with new words and new meaning, and all of a sudden I can see things clearly in the middle of the night, deep in the darkness.

MOTHER: That doesn't make sense.

DAUGHTER: Yes, it does… (*Pause.*) I have seen the girl next door running away from her house.

MOTHER: You're imagining things.

DAUGHTER (*Firmly, a step forward.*): "Once upon a time…" "Once upon a future…"

MOTHER (*Weakly, a step backward.*): No…no…

DAUGHTER (*Firmly.*): "Once upon a time, Mother." "Once upon a future."

Third sequence of "Once Upon a Time." Light change.

DAUGHTER: Last night, she dropped a letter through the window.

MOTHER: You spend your time weaving intricate webs to trap me in. Your old mother. Your poor, old, unhappy mother.

DAUGHTER: The girl has escaped, Mamá.

MOTHER: Lies have become an obsession with you, particularly when you're getting older.

DAUGHTER: A little rebellious girl.

MOTHER (*Stronger.*): But you know her grandmother. She is old, but strong as an ox. She comes from a stock that doesn't yield easily. She rules with a stick. You'll see. You'll see.

DAUGHTER: The girl has escaped. She told me in a whisper when you were napping in the armchair. Her journey...

MOTHER: Many have died on that journey.

DAUGHTER: She slipped her body through the trellis. I saw her among the shadows. She managed to escape.

MOTHER: Dreams, that's what they are. Fantasies... Wishes... Your most secret, obscure desires... Rapes... Sexual fantasies... Don't you realize that you're sinning and that you'll burn in Hell? The Priest told you when you...when you were dreaming.

DAUGHTER: That's not true.

MOTHER: Besides, you have never seen that girl because she does not exist.

DAUGHTER: She does too exist! She exists and escaped last night.

MOTHER: You have become delirious. At night you can't distinguish one face from another. Those are ravings of your imagination.

DAUGHTER: She tried many times before and failed, but this time she succeeded. She is definitely gone.

MOTHER: She is just a cheap little devil that will end up a tramp.

DAUGHTER: You're deceiving yourself, because you are afraid, Mamá. You know what it's all about. She escaped every night and returned at dawn, trembling, as if they were going to kill her when they found out what she was up to.

MOTHER: It's natural.

DAUGHTER: Last night, I barely spoke to her...I was afraid that you would wake up and discover me, and that you would torture me and throw me in the basement and that the Chief of Police would come back again and would rape me, because that was what he was always thinking.

MOTHER: You are becoming an obscene old maid... Of course, within these walls nothing is known for sure... What certainty do you have? We are mixing up... Well, you are mixing up dreams and reality...mixing them up... How strange! Maybe nothing is real anymore.

DAUGHTER: I'm inventing things then?

MOTHER: Be sure of that. You're inventing everything, which is boring, but safe. There is nothing wrong with that. After all, now that we are all alone, it is necessary to pass the time...playing... I give up... I no longer have the Police Chief, who used to amuse me so much

and make me laugh… But, I must confess, remembering the past overwhelms me… Let's go to sleep.
DAUGHTER: Once more, Mamá. "Once upon a future…"

Blue light.

DAUGHTER: Last night, when you were napping next to
the window, she approached me again. She had a new
story and explained it all to me slowly, like a lesson…
A lesson in revolt… As if we were in a confessional
and finally the truth were spoken.
MOTHER: You're boring me… It's nonsense… That
doesn't make any sense.
DAUGHTER: In the early evening the whole family was
there together in the living room. It was almost seven,
and everyone had to go to bed because that was the
law. Her grandmother, at the table with her uncle, was
talking about the General.
MOTHER: Her grandmother is an extraordinary woman,
old-fashioned, unique and in a class all her own. What
a character! What a way to govern a house. She rules it.
The servants don't breathe. They don't rest. Everyone
respects her and no one moves a muscle when she
strikes her cane against the floor. (*The* Mother *strikes the
floor.*)
DAUGHTER: She was listening. She was attentive to
everything they had to say. But she was trembling from
head to toe.
MOTHER (*On the sofa, changing her voice.*): "Last night,
around eleven o'clock, I felt the heat surrounding me.
It was a hot breeze coming from somewhere. Hot, very
hot, not the least bit cool. I thought that maybe a window was being opened. I became suspicious. I had no
idea what was going to happen next. Maybe the terror-

ists were already inside the house... (*Pause, gesture.*) I placed my hand on the rifle in case I had to use it. You never know. I suppose it was just the wind, but, how could I be sure? These are dangerous times. We should be alert. Ready to kill. We must lock the house. We have no choice.

DAUGHTER: She knew that they were watching her closely. At any moment they could lock her up within the four walls of her bedroom, without windows and only an opening in the roof.

MOTHER: A very practical room, of course.

DAUGHTER: The grandmother asked for a cigar.

MOTHER (*Changing her voice.*): "A cigar... A cigar... It's been days since I've smoked."

DAUGHTER: The cigars were on a little table not very far from the window. She reached for them. But first she looked through the Venetian blinds and watched the streets, open and free. An old man with a bloodied jasmine in hand was looking toward the window. (*Pause.*) The grandmother spoke about the terrorist, about the war, about the bombings. (*The* Daughter *approaches the little table on the other side of the set. The* Mother *is on the sofa. She is reclined in such a way that she doesn't see what the* Daughter *is doing. The* Daughter *brings her* Mother *the cigar and the matchbox. The cigar and the matchbox don't appear physically on the set. The* Mother *lights the cigar.*)

MOTHER (*Voice change, acting as if she is smoking.*): "Let them burn the sugarcane, let them burn everything, let nothing remain but ashes and salt!"

DAUGHTER: Everybody began to laugh. She was about to fall and reclined her head next to the Venetian blinds. She looked at the street again, furtively, with fear and hope, being careful that no one noticed. No one did. They were all in their own world. It was as if she had disappeared from the rest of them. It was then that they asked her for some wine. She took a few steps. She was tired of those centuries of oppression, of silence, of words never spoken. She approached the table again and saw the empty glasses... A chalice that she had to fill...

DAUGHTER (*Next to the little table, takes the wineglass like a chalice. Serves the wine, looks for the poison in the cabinet and dissolves it in the wineglass, carrying it afterward to her* Mother.): Then she remembered the poison that her grandmother had hidden in the cabinet. The same one she used on the cats. Her grandmother had enjoyed those deaths so much! She took it in her hand. It seemed like she had learned a lesson.

MOTHER (*Voice change.*): "And there are thieves, besides. What can one do with the thieves but set fire to them?"

DAUGHTER: She served a glass of wine. The poison dissolved slowly. She had suffered so much that she had forgotten the pain.

MOTHER: "The wine! Haven't I already asked you for it? What happened to the wine?"

The lights begin to change.

DAUGHTER: That woman was detestable. I never met her. But she had spoken to me so many times and she had cried so much that I felt like I knew her, as if she had buried her claws in me throughout my whole life... Domineering... Almost insane... Her cruel voice... Her harsh gestures... The shouts at the slaves on the plantation... Your necklaces... Your jewelry... Your money... Your arrogance... Your abominable pride...

Your friends... Your card games... Your Chief of Police... Your basement full of blood... All dead and buried... (*Long pause. The* Mother *and the* Daughter *look at each other.*) She looked at her with hate, she told me... A last hateful look. She lacked pity. That woman only understood the language of the whip and the cane. (*The* Mother *strikes the floor with the cane several times.*)

End of "Once Upon a Time" sequence. Lighting change.

DAUGHTER (*The* Mother *has the wineglass in her hand. The* Daughter *turns toward the window.*): A long day, too long for me... Who am I? My life has been so sad that I don't know if I have a right to anything... I gave her the wineglass, but she didn't understand. She was bound to survive.

MOTHER (*She drinks.*): It has a strange taste.

DAUGHTER: Those were her exact words.

MOTHER: What's happening? What has happened? It's a trick. A damned trick. You must call a doctor! Now! Right now! A doctor, damn you, a doctor! A moment of hesitation and my damned sand castle has tumbled down!

DAUGHTER: You're acting out a role. You're playing.

MOTHER: It's a crime! An assassination!

DAUGHTER: No, it's something more simple. It's freedom.

MOTHER: Revolution and war! The rebellion of the slaves! Kill all of them! I'm the owner of Heaven and Earth!

DAUGHTER (*Confused.*): But... What are we? Who is she? Where am I? Where has all this happened?

MOTHER: I'm suffocating. I need a little air.

DAUGHTER: I'll open the window.

MOTHER: Open it, open it all the way! Your freedom won't be easy. (*The* Mother *dies. Slowly, almost hesitant, the* Daughter *opens the window.*)

Blackout.

COSER Y CANTAR*

✄ Dolores Prida ✄

CHARACTERS

ELLA (una mujer)
SHE (the same woman)

The action takes place in an apartment in New York City in the present/past.

SET

A couch, a chair, and a dressing table with an imaginary mirror facing the audience is on each side of the stage. A low table with a telephone on it is upstage center. In the back, a low shelf or cabinet holds a record player, records and books. There are back exits on stage right and stage left.

Stage right is Ella's area. Stage left is She's. Piles of books, magazines and newspapers surround She's area. A pair of ice skates and a tennis racket are visible somewhere. Her dressing table has a glass with pens and pencils and various bottles of vitamin pills. SHE wears jogging shorts and sneakers.

Ella's area is somewhat untidy. Copies of Cosmopolitan, Vanidades *and* TV Gíuas *are seen around her bed. Ella's table is crowded with cosmetics, a figurine of the Virgen de la Caridad and a candle. A large conch and a pair of maracas are visible. Ella is dressed in a short red kimono.*

---

*From *Beautiful Señoritas*

IMPORTANT NOTE FROM THE AUTHOR

This piece is really one long monologue. The two women are one and are playing a verbal, emotional game of pingpong. Throughout the action, except in the final confrontation, Ella and She never look at each other, acting independently, pretending the other one does not really exist, although each continuously trespasses on each other's thoughts, feelings and behavior.
This play must NEVER be performed in just one language.

Coser y Cantar was first performed at Duo Theater in New York City on June 25, 1981 with the following cast:

ELLA ....Elizabeth Peña
SHE ....María Normán

It was directed by María Norman. The play has had many subsequent productions throughout the U.S. and in Puerto Rico. It was first published in *Tramoya*, the theater magazine of Universidad Veracruzana and Rutgers University, Issue No. 22, Jan.-Mar. 1990.

ACT I

In the dark we hear "Qué sabes tú", a recording by Olga Guillot. As lights go up slowly on Ella's couch we see a naked leg up in the air, then a hand slides up the leg and begins to apply cream to it. Ella puts cream on both legs, sensually, while singing along with the record. Ella sits up in bed, takes a hairbrush, brushes her hair, then using the brush as a microphone continues to sing along. Carried away by the song, Ella gets out of bed and "performs" in front of the imaginary mirror by her dressing table. At some point during the previous scene, lights will go up slowly on the other couch. She is reading Psychology Today *magazine. We don't see her face at the beginning. As Ella is doing her act by the mirror,* She's *eyes are seen above the magazine. She stares ahead for a while. Then shows impatience. She gets up and turns off the record player, cutting off* Ella's *singing in mid-sentence. She begins to pick up newspapers and magazines from the floor and stacks them up neatly.*

ELLA (*With contained exasperation.*): ¿Por qué haces eso? ¡Sabes que no me gusta que hagas eso! Detesto que me interrumpas así. ¡Yo no te interrumpo cuando tú te imaginas que eres Barbra Streisand!

SHE (*To herself, looking for her watch.*): What time is it? (*Finds watch.*) My God, twelve thirty! The day half-gone and I haven't done a thing.... And so much to be done. So much to be done. (*Looks at one of the newspapers she has picked up.*) ...Three people have been shot already. For no reason at all. No one is safe out there. No one. Not even those who speak good English. Not even those who know who they are...

ELLA (*Licking her lips.*): Revoltillo de huevos, tostadas, queso blanco, café con leche. Hmmm, eso es lo que me pide el estómago. Anoche soñé con ese desayuno.

Ella *goes backstage singing "Es mi vivir una linda guajirita." We hear the sound of pots and pans over her singing. At the same time,* She *puts on the Jane Fonda exercise record and begins to do exercises in the middle of the room. Still singing,* Ella *returns with a tray loaded with breakfast food and turns off the record player.* Ella *sits on the floor, Japanese-style and begins to eat.* She *sits also and takes a glass of orange juice.*

SHE: Do you have to eat so much? You eat all day, then lie there like a dead octopus.

ELLA: Y tù me lo recuerdas todo el día, pero si no fuera
    por todo lo que yo como, ya tú te hubieras muerto de
    hambre. (Ella *eats. She* sips her orange juice.)
SHE (*Distracted.*): What shall I do today? There's so much
    to do.
ELLA (*With her mouth full.*): Sí, mucho. El problema siem-
    pre es, por dónde empezar.
SHE: I should go out and jog a couple of miles.
ELLA (*Taking a bite of food.*): Sí. Debía salir a correr. Es
    bueno para la figura. (*Takes another bite.*) Y el corazón.
    (*Takes another bite.*) Y la circulación. (*Another bite.*) A cor-
    rer se ha dicho. (Ella *continues eating. She* gets up and
    opens an imaginary window facing the audience. She *looks
    out, breathes deeply, stretches.*)
SHE: Aaah, what a beautiful day! It makes you so...so
    happy to be alive!
ELLA (*From the table, without much enthusiasm.*): No es para
    tanto.
SHE (*Goes to her dressing table, sits down, takes pen and pa-
    per.*): I'll make a list of all the things I must do. Let's
    see. I should start from the inside.... Number one,
    clean the house...
ELLA (*Still eating.*): Uno, limpiar la casa.
SHE: Two, take the garbage out.
ELLA: Dos, sacar la basura.
SHE: Then, do outside things. After running, I have to do
    something about El Salvador.
ELLA: Salvar a El Salvador.
SHE: Go to the march at the U.N.
ELLA (*Has finished eating, picks up tray, gets enthusiastic about
    the planning.*): Escribir una carta el editor del *New York
    Times.*

SHE: Aha, that too. (*Adds it to the list.*) How about peace in the Middle East?

ELLA: La cuestión del aborto.

SHE: Should that come after or before the budget cuts?

ELLA (*With relish.*): Comprar chorizos mexicanos para unos burritos.

SHE (*Writing.*): See that new Fassbinder film. (Ella *makes a "boring" face.*) Find the map... (She *writes.*)

ELLA (*Serious.*): Ver a mi madrina. Tengo algo que preguntarle a los caracoles. (*Splashes Florida Water around her head.*)

SHE (*Exasperated.*): Not again!... (*Thinks.*) Buy a fish tank. (*Writes it down.*)

ELLA: ¿Una pecera?

SHE: I want to buy a fish tank, and some fish. I read in *Psychology Today* that it is supposed to calm your nerves to watch fish swimming in a tank.

ELLA (*Background music begins.*): Peceras. (*Sits at her dressing table. Stares into the mirror. Gets lost in memories.*) Las peceras me recuerdan el aeropuerto cuando me fui... los que se iban, dentro de la pecera. Esperando. Esperando dentro de aquel cuarto transparente. Al otro lado del cristal, los otros, los que se quedaban: los padres, los hermanos, los tíos.... Allí estábamos, en la pecera, nadando en el mar que nos salía por los ojos... Y los que estaban dentro y los que estaban afuera solo podían mirarse. Mirarse las caras distorcionadas por las lágrimas y el cristal sucio—lleno de huellas de manos que se querían tocar, empañado por el aliento de bocas que trataban de besarse a través del cristal.... Una pecera llena de peces asustados, que no sabían nadar, que no sabían de las aguas heladas...donde los tiburones andan con pistolas...

SHE (*Scratches item off the list forcefully.*): Dwelling in the past takes energies away.

ELLA (*Looks for the map among objects on her table. Lifts the Virgen de la Caridad statue.*): ¿Dónde habré puesto el mapa? Juraría que estaba debajo de la Santa... (*Looks under the bed. Finds one old and dirty tennis shoe. It seems to bring back memories.*) Lo primerito que yo pensaba hacer al llegar aquí era comprarme unos tenis bien cómodos y caminar todo Nueva York. Cuadra por cuadra. Para saber dónde estaba todo.

SHE: I got the tennis shoes—actually, they were basketball shoes... But I didn't get to walk every block as I had planned. I wasn't aware of how big the city was. I wasn't aware of muggers either... I did get to walk a lot, though...in marches and demonstrations. But by then, I had given up wearing tennis shoes. I was into boots....

ELLA: ...Pero nunca me perdí en el subway...

SHE: Somehow I always knew where I was going. Sometimes the place I got to was the wrong place, to be sure. But that's different. All I had to do was choose another place...and go to it. I have gotten to a lot of right places too.

ELLA (*With satisfaction.*): Da gusto llegar al lugar que se va sin perder el camino.

Loud gunshots are heard outside then police sirens, loud noises, screams, screeches. Both women get very nervous and upset. They run to the window and back, not knowing what to do.

SHE: There they go again! Now they are shooting the birds on the trees!

ELLA: ¡Están matando las viejitas en el parque...

SHE: Oh, my God! Let's get out of here!

ELLA: …Y los perros que orinan en los hidrantes!

SHE: No, no. Let's stay here! Look! They've shot a woman riding a bicycle…and now somebody is stealing it!

ELLA: ¡La gente corre, pero nadie hace nada!

SHE: Are we safe? Yes, we are safe. We're safe here… No, we're not! They can shoot through the window!

ELLA: ¡La gente grita pero nadie hace nada!

SHE: Get away from the window!

ELLA (*Pause.*): Pero, ¿y todo lo que hay que hacer?

They look around undecided, then begin to do several things around the room but then drop them immediately. She *picks up a book.* Ella *goes to the kitchen. We hear the rattling of pots and pans.* Ella *returns eating leftovers straight from a large pot.* Ella *sits in front of the mirror, catches sight of herself. Puts pot down, touches her face, tries different smiles, none of which is a happy smile.* She *is lying on the couch staring at the ceiling.*

ELLA: Si pudiera sonreír como la Mona Lisa me tomarían por misteriosa en vez de antipática porque no enseño los dientes…

SHE (*From the couch, still staring at the ceiling.*): That's because your face is an open book. You wear your emotions all over, like a suntan… You are emotionally naive…or rather, emotionally primitive…perhaps even emotionally retarded. What you need is a…a certain emotional sophistication…

ELLA: …sí, claro, eso…sofisticación emocional… (*Thinks about it.*) …sofisticación emocional… ¿Y qué carajo es sofisticación emocional? ¿Ser como tú? ¡Tú, que ya ni te acuerdas como huele tu propio sudor, que no reconoces el sonido de tu propia voz! ¡No me jodas!

SHE: See what I mean! (*Gets up, goes to her dressing table, looks for the map.*)

ELLA (*Exasperated.*): ¡Ay, Dios mío, ¿qué habré hecho yo para merecérmela? Es como tener un...un pingüino colgado del cuello!

SHE: An albatross...you mean like an albatross around your neck. Okay, okay...I'll make myself light, light as a feather...light as an albatross feather. I promise. (*Continues to look for the map.*) Where did I put that map? I thought it was with the passport, the post-cards...the traveling mementos... (*Continues looking among papers kept in a small box. Finds her worry beads. That brings memories. She plays with the beads for a while.*) ...I never really learned how to use them... (*Ella continues searching elsewhere.*) Do you know what regret means?

ELLA (*Absentmindedly.*): Es una canción de Edith Piaff.

SHE: Regret means that time in Athens, many years ago...at a cafe where they played bouzouki music. The men got up and danced and broke glasses and small dishes against the tiled floor. The women did not get up to dance. They just watched and tapped their feet under the tables...now and then shaking their shoulders to the music. One Greek man danced more than the others. He broke more glasses and dishes than the others. His name was Nikos. It was his birthday. He cut his hand with one of the broken glasses. But he didn't stop, he didn't pay any attention to his wound. He kept on dancing. He danced by my table. I took a gardenia from the vase on the table and gave it to him. He took it, rubbed it on the blood dripping from his hand and gave it back to me with a smile. He danced away to other tables.... I wanted to get up and break some dishes and dance with him. Dance away, out the door, into the street, all the way to some cheap hotel by the harbor, where next morning I would hang the bed sheet stained with my blood out the window. But I didn't get up. Like the Greek women, I stayed on my seat, tapping my feet under the table, now and then shaking my shoulders to the music…a bloodied gardenia wilting in my glass of retsina…

ELLA: No haber roto ni un plato. That's regret for sure.

The clock strikes the hour. Alarmed, they get up quickly and look for their shoes.

SHE (*Putting boots on. Rushed, alarmed.*): I have to practice the speech!

ELLA (*Puts on high heels.*): Sí tienes que aprender a hablar más alto. Sin micrófono no se te oye. Y nunca se sabe si habrá micrófono. Es mejor depender de los pulmones que de los aparatos. Los aparatos a veces fallan en el momento más inoportuno.

They stand back to back facing stage left and stage right respectively. They speak at the same time.

SHE (*In English.*): A E I O U.
ELLA (*In Spanish.*): A E I O U.
ELLA: Pirámides.
SHE: Pyramids.
ELLA: Orquídeas.
SHE: Orchids.
ELLA: Sudor.
SHE: Sweat.
ELLA: Luz.
SHE: Light.
ELLA: Blood.

SHE: Sangre.
ELLA: Dolphins.
SHE: Delfínes.
ELLA: Mountains.
SHE: Montañas.
ELLA: Sed.
SHE: Thirst.

> *Freeze. Two beats. They snap out of their concentration.*

ELLA: Tengo sed.
SHE: I think I'll have a Diet Pepsi.
ELLA: Yo me tomaría un guarapo de caña. (She *goes to the kitchen.*)
ELLA (*Looking for the map. Stops before the mirror and looks at her body, passes hand by hips, sings a few lines of Macorina and continues to look for the map behind furniture, along the walls, etc. Suddenly it seems as if* Ella *hears something from the apartment next door.* Ella *puts her ear to the wall and listens more carefully. Her face shows confusion.* Ella *asks herself, deeply, seriously intrigued.*): ¿Por qué sería que Songo le dió a Borondongo? ¿Sería porque Borondongo le dío a Bernabé? ¿O porque Bernabé le pegó a Muchilanga? ¿O en realidad sería porque Muchilanga le echo burundanga? (*Pause.*) …¿Y Monina? ¿Quien es Monina? ¡Ay, nunca lo he entendido…el gran misterio de nuestra cultura! (She *returns drinking a Diet Pepsi. Sits on the bed and drinks slowly, watching the telephone with intense concentration.* Ella's *attention is also drawn to the telephone. Both watch it hypnotically.*) El telefono no ha sonado hoy.
SHE: I must call mother. She's always complaining.
ELLA: Llamadas. Llamadas. ¿Por qué no llamará? Voy a concentrarme para que llame. (*Concentrates.*) El telé-

fono sonará en cualquier momento. Ya. Ya viene.
Suena. Sí. Suena. Va a sonar.

SHE (*Sitting in the lotus position, meditating.*): Ayer is not the
same as yesterday.

ELLA: Estás loca.

SHE: I think I'm going crazy. Talking to myself all day.

ELLA: It must be. It's too soon for menopause.

SHE: Maybe what I need is a good fuck after all.

ELLA: Eres una enferma.

SHE: At least let's talk about something important—exercise our intellects.

ELLA: ¿Como qué?

SHE: We could talk about...about...the meaning of life.

ELLA: Mi mamá me dijo una vez que la vida, sobre todo la
vida de una mujer, era coser y cantar. Y yo me lo creí.
Pero ahora me doy cuenta que la vida, la de todo el
mundo: hombre, mujer, perro, gato, jicotea, es, en realidad, comer y cagar...¡en otras palabras, la misma mierda!

SHE: Puke! So much for philosophy.

Both look among the books and magazines. Ella *picks up*
Vanidades *magazine, flips through the pages.* She *starts reading*
Self *magazine.*

ELLA: No sé que le ha pasado a *Corín Tellado.* Ya sus nove-
las no son tan románticas como antes. Me gustaban
más cuando ella, la del sedoso cabello castaño y los
brazos torneados y los ojos color violeta, no se entrega-
ba así, tan fácilmente, a él, el hombre, que aunque más
viejo, y a veces cojo, pero siempre millonario, la desea-
ba con locura, pero la respetaba hasta el día de la
boda...

SHE: I can't believe you're reading that crap.

ELLA (*Flipping through the pages some more.*): Mira, esto es interesante: ¡un test! "Usted y sus Fantasías". A ver, lo voy hacer. (*Gets a pencil from the table.*) Pregunta número uno: ¿Tienes fantasías a menudo? (*Piensa.*)

SHE: Yes. (Ella *writes down answer.*)

ELLA: ¿Cuán a menudo? (*Thinks.*)

SHE: Every night...and day.

ELLA (*Writes down answer.*): ¿Cuál es el tema recurrente de tus fantasías?

SHE (*Sensually mischievous.*): I am lying naked. Totally, fully, wonderfully naked. Feeling good and relaxed. Suddenly, I feel something warm and moist between my toes. It is a tongue! A huge, wide, live tongue! The most extraordinary thing about this tongue is that it changes. It takes different shapes... It wraps itself around my big toe...then goes in between and around each toe...then it moves up my leg, up my thigh...and into my...

ELLA: ¡Vulgar! No se trata de esas fantasías. Se trata de...de...de ¡Juana de Arco!

SHE: I didn't know that Joan of Arc was into...

ELLA: Ay, chica, no hablaba de fantasías eróticas, sino de fantasías *heróicas*...a lo Juana de Arco. A mí Juana de Arco me parece tan dramática, tan patriótica, tan sacrificada...

SHE: I don't care for Joan of Arc—too hot to handle! ...ha, ha, ha. (*Both laugh at the bad joke.*)

ELLA (*Picking up the chair and lifting it above her head.*): Mi fantasía es ser una superwoman: ¡Maravilla, la mujer maravilla! (*Puts chair down and lies across it, arms and legs kicking in the air, as if swimming.*) ...Y salvar a una niña que se ahoga en el Canal de la Mancha, y nadar, como Esther Williams, hasta los blancos farallones de

Dover... (*Gets up, then rides astride the chair.*) ¡Ser una heroína que cabalgando siempre adelante, hacia el sol, inspirada por una fe ciega, una pasión visionaria, arrastre a las multitudes para juntos salvar al mundo de sus errores!

SHE: Or else, a rock singer! They move crowds, all right. And make more money. How about, La Pasionaria and her Passionate Punk Rockers!

ELLA (*Disappointed.*): Tú nunca me tomas en serio.

SHE: My fantasy is to make people happy. Make them laugh. I'd rather be a clown. When times are as bad as these, it is better to keep the gathering gloom at bay by laughing and dancing. The Greeks do it, you know. They dance when they are sad. Yes, what I really would like to be is a dancer. And dance depression... inflation...and the NUCLEAR THREAT...AWAY!

ELLA (*To herself disheartened.*): Pero tienes las piernas muy flacas y el culo muy grande.

SHE (*Ignoring Ella's remarks.*): Dancing is what life is all about. The tap-tapping of a hundred feet on Forty-Second Street is more exciting than an army marching off to kill the enemy.... Yes! My fantasy is to be a great dancer...like Fred Astaire and Ginger Rogers!

ELLA: ¿Cuál de ellos, Fred Astaire o Ginger Rogers?

SHE: Why can't I be both?

ELLA: ¿Será que eres bisexual?

SHE (*Puts her head between her legs as if exercising.*): No. I checked out. Just one.

ELLA: ¿Nunca has querido ser hombre?

SHE: Not really. Men are such jerks.

ELLA: Pero se divierten más. ¿De veras que nunca te has sentido como ese poema?: " ...Hoy, quiero ser hombre. Subir por las tapias, burlar los conventos, ser todo un

Don Juan; raptar a Sor Carmen y a Sor Josefina, rendirlas, y a Julia de Burgos violar..."

SHE: You are too romantic, that's your problem.

ELLA: ¡Y tú eres muy promiscua! Te acuestas con demasiada gente que ni siquiera te cae bien, que no tiene nada que ver contigo.

SHE (*Flexing her muscles.*): It keeps me in shape. (*Bitchy.*) And besides, it isn't as corny as masturbating, listening to boleros.

ELLA (*Covering her ears.*): ¡Cállate! ¡Cállate! ¡Cállate! (*Goes to the window and looks out.*) (*Pause.*) Está nevando. No se ve nada allá afuera. Y aquí, estas cuatro paredes me están volviendo...¡bananas! (Ella *goes to the table, takes a banana and begins to eat it.* She *plays with an old tennis racket.*) Si por lo menos tuviera el televisor, podría ser una película o algo...pero, no...

SHE: Forget about the TV set.

ELLA: ¡Tuviste que tirarlo por la ventana! Y lo peor no es que me quedé sin televisor. No. Lo peor es el caso por daños y perjuicios que tengo pendiente.

SHE: I don't regret a thing.

ELLA: La mala suerte que el maldito televisor le cayera encima al carro de los Moonies que viven al lado. ¿Te das cuenta? ¡Yo, acusada de terrorista por el Reverendo Sun Myung Moon! ¡A nadie le pasa esto! ¡A nadie más que a mí! ¡Te digo que estoy cagada de aura tiñosa!

SHE. You are exaggerating. Calm down.

ELLA: Cada vez que me acuerdo me hierve la sangre. Yo, yo, ¡acusada de terrorista! ¡Yo! ¡Cuando la víctima he sido yo! ¡No se puede negar que yo soy una víctima del terrorismo!

SHE: Don't start with your paranoia again.

ELLA: ¡Paranoia! ¿Tú llamas paranoia a todo lo que ha pasado? ¿A lo que pasó con los gatos? ¡Mis tres gatos, secuestrados, descuartizados, y luego dejados en la puerta, envueltos en papel de regalo, con una tarjeta de Navidad!

SHE: You know very well it didn't happen like that.

ELLA: ¿Y la cobra entre las cartas? How about that snake in the mail box? Who put it there? Who? Who? Why?

SHE: Forget all that. Mira como te pones por gusto... Shit! We should have never come here.

ELLA (*Calming down.*): Bueno, es mejor que New Jersey. Además ¿cuál es la diferencia? El mismo tiroteo, el mismo cucaracheo, la misma mierda...coser y cantar, you know.

SHE: At least in Miami there was sunshine...

ELLA: Había sol, sí, pero demasiadas nubes negras. Era el humo que salía de tantos cerebros tratando de pensar. Además, aquí hay más cosas que hacer.

SHE: Yes. Más cosas que hacer. And I must do them. I have to stop contemplating my navel and wallowing in all this...this... Yes, one day soon I have to get my caca together and get out THERE and DO something. Definitely. Seriously. (*Silent pause. Both are lost in thought.*)

ELLA: I remember when I first met you...there was a shimmer in your eyes...

SHE: Y tú tenías una sonrisa...

ELLA: And with that shimmering look in your eyes and that smile...

SHE: ...pensamos que íbamos a conquistar el mundo...

ELLA: ...But...

SHE: ...I don't know... (*Goes to her table and picks up a bottle of vitamins.*): Did I take my pills today?

ELLA: Sí.

SHE: Vitamin C?
ELLA: Sí.
SHE: Iron?
ELLA: Sí.
SHE: Painkiller?
ELLA: Of course…because camarón que se duerme se lo
lleva la corriente.
SHE: A shrimp that falls asleep is carried away by the cur-
rent?
ELLA: No…that doesn't make any sense.
SHE: Between the devil and the deep blue sea?
ELLA: …No es lo mismo que entre la espada y la pared,
porque del dicho al hecho hay un gran trecho.
SHE: Betwixt the cup and the lip you should not look a gift
horse in the mouth.
ELLA: A caballo regalado no se le mira el colmillo, pero
tanto va el cántaro a la fuente, hasta que se rompe.
SHE: An eye for an eye and a tooth for a tooth.
ELLA: Y no hay peor ciego que el que no quiere ver. (*Both
are lethargic, about to fall asleep.*)
SHE (*Yawning.*): I have to be more competitive.
ELLA (*Yawning.*): Despues de la siesta.

*They fall asleep. Lights dim out. In the background music
box music comes on and remains through* Ella's *entire monologue.*

ELLA (*Upset voice of a young child.*): Pero, ¿por qué tengo
que esperar tres horas para bañarme? ¡No me va a
pasar nada!… ¡Los peces comen y hacen la digestión
en el agua y no les pasa nada!… Sí, tengo muchas
leyes. ¡Debía ser abogada! ¡Debía ser piloto! ¡Debía ser
capitán! ¡Debía ser una tonina y nadar al otro lado de
la red, sin temer a los tiburones! (*Pause. Now as a rebel-*

lious teenager.) ¡Y no voy a caminar bajo el sol con ese paraguas! ¡No me importa que la piel blanca sea mas elegante!… ¡No se puede tapar el sol con una sombrilla! ¡No se puede esperar que la marea baje cuando tiene que subir! (*As an adult.*) …No se puede ser un delfín en las pirámides. No se le puede cortar la cabeza al delfín y guardarla en la gaveta, entre las prendas más íntimas y olvidar el delfín. Y olvidar que se quiso ser el delfín. Olvidar que se quiso ser la niña desnuda, cabalgando sobre el delfín…

SHE (*Lights up on She. Needling.*): So, you don't have dreams. So, you can't remember your dreams. So, you never talk about your dreams. I think you *don't want* to remember your dreams. You always want to be going somewhere, but now you are stuck here with me, because outside it's raining blood and you have been to all the places you can possibly ever go to! No, you have nowhere to go! Nowhere! Nowhere! (Ella *slaps* She *with force. The clock strikes twice. They awaken. Lights come up fully.* She *slaps herself softly on both cheeks.*) A nightmare in the middle of the day!

ELLA: Tengo que encontrar ese mapa. (*They look for the map.*)

SHE (*Picks up a book, fans the pages. Finds a marker in one page. Reads silently, then reads aloud.*): "Picasso's gaze was so absorbing one was surprised to find anything left on the paper after he looked at it…" (*Thinks about this image. Then softly.*) Think about that…

ELLA: Sí. Claro. Así siento mis ojos en la primavera. Después de ver tanto árbol desnudo durante el invierno, cuando salen las primeras hojas, esas hojitas de un verde tan tierno, me da miedo mirarlas mucho porque temo que mis ojos le vayan a chupar todo el color.

SHE: I miss all that green. Sometimes I wish I could do like Dorothy in "The Wizard of Oz," close my eyes, click my heels and repeat three times, "there's no place like home"…and, puff! be there.

ELLA: El peligro de eso es que una pueda terminar en una finca en Kansas.

SHE: …I remember that trip back home…I'd never seen such a blue sea. It was an alive, happy blue. You know what I mean?

ELLA: A mí no se me había olvidado. Es el mar más azul, el más verde…el más chévere del mundo. No hay comparación con estos mares de por aquí.

SHE: …It sort of slapped you in the eyes, got into them and massaged your eyeballs…

ELLA: Es un mar tan sexy, tan tibio. Como que te abraza. Dan ganas de quitarse el traje de baño y nadar desnuda…lo cual, por supuesto, hiciste a la primera oportunidad…

SHE: …I wanted to see everything, do everything in a week…

ELLA (*Laughing.*): …No sé si lo viste todo, pero en cuanto a hacer…¡el trópico te alborotó, chiquitica! ¡Hasta en el Malecón! ¡Qué escándalo!

SHE (*Laughing.*): I sure let my hair down! It must have been all that rum. Everywhere we went, there was rum and "La Guantanamera"… And that feeling of belonging, of being home despite…

ELLA (*Nostalgic.*): ¡Aaay!

SHE: ¿Qué pasa?

ELLA: ¡Ay, siento que me viene un ataque de nostalgia!

SHE: Let's wallow!

ELLA: ¡Ay, sí, un disquito!

She *puts a record on. It is "Nostalgia habanera" sung by Olga Guillot. Both sing and dance along with the record for a while. The music stays on throughout the scene.*

BOTH (*Singing.*):

"Siento la nostalgia de volver a ti
más el destino manda y no puede ser
Mi Habana, mi tierra querida
cuándo yo te volveré a ver
Habana, como extraño el sol indiano de tus calles
Habana etc...."

ELLA: ¡Aaay, esta nostalgia me ha dado un hambre!

SHE: That's the problem with nostalgia—it is usually loaded with calories! How about some steamed broccoli...

ELLA: Arroz...

SHE: Yogurt...

ELLA: Frijoles negros...

SHE: Bean sprouts...

ELLA: Plátanos fritos...

SHE: Wheat germ...

ELLA: Ensalada de aguacate...

SHE: Raw carrots...

ELLA: ¡Flan!

SHE: Granola!

ELLA: ¿Qué tal un arroz con pollo, o un ajiaco?

SHE: Let's go!

They exit out to the kitchen. Lights out. Record plays to the end. We hear rattling of pots and pans. When lights go up again they lie on their respective beds.

ELLA: ¡Qué bien! ¡Qué rico! Esa comida me ha puesto erótica. I feel sexy. Romántica.

SHE (*With bloated feeling.*): How can you feel sexy after rice and beans?... I feel violent, wild. I feel like...chains, leather, whips. Whish! Whish!

ELLA: No, no, no! Yo me siento como rosas y besos bajo la luna, recostada a una palmera mecida por el viento...

SHE: Such tropical, romantic tackiness, ay, ay, ay.

ELLA: Sí,...y un olor a jasmines que se cuela por la ventana...

SHE: I thought you were leaning on a swaying coconut tree.

ELLA: ...Olor a jasmines, mezclado con brisas de salitre. A lo lejos se escucha un bolero: (*Sings.*)
"Te acuerdas de la noche de la playa
Te acuerdas que te di mi amor primero..."

SHE: ...I feel the smell of two bodies together, the heat of the flesh so close to mine, the sweat and the saliva trickling down my spine... (*Both get progressively excited.*)

ELLA: ...y unas manos expertas me abren la blusa, me sueltan el ajustador, y con mucho cuidado, como si fueran dos mangos maduros, me sacan los senos al aire...

SHE: ...And ten fingernails dig into my flesh and I hear drums beating faster and faster and faster!

They stop, exhaling a deep sigh of contentment. They get up from bed at different speeds and go to their dressing tables. Ella lights up a cigarette sensually. She puts cold cream on her face, slowly and sensually. They sing in a sexy, relaxed manner.

ELLA: "Fumar es un placer...
SHE: ...Genial, sensual...
ELLA: ...Fumando espero...
SHE: ...Al hombre que yo quiero...

ELLA: ...Tras los cristales...

SHE: ...De alegres ventanales...

ELLA: ...Y mientras fumo..."

SHE (*Half laughs.*): ...I remember the first time...

ELLA: Ja ja...a mí me preguntaron si yo había tenido un orgasmo alguna vez. Yo dije que no. No porque no lo había tenido, sino porque no sabía lo que era... Pensé que orgasmo era una tela.

SHE: I looked it up in the dictionary: orgasm. Read the definition, and still didn't know what it meant.

ELLA: A pesar del diccionario, hasta que no tuve el primero, en realidad no supe lo que quería decir...

SHE: It felt wonderful. But all the new feelings scared me...

ELLA (*Kneeling on the chair.*): ...Fuí a la iglesia al otro día... me arrodillé, me persiné, alcé los ojos al cielo—es decir al techo—muy devotamente, pero cuando empecé a pensar la oración...me di cuenta de que, en vez de pedir perdón, estaba pidiendo...aprobación! ...permiso para hacerlo otra vez!

SHE: ...Oh God, please, give me a sign! Tell me it is all right! Send an angel, una paloma, a flash of green light to give me the go ahead! Stamp upon me the Good Housekeeping Seal of Approval, to let me know that fucking is okay!

ELLA: ¡Ay, Virgen del Cobre! Yo tenía un miedo que se enterara la familia. ¡Me parecía que me lo leían en la cara!

They fall back laughing. The telephone rings three time. They stop laughing abruptly, look at the telephone with fear and expectation. After each ring each one in turn extends the hand to pick it up, but stops midway. Finally, after the third ring, She *picks it up.*

SHE: Hello?... Oh, hiii, how are you?... I am glad you called... I wanted to... Yes. Okay. Well, go ahead... (*Listens.*) Yes, I know...but I didn't think it was serious. (*Listens.*) ...You said our relationship was special, untouchable... (*Whimpering.*) Then how can you end it just like this...I can't believe that all the things we shared don't mean anything to you anymore... (*Listens.*) What do you mean, it was meaningful while it lasted?! ...Yes, I remember you warned me you didn't want to get involved...but, all I said was that I love you... Okay. I shouldn't have said that... Oh, please, let's try again!... Look...I'll...I'll come over Saturday night... Sunday morning we'll make love...have brunch: eggs, croissants, Bloody Marys...we'll read the *Times* in bed and...please, don't...how can you?...

ELLA (*Having been quietly reacting to the conversation, and getting angrier and angrier* Ella *grabs the phone away from* She.): ¿Pero quién carajo tú te crees que eres para venir a tirarme así, como si yo fuera una chancleta vieja? ¡Qué huevos fritos ni ocho cuartos, viejo! ¡Después de tanta hambre que te maté, los buenos vinos que te compré! ¡A ver si esa putica que te has conseguido cocina tan bien como yo! ¡A ver si esa peluá te va a dar todo lo que yo te daba! ¡A ver si esa guaricandilla... (*Suddenly desperate.*) Ay, ¿como puedes hacerme esto a mí? ¡A mí que te adoro ciegamente, a mí, que te quiero tanto, que me muero por ti!... Mi amor...ay, mi amor, no me dejes. Haré lo que tú quieras. ¡Miénteme, pégame, traicióname, patéame, arrástrame por el fango, pero no me dejes! (*Sobs. Listens. Calms down.*

Now stoically melodramatic and resigned.) Está bien. Me
clavas un puñal. Me dejas con un puñal clavado en el
centro del corazón. Ya nunca podré volver a amar. Mi
corazón se desangra, siento que me desvanezco... Me
iré a una playa solitaria y triste, y a media noche, como
Alfonsina, echaré a andar hacia las olas y... (*Listens for
three beats. Gets angry.*) ¿Asi es como respondes cuando
vuelco mi corazón, mis sentimientos en tu oído?
¡¿Cuando mis lágrimas casi crean un corto circuito en
el teléfono?! ¡Ay, infeliz! ¡Tú no sabes nada de la vida!
Adiós, y que te vaya bien. De veras...honestamente,
no te guardo rencor...te deseo lo mejor...¿Yo?...yo
seguiré mi viaje. Seré bien recibida en otros puertos. Ja,
ja, ja... De veras, te deseo de todo corazón que esa tipa,
por lo menos, ¡sea tan BUENA EN LA CAMA COMO
YO! (*Bangs the phone down. Both sit on the floor back to
back. Long pause. Ella fumes. She is contrite.*)
SHE: You shouldn't have said all those things.
ELLA: ¿Por qué no? Todo no se puede intelectualizar. You
    can't dance everything away, you know.
SHE: You can't eat yourself to numbness either.
ELLA: Yeah.
SHE: You know what's wrong with me? I can't relate any
    more. I have been moving away from people. I stay
    here and look at the ceiling. And talk to you. I don't
    know how to talk to people anymore. I don't know if I
    want to talk to people anymore!
ELLA: Tu problema es que ves demasiadas películas de
    Woody Allen, y ya te crees una neoyorquina neurótica.
    Yo no. Yo sé como tener una fiesta conmigo misma. Yo
    me divierto sola. Y me acompaño y me entretengo. Yo
    tengo mis recuerdos. Y mis plantas en la ventana. Yo

tengo una solidez. Tengo unas raíces, algo de que agar-
rarme. Pero tú…¿tú de qué te agarras?

SHE: I hold on to you. I couldn't exist without you.

ELLA: But I wonder if I need you. Me pregunto si te nece-
sito..robádome la mitad de mis pensamientos, de mi
tiempo, de mi sentir, de mis palabras…como una san-
guijuela!

SHE: I was unavoidable. You spawned me while you swam
in that fish tank. It would take a long time to make me
go away!

ELLA: Tú no eres tan importante. Ni tan fuerte. Unos
meses, tal vez unos años, bajo el sol, y, ¡presto!…desa-
parecerías. No quedaría ni rastro de ti. Yo soy la que
existo. Yo soy la que soy. Tú…no sé lo que eres.

SHE: But, if it weren't for me you would not be the one you
are now. No serías la que eres. I gave yourself back to
you. If I had not opened some doors and some windows for you, you would still be sitting in the dark,
with your recuerdos, the idealized beaches of your
childhood, and your rice and beans and the rest of
your goddamn obsolete memories! (*For the first time
they face each other, furiously.*)

ELLA: Pero soy la más fuerte!

SHE: I am as strong as you are! (*With each line, they throw
something at each other, pillows, books, papers, etc.*)

ELLA: ¡Soy la más fuerte!

SHE: I am the strongest!

ELLA: ¡Te robaste parte de mí!

SHE: You wanted to be me once!

ELLA: ¡Estoy harta de ti!

SHE: Now you are!

ELLA: ¡Ojalá no estuvieras!

SHE: You can't get rid of me!

ELLA: ¡Alguien tiene que ganar!
SHE: No one shall win!

*Loud sounds of sirens, shots, screams are heard outside.
They run towards the window, then walk backwards in fear,
speaking simultaneously.*

SHE: They are shooting again!
ELLA: ¡Y están cortando los árboles!
SHE: They're poisoning the children in the schoolyard!
ELLA: ¡Y echando la basura y los muertos al río!
SHE: We're next! We're next!
ELLA: ¡Y no salgo de aquí!
SHE: Let's get out of here! (*Another shot is heard. They look at
     each other.*)
ELLA: El mapa…
SHE: Where's the map?

Blackout.

MEMORIES OF MY FATHER'S FAMILY DURING HIS SELF-IMPOSED EXILE*

Omar Torres

ACT I

Scene 1

A dining area and living room in a middle-class home. Mario *is sitting by the radio, listening to a waltz by Strauss.* Ana *is doing housework in the kitchen.* Elena *enters.*

ELENA: You're here already? It must be lunchtime.

ANA (*From the kitchen.*): You're having breakfast? (Elena *picks up articles of clothing from the furniture.*) It's almost noon. Everyone eats whenever they want. What do they care.

ELENA: A mother who talks to herself, a brother who doesn't talk. The three of us can make great conversation together.

ANA (*Talking to herself.*): I'm tired of making breakfast, of asking people if they want breakfast. (*Shouting at* Elena.) I asked you if you want breakfast?

ELENA: Of course I want breakfast.

MARIO (*Talking to himself aloud.*): Have you ever noticed how your hair sticks up in the back when you get up in the morning? If I don't wet my hair in the morning, I can't comb it. It goes to one side, like this, as if my head were a crooked pyramid.

ELENA (*Sitting at the table.*): It is.

From *Fallen Angels Sing*

MARIO: But I only wash it twice a week; the other days I just wet it.

ANA (*Coming into the room.*): I don't know what to make for lunch. Beto always wants chicken with rice. It's enough to have it on Sundays. I'll make *picadillo*. (*To* Elena.) You want *picadillo* for lunch?

ELENA: You know very well I never eat *picadillo*. In thirty-five years I have never had *picadillo*. Why do you ask me if I want *picadillo*?

MARIO: We heard you. You don't want *picadillo*.

ANA: Well, I'll make *picadillo*.

ELENA: I have such a headache. Why doesn't Otilio come with my prescription? I don't know why they trust a drunk with medicine.

ANA: He's not a drunk. He drinks a little, but that doesn't mean he is a drunk. Dr. Pérez gave him a place to live, and Otilio runs errands for him.

ELENA (*Having breakfast.*): Where's Lundi?

ANA: At five this morning he ran out of the house.

ELENA: If he continues like this, we'll have to put him in an institution.

ANA: We're not going to put him anywhere; what's gotten into you?

ELENA: Nothing has gotten into me. I'm just sick and tired of being the only one who works in this house. Do you know how many dresses and blouses I have to sell in that dump to keep this house going?

ANA: Roberto also gives money.

ELENA: Oh, yes! Roberto also gives money. When he wins at poker or blackjack. How about when he loses? Should we sit with a rosary, and pray for him to win? We're going to need lots of praying. This last year he's had a hell of a losing streak.

MARIO: That's strange! Roberto is a good gambler, he used to win all the time.

ANA: Leave him alone. You're always picking on your brothers. Stop it!

MARIO: A man was killed last night.

ELENA: I should put a stop to it. We'll all starve. How long has it been since Beto stopped working? What am I saying? He has never worked.

MARIO: In the middle of the night.

ANA: He worked when we had the farm.

ELENA: What are you talking about? He was the only farmer I knew who never got dirt on his hands.

MARIO: I think they said it was something he ate.

ELENA: You know very well he sold the farm so that he wouldn't have to look for any more excuses not to work.

MARIO: What was it? I think it was *picadillo*. Pancho told me this morning. Do you know he lost his job? Pancho, I mean.

ELENA: I can't stand it when you do that.

MARIO: Do what?

ELENA: Start to say something, and then go into something else.

MARIO: I never do that.

ELENA: You just did it.

MARIO: The thing is that his wife said she made *picadillo* for dinner, that it was quite good, that she is a great cook and so on and so forth. But she also said that her husband was complaining it was too salty. And there's nothing worse than a salty *picadillo*. Well, to make a long story short...

ELENA: Thank God for small favors. You never speak, but when you do...

MARIO: To make a long story short...

ELENA: I wonder where Lundi is.

MARIO: He ate the *picadillo*. In the middle of the night, the salty *picadillo* began to take revenge on him. He had to get up to go to the kitchen and get a glass of water. The usual nightly shooting that we've been having lately took place precisely at that moment. How lucky can you get? A bullet went through the kitchen window, and poor Chucho got it between the salty *picadillo* and the glass of water.

ANA: Is that the Chucho that's married to Felicia?

ELENA: Ana, the one that was married to Felicia, died two years ago.

ANA: How can that be?

ELENA: He was run over by a truck.

MARIO: Ana, watch the salt!

ELENA: If it's on account of the salt, no one will ever get shot in this house. She never uses salt.

ANA: Who says I don't use salt? Of course I use salt. How can I cook without salt. The thing is that in this house no one is ever satisfied.

ELENA: Salt or no salt your cooking leaves a lot to be desired. (Lundi *enters running*.)

LUNDI: It exploded. There was an explosion. Boom! An explosion. Didn't you hear it?

ELENA: What explosion?

ANA: I did hear something this morning.

LUNDI: An explosion, boom. I was there.

MARIO: I heard it on the news a little while ago.

LUNDI: People were running.

MARIO: Did anyone get killed?

ELENA: One day we'll all be blown to pieces. (*Leaving*.) My head is splitting.

LUNDI: Mario, did you hear about the explosion?

MARIO: Yes, I heard about it on the radio. Did you hear about the shootings? They shot Chucho in the middle of the night.

LUNDI: In the middle of the night? I'm not sleeping anymore. No sir, not me. I'm not crazy. I'm going to be awake all night. All night. With my eyes open. Can you sleep with your eyes open? I better not, just in case. I have a better idea: I won't sleep anymore. Can I do that, Mario? Ana, Ana, can't I stop sleeping? Come on, Ana, help me to stop sleeping.

ANA: You can stop sleeping.

LUNDI: I'll just sit up all night. Mario, are you going to stop sleeping also? Eh, Mario, are you going to sit up all night?

ANA: Lundi, you have to go to the butcher.

LUNDI: To the butcher? You want meat?

ANA: No, I want potatoes.

LUNDI: The butcher doesn't sell potatoes, Ana. You're going crazy.

ANA: You're driving me crazy. You're driving everyone around here crazy. Now, listen. Stay put, and listen. Get a pound-and-a-half of ground beef for the *picadillo*.

LUNDI: Ground beef. A pound-and-a-half.

ANA: A pound-and-a-half.

LUNDI: Ground beef.

ANA: Yes.

LUNDI: A pound-and-a-half.

ANA: Of ground beef.

LUNDI: Ana, you sound like a broken record. Yes, a pound-and...

ANA: Hurry up, it's for lunch. (Lundi *leaves, running.* Beto *enters. He's slender, pale. He's always whistling or making some sort of sound with his mouth. He wears a hat too small for his head.*)

BETO: One day that boy is going to stomp over someone. Where's he going?

ANA: To the butcher.

BETO: At this hour?

ANA: There was no one else.

BETO: Are we having chicken with rice?

ANA: We're having *picadillo*.

MARIO (*Getting up.*): Watch the salt.

BETO: What's with the salt?

ANA: Don't pay any attention to him.

BETO: Listening to so much music is making him stupid. (Otilio *enters. He's unshaven. He's wearing very old clothes, but clean. He's drunk.*)

OTILIO: Good people of Oriente. Permit me to call you Orientals, although if that were the case…

ANA: Good morning, Otilio.

BETO: How did you come in?

OTILIO: My good man, permit me to call you inquisitive. Through the door, of course. (Elena *enters.*)

ELENA: You certainly took your time getting here. Did you bring my pills?

OTILIO: You may change that question into an affirmative statement.

ELENA: Thank God.

OTILIO: Do you believe that a Christian in harmony with God would need to consume such a fertile amount of manmade relief?

ELENA: What have you been drinking?

OTILIO: The nectar of forgiveness.

ELENA: Is that what they call it now?

OTILIO: Permit me to call you a pill freak.

ELENA: Otilio, I'm not in the mood.

OTILIO: My dear woman, that is the story of every mortal soul. One is never in the mood for what one gets. But one gets it anyway. Your days have been carved in the tree of life.

ELENA: Who do you think you are, the Aristotle of the Caribbean?

BETO: Otilio, for a Saturday morning you are really a pain in the neck.

OTILIO: Saturday mornings are no different than Wednesday afternoons, or Tuesday evenings.

ANA: You can say that again.

OTILIO: You are born into a circle.

ANA: You want some coffee?

OTILIO: That is poison. Although, if you have a bit of spirits.

BETO: There's no liquor in the house.

ANA: No one drinks here.

OTILIO: Allow me to call you cheap and dry.

ELENA: You have no place to go?

OTILIO: We are all confined to the place we inhabit. There's no escape, we're trapped.

ELENA: The door is open.

OTILIO (*Takes a bottle from his coat pocket, pours into the cap and drinks.*): Permit me to fertilize my soul. As I was saying, doors are deceiving. Sometimes even open doors cannot let you escape, sometimes open doors trap you.

ELENA: Otilio, I have a headache.

OTILIO: That is just what I mean.

ELENA: Nothing that silence won't cure.

OTILIO: Words are incommunicable anyhow. Just sit back and relax.

ELENA: I wasn't talking about my silence. I was talking about yours.

ANA: Nena, don't be rude.

OTILIO: It's quite all right. We must all speak our piece sometime. I was leaving anyway. (*He starts to walk out.*) I shall remember your faces as I see them now. (*To* Elena.) Permit me to call you a winter frog. Winter frogs are always lonely and make horrible sounds. (Otilio *leaves.*)

ELENA: I can't stand that man.

BETO: You can't stand anybody.

ELENA: I simply cannot stand drunks.

BETO: You simply hate people.

ANA: Nena always gets annoyed at the slightest thing.

BETO: I have never come across a man you happen to like.

ELENA: Certainly not in this house.

ANA: She was quite taken by that man, what was his name? Carlitos? Julito? You know, the nephew of Modesto, the barber.

ELENA: Let's not bring that up again.

BETO: That's who she likes: nobodies.

ELENA: Sure, that's the type I like, but you don't like any type. No one is good enough for you. Every time I met someone, you rejected him. You always found some fault. (Lundi *enters.*)

ANA: Nena, the truth is you never met anyone who was worth anything.

ELENA: What am I supposed to be? A Cuban princess?

BETO: You may not be a princess, but you come from a good family.

ELENA: That's a laugh. All I know is that I am thirty-five and counting.

LUNDI: And counting fast. Thirty-five, thirty-six, thirty-seven. Am I good enough for you, Nena? Am I?

ELENA: Sure you are, Lundi.

BETO: If you haven't married it's your own fault.

ELENA: Let's drop it.

BETO: It's true.

ELENA: I don't know why you were always so particular about my going out with anyone. You are a disgrace yourself.

ANA: Elena.

LUNDI: Elena.

BETO: There's no more respect in this house.

ANA: You have no right to speak to him like that.

ELENA: It's the truth. What does he have to be so proud of? The only thing he has ever done is gamble at that club. He hasn't done an honest day's work in his life. And Roberto? A chip off the same block, a gambler like his father. Who's kidding whom?

BETO: You always had everything.

ELENA: Hell is what I've always had.

LUNDI (*Singing.*): Hell, hell, hell. Hell for everyone.

ANA: I better make lunch. Roberto is coming in a little while.

ELENA: Why don't you ask him to get married and work like any decent man should do. Oh, no! Not King Roberto. King Roberto is our beloved forty-year-old money-getter; the quickest hands in the tropics, the wizard of dominoes, our poker perfectionist.

ANA: Leave Roberto alone. He hasn't done anything to you.

ELENA: No, he hasn't done anything to me. He simply hasn't done anything. Why do you protect him all the time? Why do you always take sides with him?

ANA: I never take sides.

ELENA: You always do.

BETO: All right. All right. That's enough.

ELENA: It's not enough.

BETO: I said that's enough. (Elena *rushes out*.)

LUNDI: Beto, did you hear the explosion?

ANA: Lundi, cut it out.

BETO: What explosion?

LUNDI: There was an explosion, it went BOOM! You didn't hear it? You were probably asleep. Everybody else in town heard it, except you. But I swear, Beto, I had nothing to do with it.

ANA: Lundi, you have to get a haircut. Beto, give Lundi some money to get a haircut.

BETO: He looks fine to me.

LUNDI: I look fine.

ANA: If you don't get a haircut, you're not having lunch.

LUNDI: Beto, give me the money. Did I tell you about the explosion? Beto, I swear I had nothing to do with it.

BETO: I'm sure you didn't.

LUNDI: You believe me, Beto, don't you?

BETO: Why shouldn't I believe you?

LUNDI: I just wanted to make sure. (*Pause.*) Do you know what I learned today? I learned that the rebels are in town.

BETO: Where did you hear that?

LUNDI: You know who is a rebel? Martínez, the man who works at the bank.

ANA (*Entering.*): Where did you hear that?

LUNDI: I heard it, I heard it. There's going to be such an explosion. I heard everything.

ANA: My head is what's going to explode.

LUNDI: Ana, you know they say that the jails are full. Full, full, full, full. And you know what? They pull out their fingernails to make them talk.

ANA: Where have you been that you heard all this?

LUNDI: I know.

BETO: If some rebels get caught, I'm sure they'll do anything to make them say whatever they want to hear. That's war.

ANA: What war?

BETO: Ana, people are getting killed all over. Look what happened to that guy Chucho. He got killed in his own home, drinking a glass of water.

ANA: That's no war, it's just a bunch of crazy soldiers.

LUNDI: I'll talk. If they ask me, I'll talk.

ANA: You have nothing to say, you know nothing.

LUNDI: Yes I do. I heard the explosion. I saw everything.

ANA: You were imagining things.

LUNDI: I wasn't imagining things. Beto, do you believe I was imagining things? You said you believed me, didn't you?

BETO: Yes, I believe you, Lundi, but you can't go around telling people you know anything.

LUNDI: But, if they send me to jail?

ANA: Nobody is going to send you any place, except to take out the garbage.

LUNDI: But if they send me to jail, I'll talk. No, you're right, I don't know anything. I won't talk. Right, Beto?

ANA: I want to know where you've been.

LUNDI: Here and there.

ANA: You should spend more time here, instead of running around the city looking for bombs.

BETO: Lundi, you have nothing to worry about, the white horse hasn't been seen yet.

ANA: You fantasize more than he does.

LUNDI: What white horse, Beto?

BETO: You don't know the legend of the white horse?

LUNDI: No, but I want to know. Tell me about it, Beto. Tell me, tell me.

BETO: Well, the story goes like this: When the Spanish first started to settle in Cuba, they sent a man called Don Alfonso de Ojeda to our town. Well, this guy Don Alfonso had a very beautiful daughter. Then there was this Indian, a very handsome man. He used to ride a white horse every afternoon. The Spanish made the Indians work all day, but since Cueiba was a very strong Indian, he would always finish early, and then he would go around town on his beautiful white horse. One day he saw the daughter of Ojeda, and he fell in love with her, and she also fell in love with him. But it was an impossible love. So one night he ran away with her, and he was caught.

LUNDI: Did they pull out his fingernails?

BETO: Forget about the fingernails. He was beheaded. They cut off his head.

LUNDI: I don't want them to cut off my head.

BETO: Will you listen? Well, after that, the beheaded Indian rode around town on his white horse. Now, every time that something happens, some tragedy or something, they say they see the white horse prancing along Francisco Vega Street.

LUNDI: I don't know, Beto, but I don't have a white horse. I don't want them to cut off my head. Beto, don't let them cut off my head.

ANA: Now you've really fixed things.

LUNDI: I would look horrible without my head. (Lundi *starts to leave.*) I want my head. I want my head. I want… (Lundi *runs out shouting.*)

ANA: Lundi, come back here.

BETO: Let him go.

ANA: How can I let him go? He's going to get into trouble. Lundi! Beto, go after him. Lundi! Beto, go and get him back.

BETO: I have to work on my list, it's been a slow day.

ANA: I don't care, go after him. Beto, he has to go to the butcher. Go after him or there will be no lunch.

BETO (*Getting up.*): When it isn't lunch, dinner; it's always something. (*He walks out.*)

ANA: I would be very happy if I didn't have to cook. We can forget about it right now. Less work for me. Forty years cooking three meals a day. How many meals is that? If I only knew. I wonder why women want to get married; you're either a housewife, an old maid or a prostitute. I don't know which is worse. (*Pause.*) Don't go to the store. Don't do anything. Leave it to me. I do the cooking, the cleaning, the laundry. (Elena *enters.*)

ELENA: You're talking to yourself again.

ANA: I'm talking to your father.

ELENA: Where is he?

ANA: He's around.

ELENA: There's no one here.

ANA: That's the way he solves everything, by leaving. He has spent his whole life walking away from everything.

ELENA: You're in good form today.

ANA: The best thing you can do is never to marry anyone.

ELENA: The prospects are not very good, so you don't have to worry.

ANA: You're better off.

ELENA: Sure, I'm better off. I spend my days working in a rathole of a store, and my evenings sitting on that porch watching people go by, watching my life go by. I'm a professional spectator. Everything passes me by.

ANA: It could be worse.

ELENA: Certainly it could be worse. You tell me how it could be worse. I am thirty-five years old. Thirty-five years old and I have never felt a caress. Not once has a man touched my hair.

ANA: Why do you want anybody to touch your hair?

ELENA: I don't know what it is to have someone hold my hand. To have someone talk to me.

ANA: Here everybody talks to you.

ELENA: Here everybody talks to himself. Besides, what everyone says around here is not worth hearing.

ANA: Believe me, you've missed nothing. I remember the first time your father held my hand. He didn't say a word. Well, he has never said much, that's nothing new. We were walking in the park on a Sunday afternoon. The municipal band was playing. You know that the men walk in one direction and the women in the opposite direction. Well, we had gone around the park six or seven times. Every time we passed each other he would smile. He was wearing his little hat, just like the one he wears now. About the eighth time he said something, I don't know what. He just mumbled something. The next time around we stopped as we were about to pass each other by. He mumbled something again, and grabbed one of my fingers. I nearly died. I was petrified. Everybody was looking at us. I pulled my hand back and walked away as fast as my legs could carry

me. I was almost running. My face was red as a toma-
to. But after that, it was all downhill.

ELENA: I would have been happy with just that moment.
(*Fadeout*.)

Scene 2

That evening, Elena, Ana, Beto *and* Robinson *are seated on the porch, watching people go by.*

ROBINSON: People are all the same. You've seen how the situation has deteriorated in the last two years; nobody seems to mind. They go about their business, as if nothing is happening. Everyone works, plays, drinks. Nothing bothers the people here.

BETO: Talking about playing, Nico owes me $2.50. He played a pretty combination.

ROBINSON: What was it?

BETO: He dreamed he was taking a long voyage by sea, but there was no ship. All there was was a horse. So, what did he do? He bets on #1 and #3; horse and sailor, a great combination.

ANA: That's really far-fetched.

ROBINSON: It's a common dream.

ANA: Going to sea on a horse?

ROBINSON: Everyone has a story.

BETO: There was nothing wrong with the combination, although it didn't win.

ROBINSON: Take me, for instance.

ELENA: Who would want to take you, Robinson?

ROBINSON: One day I'm reading the newspaper, and what do I find? Right there, on page seven I read that I'm dead. Dead. No more, no less.

BETO: You should play number sixty-four: "Big-dead-man," and number four for cat, with nine lives. That's a pretty combination: four and sixty-four.

ROBINSON: I mean, how would you feel reading that you're dead?

ELENA: We're all dead, we've all been dead forever. Everyone in this town. Life never came here.

ANA: Nena, you say such things.

BETO: Maybe you should play eight, instead of sixty-four.

ELENA: Stop it with your numbers. All you think about is numbers, combinations, gambling, cockfights.

BETO: Just because you play every day and never win is no reason to criticize the ones who do.

ELENA: Some people are not lucky at gambling, but they're lucky at love, or vice-versa. I lost on both counts.

ROBINSON: As I was saying, I was reading this newspaper, and there I found my name: Raul Robinson, dead.

ANA: You don't look dead to me, Robinson.

ROBINSON: Thank God.

ELENA: Someone probably took a look at you, and decided you had one foot on the other side.

ROBINSON: No, really, I'm not kidding.

ANA: But how can that be?

ROBINSON: Well, I left Havana quite some time ago, and I never went back.

ANA: That's no reason to kill you.

ROBINSON: No, but I never wrote back. I never got in touch with anyone.

BETO: Well, that was very foolish.

ELENA: Come to think of it, why did you come here in the first place? Of all the places to go, you came here.

ROBINSON: I wanted to get away from everything.

ELENA: You came to the right place.

ANA: What made you want to get away?

ROBINSON: My wife died. I...I sort of went crazy. I didn't have anyone else. We didn't have any children. We were always together, for thirty years.

BETO: I didn't have such luck.

ANA: I don't know what you would have done without me.

ELENA: The same thing he has done with you. Nothing.

BETO: But you were very well-known, weren't you, Robinson?

ROBINSON: Yeah, I made a name for myself. I was a composer.

ANA: Of music?

BETO: Sure. You had some pieces that were famous.

ROBINSON: Well, from this incident that I told you about, I wrote a *danzón* that became very popular: "Alive and Kicking," that was the title.

BETO: I have danced to that many times.

ANA: Not with me.

BETO: That was before your time.

ANA: I've never danced in my life.

ELENA: That's one thing we have in common.

ROBINSON: That's a shame. My wife and I used to go dancing every week.

ANA: Maybe you two can go out dancing sometime?

ELENA: You must be crazy.

ROBINSON: That's not a bad idea. I can still get around the dance floor.

BETO: I wonder what number is dancing.

ANA: I don't think dancing has a number.

ROBINSON: Dancing? Three-quarter.

ANA: Three-quarter?

ROBINSON: Sure. Three-quarter, like a waltz. La, la-la, la, la-la.

ELENA: Speaking of waltzes, your music-loving son didn't come to dinner tonight.

ANA: He wasn't feeling well.

ELENA: Could it have been from indigestion?

ANA: He has a great stomach.

ELENA: That, I'll agree with you.

ROBINSON: That's Mario you're talking about? He knows his music all right.

ELENA: That's the only thing he knows.

ANA: He knows a lot about electricity.

ROBINSON: It's hard to make a living in this town.

ELENA : If you want to work, you can find it.

ROBINSON: Not me, I'm okay. I have a few pennies in the bank.

ANA: Nena should have married a responsible man like you, Robinson. (ROBINSON *chuckles,* ELENA *gives a piercing glance at her mother.*)

BETO: The house has been quiet without Lundi.

ROBINSON: He hasn't shown up yet?

ANA: He vanished. No one has seen him, no one knows anything.

BETO: It was going to happen sooner or later. A crazy boy running around town day and night with the way things are. Maybe he went to the mountains to join the rebels?

ANA: What does he know about rebels?

BETO: The same thing that we do: nothing. Nena, don't you think it's possible?

ELENA: I don't want to talk about it. If anything happens to him, it's our fault.

ANA: Why is it our fault?

ELENA: We drove him crazy.

ANA: What's this guilt feeling that's come over you?

ELENA: You disgust me.

ANA: Stop it, we have visitors.

ELENA: Robinson knows what goes on in this house. Besides, I have been stopping all my life. I'm tired of living with lies.

ANA: You live the life you want to live.

ELENA: I have lived the life you made me live.

ANA: What would you have done without me?

ELENA: Been a normal human being. You made freaks of us all.

ANA: Blame me for everything. I'm sure you're going to blame me for Lundi's madness also?

ELENA: Yes, I'll blame you for everything. We were all your scapegoats. Don't play victim with me. You've been doing that for too long.

BETO: You have no reason to say that.

ELENA: Don't you preach to me. It's too late for that. You're too old to begin to act like a man now. (*Pause.*)

ANA: Robinson, don't get the wrong impression, we all loved Lundi. He grew up in our house. When he was little, his parents moved to Havana. They were living in a small apartment, so they asked us to attend to him for a few weeks, until they got settled. Since he was the brother-in-law of Hilda, my daughter, we said yes. So he came to live with us. It was supposed to be temporary. His parents left for the United States, and he's been here ever since. Ah, Robinson... (*Shots are heard at a distance.*)

ROBINSON: There go the shootings again. Do you know that Polanco put some hooks on the bathroom walls to hang mattresses when the shootings start? They're living half their lives in the bathroom. We're all nervous. Myself? I stare at the walls at night. I can't sleep.

ELENA: Lundi used to stare at the walls.

ANA: Let's stop talking about Lundi. (*Leaving.*) Good night.

ELENA: Yes, let's stop talking about Lundi. Let's simply stop talking.

ANA: You're becoming impossible. (*Pause.*)

ROBINSON: Well, I must be going. It's getting late, and you know it's not safe to walk the streets at night.

BETO: Yeah, I think I'm going to turn in also.

ROBINSON (*Leaving.*): Good night.

BETO (*Leaving in the opposite direction.*): Good night, Robinson. Remember, tomorrow is Saturday. Try to dream of a winner.

ANA: Good night. (*To* Elena.) You should be ashamed of yourself.

ELENA: For saying the truth? It's strange to hear the truth around here. It's about time we started, don't you think? Or I should say, it's about time you all started because I won't be here.

ANA: What do you mean?

ELENA: I mean I'm leaving.

ANA: Leaving for where?

ELENA: Leaving. Leaving for good. I'm going to the North.

ANA: You're crazy.

ELENA: Just like Lundi. (Beto *enters.*)

BETO: Ana, my milk.

ANA: Beto, Elena's going to the North.

BETO: Yes, she needs to get away for a while.

ELENA: Not for a while, I have to do something with my life.

BETO: You have your job.

ELENA: Oh, yes, I should treasure selling old-fashioned dresses to old-fashioned women.

ANA: You have lots of friends.

ELENA: Three ugly women with whom I play *canasta*. I can always invite myself to some neighbor's house to watch television, or sit here and watch people go by.

BETO: Well, you're old enough. You do what you think you have to do. I won't stop you.

ANA: What are people going to say? A woman traveling alone to the United States.

ELENA: You're in another century. This town, this country is in another century. There's a revolution going on out there. People are getting killed everyday. We have to sleep on the floor most of the time. They shoot at our houses. Everything's falling down, and you're still worried about my traveling alone, about what people are going to say. Damn the people, damn this town, this country, this revolution. Damn you, I'm leaving. (*She rushes out.*)

ANA: I don't know what's come over this girl. (Beto *sits next to* Ana.)

BETO: We wanted the best for her. We loved her. Didn't we?

ANA: She'll get over it in the morning.

BETO: She won't. She's been holding back for too many years. You know, Ana, I haven't mingled much in the affairs of this house, but I know what's been going on. I know she resents me. (*Pause.*) I don't want to die knowing my daughter hates me. (*She holds his hand.*)

ANA: Don't you start now. She's just tired. It will be all right. (Beto *gets up and walks out slowly. She stares into the distance and talks to herself.*) Elena is right, this is a house of lunatics.

Scene 3

Next morning. Dining room area. Elena *and* Mario *are having breakfast.* Otilio *enters.*

OTILIO: Good people of Oriente, permit me...

ELENA: Otilio, you have great visiting hours.

OTILIO: As the Chinese philosopher once said...

ELENA: Otilio, it's too early for philosophy.

OTILIO: Permit me to call you tired sun, for you are a slow riser.

ELENA: Permit me to show you to the door, for you are leaving.

MARIO: Jesus, I can't even have breakfast in peace.

ELENA: I'm kidding, Otilio.

OTILIO: I know, I know... (*Pause.*) Is it true that you're leaving?

ELENA: It's true.

MARIO: I don't think that's a good idea.

ELENA: You simply don't think.

MARIO: Listen to our precocious old maid.

ELENA: Why don't you just worry about your own family? Your wife is pregnant again, and still washing clothes to feed your children. How can you sit there like a tropical Buddha?

MARIO: And you are so pure! You are the one to be blamed for Lundi. Always complaining about him. Have you forgotten how you made fun of him, how you imitated him, how you used to put live frogs in his bed?

ELENA: Stop it.

MARIO: I thought you wanted to talk about Lundi?

ELENA: Stop it.

MARIO: Remember the time you were taking a shower, and you called Lundi to bring you a towel, and you let him see you naked, and then laughed at him?

ELENA: Stop it.

MARIO: You drove him crazy.

ELENA: Stop it, stop it.

MARIO: You want me to stop now?

ELENA: Mario. (Ana *and* Beto *enter carrying groceries.*)

ANA: What's all this shouting? (*Pause.*) We were just at the market. No one knows anything.

BETO: I want my steak medium rare.

ANA: We're not having steaks.

BETO: For forty years I've been telling her that I like my steaks medium-rare. I cannot eat a well-done steak. Elena, you know I cannot chew.

ANA: I wish Roberto were here.

BETO (*Going to the bedroom.*): Remember, medium-rare. (*A car is heard coming to a full stop. Doors slam. Voices are heard. The car skids off.* Lundi *enters, with both hands bandaged, and full of blood stains.*)

LUNDI: I didn't tell them.

ANA: Lundi, my God!

LUNDI: I didn't tell them, I didn't tell them, and they said I was lying. I didn't tell them, and they pulled out my fingernails. Ana, Beto, Nena, I didn't tell them, I didn't tell them. (Lundi *collapses.*)

ELENA: Lundi! (*Blackout.*)

ACT II

Scene 1

Miami, Florida, five years later. The living room of a small apartment. Roberto is sitting at a desk, writing. Elena is sitting on the sofa, reading a magazine.

ELENA: Do you know what day it is today?

ROBERTO: Saturday.

ELENA: I mean, what day of the week?

ROBERTO: 17th.

ELENA: December 17th.

ROBERTO: So?

ELENA: Five years ago today Lundi died.

ROBERTO: It's been five years already?

ELENA: We arrived in Miami almost four years ago. It's funny how things worked out. I was going to leave Cuba in December of '58; then Lundi died; then Beto became ill; then the Revolution triumphed; then Beto also died, and then all of us left. Lundi was crazy, and yet he was the only one in our house who saw what was happening in Cuba.

ROBERTO: I knew what was happening. As it turned out, all the fighting was for nothing, that son-of-a-bitch turned communist on us. He really fooled everybody, didn't he?

ELENA: You kept your secret pretty well. No one ever suspected that you were a rebel. How could you keep something like that from us?

ROBERTO: I had to. I was doing sabotage, putting bombs all over Oriente. That was no child's play. They would have shot me on sight.

ELENA: How long did you do that?

ROBERTO: Since the middle of '57. Fidel was just sitting there in the mountains, nothing was happening, so we decided to take the fight to the towns. It was actually the sabotage in the cities that finally brought Batista's downfall.

ELENA: What do you mean?

ROBERTO: The soldiers began taking reprisals; in the process they hurt lots of innocent people. They began torturing people, some died. You never heard the cries in the night?

ELENA: No.

ROBERTO: They got very vicious.

ELENA: Pulling out people's fingernails?

ROBERTO: That was just the beginning.

ELENA: That's what happened to Lundi.

ROBERTO: It's always the innocents...

ELENA: Did he know anything?

ROBERTO: About what?

ELENA: About anything: the rebels? You?

ROBERTO: What do you mean?

ELENA: You know what I mean. Did Lundi know that you were a rebel? Did he know that you were doing sabotage?

ROBERTO: What do I know? He was always showing up everywhere.

ELENA: Did Lundi ever see you plant a bomb? Remember when he came to the house screaming about an explosion? Was that you? Did he see you?

ROBERTO: Maybe he saw me, I don't know.

ELENA: Maybe he saw you, and maybe he was caught, and maybe the soldiers interrogated him, and tortured him. Maybe they pulled out his fingernails when he

didn't talk, because he knew it was you, and he wanted to protect you.

ROBERTO (*Angry.*): Yes, he saw me. What the hell was he
doing there? He was not supposed to be there, it was
six o'clock in the morning... (*Pause.*) I took two sticks
of dynamite and placed them at the door of the court-
house...the whole place blew up; as I turned around
the corner to get into the car that was waiting for me,
there he was, looking at me with his bug eyes, and a
grin on his skinny face. I didn't say a word. I thought
that in his craziness he would not realize what had
happened...

ELENA: But, why didn't you say something?

ROBERTO: I couldn't, Nena, believe me, I couldn't. After
the triumph of the Revolution, I went to Mazorra to
find out how he died. I met the man who was in
charge of him. He just said that Lundi had gotten wild
one night, while trying to control him, somebody must
have hit him; he fell to the ground, hit his head against
the cement wall and died... I was sure that they had
actually beaten him to death. He began making fun of
the inmates, that they should all be killed... I saw that
man as a savage, I thought he had to be destroyed, the
Revolution could not afford people like that, so I took
out my pistol and shot him. I was a captain in the Revolutionary Army. I was authorized to shoot anyone
that I considered dangerous. When people came into
the room to ask what had happened, I just said that he
was a counter-revolutionary, and that I had executed
him.

ELENA: You killed him just like that?

ROBERTO: Do you realize how many people were killed in
'59 just like that? Anyone who had a grudge against

someone else simply shot him. No questions asked. If a man found out that his wife was sleeping with another man, all he had to do was accuse his wife's lover of being a *gusano*, and then he would shoot him. We were in power, the law was on our side. We were *barbudos*, we came from the mountains, and we had a gun at our side. Thousands of people were killed. Want to know something? I never forgot Lundi's eyes looking at me; not questioning, nor judging, just looking at me. I close my eyes, and I see him, even now.

ELENA: Always someone has to die before we become aware of anything. I realized I loved Lundi when he died. And Beto, boy, I really mistreated him. I used to curse him, scream at him. I don't remember ever kissing him, my own father. Then he died, and I began to reproach myself…

ROBERTO: Don't be so tough on yourself.

ELENA: Why shouldn't I? I was tough with everybody else. You were always away. We thought you were gambling, and you were planting bombs. I needed you so much.

ROBERTO: We're together now.

ELENA: I'm so tired… (*Pause.*) Ana is almost totally blind. I spoke with Dr. Porilla today. We'll have to watch her. Last night, after everyone had gone to bed I passed by her room, and she was lying in bed, crying.

ROBERTO: She must miss Beto. They got along; she knew how to handle him. They accepted each other, they understood each other. In their own way, they must have loved each other.

ELENA: I'm sure they did. Love is funny, don't you think? (*Fadeout.*)

Scene 2

Ana *is standing by the window, looking out.* Mario *enters.*

ANA: Where's Elena?

MARIO: I think she went to do the laundry. She can't stand still. Always complaining she's tired, but she doesn't stop working.

ANA: She doesn't stop because she doesn't want to have time to think. (Mario *takes her by the arm, and walks her to the sofa.*)

MARIO: About Ralph, you mean?

ANA: Since she was very young she always wanted to get married. She was always talking about marriage. Finally, she met Ralph, and she got her wish. She was so happy. I wish Beto had been alive. He felt guilty, he thought it had been his fault that Nena never married. He never showed it, but he loved all his children. He would have been so pleased to have seen Nena finally getting married. And Ralph was such a good man, so kind.

MARIO: It was the only time that I have seen her smile.

ANA: You never saw her smile because you always made her angry. You were always picking on her. She had a bad temper, she grew up too soon... Besides, she could never accept the fact that you were married, and had children, and yet you came to have lunch and dinner with us.

MARIO: You always insisted.

ANA: I didn't want you to go hungry. Your wife was a horrible cook.

MARIO: I feel sorry for her.

ANA: You feel sorry for Nena? I don't see why.

MARIO: Remember when she brought him home for the first time? She was like a little girl, she was blushing. I thought she was going to die. She spilled her coffee, he didn't know what to say, you kept on asking questions... It's a shame he died, but he always looked sick to me. Jesus, he had a green complexion.

ANA: He didn't have a green complexion.

MARIO: He didn't have pink cheeks either.

ANA: He had cancer. In Cuba I never heard of anyone having cancer. That's an American illness.

MARIO: They had cancer in Cuba. What happened is that in Cuba people died, and nobody knew from what.

ANA: People are too finicky here.

MARIO: You're too old-fashioned. Americans like things fast.

ANA: Yes, even death. (*A knock is heard at the door.*)

MARIO: Come in. (Otilio *enters wearing suit and tie, and quite sober.*)

OTILIO: Good people of Oriente, good day!

MARIO: Otilio, Good Lord! You really put on the wardrobe.

ANA: Is that Otilio?

OTILIO: Alive and kicking, as that old song that made our friend Robinson so famous.

MARIO: How come you're so elegant?

OTILIO: Well, it's Saturday. So I said to myself, what the hell, I'll get myself elegant.

MARIO: Take a seat.

ANA: I don't know what got into you, because on Saturdays everyone around here dresses just the same as any other day.

OTILIO: To tell you the truth, I've decided to join the world of the conformists.

MARIO: You're getting married?

OTILIO: Oh, no, no, no. Nothing so drastic. I'm not conforming that much.

ANA: You should get married, Otilio, you're still young.

OTILIO: No, thank you, Ana. Once is enough.

MARIO: If you're not getting married, what's the drastic change in your life?

OTILIO: I decided to go back to teaching.

ANA: You're a teacher?

OTILIO: I have always been one.

ANA: My God, the things one finds out in exile!

MARIO: That's why people used to call you professor in Tunas?

OTILIO: People called me professor to make fun of me. No, in Tunas only Dr. Pérez knew that I was a college professor before...

MARIO: Before you started drinking?

OTILIO: Before I dropped out of our gracious tropical society, and began to indulge myself in liquor. Yes, before I started drinking.

ANA: I always wondered why you drank. You seemed perfectly healthy to me; young, even good-looking. My goodness, Otilio, you ruined your life.

OTILIO: It's a long story, Ana. I don't think you want to hear it.

ANA: Sure I want to hear it. I am going blind, but people must think that I am going deaf. Nobody wants to tell me anything.

MARIO: Ana, don't start that again.

ANA: Mario, I mean it. I am bored to death.

OTILIO: Don't worry, Ana. I'll talk to you. I'll tell you the story.

MARIO (*To* Otilio.): Do you want some coffee?

OTILIO: Yes, thank you. Had someone ever told me that I was going to be in Miami drinking coffee, I would have told them that they were doubly crazy. I never touched the stuff in my life; and here I am, a coffee addict. (Mario *returns with a cup of espresso coffee.*)

MARIO: It's from this morning. I reheated it.

OTILIO: It's fine.

ANA: Otilio, I'm waiting. Tell me what happened?

OTILIO: I'm coming to that. (*He takes a sip from the coffee.*) I am not from Las Tunas, as you must know.

ANA: I didn't know that.

OTILIO: No, I was born in Las Villas, in the central part of the island. I was a philosophy teacher. I was married.

ANA: Listen to that!

OTILIO: She was beautiful, much younger than I was. She was a girl from the countryside, full of life and zest, and we were happy. My students from the university used to come to the house, and we talked all through the night about John Locke, and Mañach, and Martí, and so on and so forth. But what I didn't know was that when I was teaching during the day, some of the students came back, and it wasn't to talk about philosophy. Of course, I was the last to know. When I finally found out, it was my own wife who told me.

ANA: She told you she was being unfaithful to you?

OTILIO: Not only that. She told me she was leaving me, and she did. She went to Havana with one of my students, José del Valle. He was writing his thesis at the time: "The Concept of Liberty in the New World."

MARIO: He certainly took his liberties!

OTILIO: He not only took his liberties, he took my wife.

ANA: And what did you do?

OTILIO: I went to pieces. I couldn't teach any longer, I couldn't do anything. I took to drinking; then I lost my job at the university. Finally, I decided to leave Las Villas. So I went to the other extreme of the island, and I wound up in Tunas.

MARIO: You can't trust women.

OTILIO: I don't know about that, Mario; but my Gladys really broke my heart. Can I tell you something? Do you know that I still love her? After all these years. And if I saw her today... well... I heard that she had left Cuba.

ANA: Do you want to see her?

OTILIO: I'd give anything to see her again. Just to see her. She had long, curly hair, and laughter. Oh, God! Ana, why do you do this to me?

MARIO: My wife left me also.

OTILIO: What? I thought you left her?

MARIO: No, she left me. I shouldn't have married anyhow. I wasn't made to have a family.

OTILIO: It certainly took you a long time to figure that one out. You had four or five children, no?

MARIO: I have five. They're all still in Cuba, in the army. They're all communists.

OTILIO: I'm sure they're better off.

ANA: That's a terrible thing to say, Otilio, but you haven't told us why you're so elegant.

OTILIO: I'm going back to teaching. I got an offer to teach Spanish, grammar and so on. So, I'm celebrating my return to the classroom. I stopped drinking. Well, I drink less. I'll leave you now.

ANA: Don't go. Elena will be back in a minute; she'll be very happy to see you.

OTILIO: I'd like to see her also, Ana, but I don't think that I
　　am ready. Give me time.
ANA: As you wish; this is your home. Do come more
　　often. It would be nice having someone to talk to
　　again. I remember when you used to come to our
　　house in Tunas and talk for hours.
OTILIO: I will come more often, Ana. I promise.
MARIO: Next time I'll make you fresh coffee. (*Blackout.*)

Scene 3

Mario *is sitting by the radio.* Ana *is standing by the door,
looking out.* Elena, *wearing rubber gloves, is cleaning. The tele-
vison set is on. From the radio a waltz is heard.*

ELENA (*To* Mario.): Sooner or later you will have to get up
　　from there. I have to clean that corner.
MARIO: What for?
ELENA: What a question.
MARIO: Nobody is going to come looking under my seat.
ELENA: God help the one who does.
MARIO: So, you don't have to clean here.
ELENA: Mario, don't get me started.
MARIO: Why don't you go home?
ELENA: Yes, I should go home, and you will die in filth. If
　　it weren't for Ana...
ANA: I'll clean that later.
ELENA: You'll clean that later. You cannot accept the fact
　　that you're almost blind. How can you clean anything?
　　Mario, get up.
MARIO: Will you please be quiet? I'm listening to music.
ANA: Nena, I'll clean that.
ELENA: You're so hard-headed!
ANA: Look who's calling whom hard-headed.

ELENA (*To* Mario.): If you're not watching the TV, why do
    you have it on?
MARIO: I'm watching it.
ELENA: Without sound?
MARIO: I said I'm watching it, not listening to it.
ELENA (*Taking her mother by the arm.*): Come and sit for a
    while.
ANA: I have to make lunch for Roberto.
ELENA: Today's Saturday, he's at his numbers game.
MARIO: But he always comes home for lunch.
ELENA: For once he should make his own.
ANA: I have some meat in the refrigerator, from last night.
ELENA: I'll do it.
ANA: How Beto would have loved to have had meat on
    Saturday!
ELENA: He had his share.
ANA: We couldn't afford to buy meat more than once a
    week when he was alive.
ELENA: He had an easy enough life.
ANA: Sometimes an easy life is not easy.
ELENA: I'll take it any day!
ANA: Don't worry, we won't be here much longer.
ELENA: Stop dreaming, we're here for good.
ANA: Not me. I know I won't die here. And if I do, I
    already made your brother promise that I would be
    buried in Cuba.
ELENA: Once you're dead, what difference does it make?
ANA: It makes a lot of difference. I don't belong here. We
    don't belong here.
ELENA: We don't belong anywhere, we have lost our place
    in the world.
MARIO: Maybe you have, because you have no faith. It's
    because of people like you that we are in exile.

ELENA: We got what we deserved.

ANA: I cannot believe that we deserved this. We lost our home, our friends, our family.

ELENA: That's a small price to pay. Even now, we haven't learned our lesson.

ANA: Anyway, I am certain that by next Christmas we'll be in Cuba.

ELENA: For five years we've been saying that: Next Christmas we'll be in Cuba. Christmases come and go, but we're still here.

MARIO: We'll never be Americans.

ELENA: We'll never be anything.

ANA: I live in the past, Nena, because it's all I have, it helps me to live the present. But with you it's different, you still have a future.

ELENA: Ana, I was born out of place, out of time. Even if I wanted to, even if I tried, I couldn't get anywhere.

ANA: Of course you can. I wish I was your age.

ELENA: We always wish what we cannot be. We always want what we cannot have. Maybe it's a defense mechanism. If we wish something very remote, we'll never be disillusioned, we'll never chastise ourselves for being a failure.

ANA: You're not a failure, you're a woman. If you just stopped feeling sorry for yourself for a moment, you would see that. Fight for what you want. I haven't given you much. At least take my strength.

ELENA: That's enough. God must be punishing me. In Cuba I used to complain because you didn't talk, now you talk too much.

ANA: It's all I can do.

MARIO: You don't look well.

ELENA: You're nothing to write home about.

MARIO: You're not so old.

ELENA: Coming from you, that's quite a compliment. I really have a monopoly on tragedy, don't I? Married at 38, widowed at 40.

ANA: Ralph was ill, you have nothing to blame yourself for.

MARIO: At least you were married for two years.

ELENA: Two wonderful years. The only time in my life I was really happy. He was so good to me! He made me feel needed. It's a great feeling to be needed.

ANA: I told you that you should marry again.

ELENA: I can't do that.

MARIO: Why not? You are your own worst enemy, always defeating yourself. Stop feeling sorry for yourself.

ELENA: And you stop talking, and get up. (*Pause.*)

ANA: Miami is really much hotter than Tunas.

MARIO (*Getting up.*): I'm going to the bathroom.

ELENA: Ana, what a short memory you have. That little house we had on Lucas Ortiz Avenue was hell, a Cuban oven.

ANA: It wasn't so bad. At night there was always a breeze.

ELENA: Yes, a warm breeze. Remember when I was going to leave home and go to New York?

ANA: That was a crazy idea.

ELENA: I never got to see New York.

ANA: We came to Miami because it was the closest thing to Cuba.

ELENA: That, it is. I've come a long way: from a clothing store to a restaurant at a racetrack. A real success story.

ANA: Sit down for a while, your back is going to start hurting you again.

ELENA: I have to finish cleaning. I still have to go home and clean there, also.

ANA: You live alone because you want to. It was all right for you to move out when you got married, we had no room here for both of you. But now you could very well move back here, unless you plan to get married again.

ELENA: It's not likely. It took me almost forty years to marry the first time. If I have to wait another forty years, I don't think I'll be in the mood for it.

ANA: You're better off. Men are a nuisance.

ELENA: You ought to know. You took care of three for years. It's about time Roberto got married. He's fifty, no?

ANA: Beto? Let me see. Yes, he's the oldest.

ELENA: It's about time he left home also.

ANA: He won't know how to take care of himself.

ELENA: Beautiful.

ANA: It's not his fault; he always had someone to do things for him.

ELENA: Yes, he had you, and Amparo. Poor Amparo. For twenty years they saw each other. She cooked for him every Thursday for twenty years; she made handkerchiefs for him. Can you imagine? After twenty years of putting up with him, he leaves the country and she stays behind.

ANA: She wasn't in love with him.

ELENA: How can you say that? She was with him for twenty years, without being married to him even, and you think that she wasn't in love with him?

ANA: They were probably used to each other. People get used to each other after a while.

ELENA: She was certainly used. (Mario *comes in*.)

MARIO: Are you finished?

ELENA: Yes.

ANA: There's no milk.

MARIO: No milk?

ANA: You had what was left this morning.

MARIO: Ana, you should make sure we never run out.

ELENA: Why don't you make sure?

MARIO: Why don't you mind your own business? (*Mario leaves.*)

ANA: That boy doesn't change.

ELENA: There were always two things we could count on: Roberto's gambling and Mario's music. His wife left him, his sons grew up, two or three governments fell, we left the country, our father died, and all through it he was listening to music, to his dreamland melody.

ANA (*Getting up.*): I'm going to lie down for a while. (*She walks away, slowly, holding on to the furniture.*)

ELENA (*To Ana.*): I'll make Beto's lunch, then I'll go. (*She removes her rubber gloves.*) Look at these hands, what a mess. I was never beautiful, but I always had pretty hands. They were the only thing I could ever brag about. I don't have one decent fingernail. (*Pause.*) Maybe Mario was right, I should take care of myself. He has never been right about anything in his life. I would like to think that he was right this time, though. (*She chuckles.*) It would be a nice feeling. I'm not that old. Who am I kidding? (*She stares into the distance, and smiles.*) Somebody must like me. Maybe I should cut my hair. Maybe I should start going out a little. It's been two years since Ralph died. I don't want to end up by myself. I need someone to love. God, I have so much to give. (*She begins to run her fingers through her hair.*) I wonder what Ana would say if she saw me with short hair. She'd probably die. Mario is going to criticize me, of course, that's nothing new. What do I care?

I have had long hair all my life. It's part of my personality. I'd probably look like a different woman. That's not a bad idea! Hell, it's not too late! Yes, I think I'll cut my hair. (*The lights begin to dim very slowly as she plays with her hair. Blackout.*)

Essay

LOST IN TRANSLATION*

⊅❧ Gustavo Pérez Firmat ❧⊄

MAMBO NO. 1

Take the phrase literally. Turn the commonplace into a place. Try to imagine where one ends up if one gets lost in translation. When I try to visualize such a place, I see myself, on a given Saturday afternoon, in the summer, somewhere in Miami. Since I'm thirsty, I go into a store called Love Juices, which specializes in nothing more salacious or salubrious than milk shakes made from papayas and other tropical fruits. Having quenched my thirst, I head for a boutique called Mr. Trapus, whose name—*trapo*—is actually the Spanish word for an old rag. Undaunted by the consumerist frenzy that has possessed me, I enter another store called Cachi Bachi—a name that, in spite of its chichi sound, is a slang word for a piece of junk, *cachi-vache*. And then for dinner I go to the Versailles of Eighth Street, a restaurant where I feast on something called Tropical Soup, the American name for the traditional Cuban stew, *ajiaco*. My dessert is also tropical, Tropical Snow, which is Miamian for *arroz con leche*; and to finish off the meal, of course, I sip some Cuban-American espresso (don't go home without it). In this way I spend my entire afternoon lost in translation—and loving every minute. Translation takes you to a place where cultures divide to conga.

*All "mambos" excerpted from *Life on the Hyphen*

SPIC'N SPANISH

MAMBO NO. 2

Miami Spanish includes a term that, so far as I know, is unique to the city of sun and solecisms: *nilingüe*. Just as a bilingüe is someone who speaks two languages (say, Spanish and English), a *nilingüe* is someone who doesn't speak either: "*ni español, ni inglés.*" Such a person is a no-lingual, a nulli-glot. My example of nilingualism is Ricky Ricardo. Ricky's occasional Spanish utterances are shot through with anglicisms: *falta* for *culpa*, *introducir* for *presentar*, *parientes* for *padres*, and so on. Sometimes the anglicisms seem deliberate (so that the monolingual viewers understand what he is saying), but at other times they're plain mistakes. A curious thing: as Ricky got older, his English didn't get any better, but his Spanish kept getting worse. Equally curious: the same thing happened to Desi Arnaz. In 1983 Arnaz was picked "king" of the Cuban carnival in Miami, Open House Eight. By then, his Spanish was as frail as his health. He now had an accent in *two* languages.

In Spanish to know a language well is to "dominate" it. But my mother tongue has it backward: people don't dominate languages, languages dominate people. By reversing the power relation, English comes closer to the truth. When someone speaks English better than Spanish, we say that he or she is "English-dominant," an expression in which the language, and not the speaker, has the upper hand. But in Ricky no language achieved dominance; English and Spanish battled each other to a tie (a tongue-tie). A *nilingüe* treats his mother tongue like a foreign language and treats the foreign language like his other tongue. T. W. Adorno once said: "Only he who is not truly at home inside a language can use it as an instrument." Ricky Ricardo is a multi-instrumentalist. He is homeless in two languages.

DESI DOES IT

MAMBO NO. 3

Going through her father's house after his death, Lucie Arnaz found a box of papers and memorabilia that she donated to the Love Library at San Diego State University, where Desi had lectured several times. The Desi Arnaz Collection contains a few home movies, an old film short entitled *Jitterhumba*, several drafts of *A Book*, and assorted notes that Arnaz took when he was working on his autobiography. Originally intending to write either a sequel to *A Book* (to be called *Another Book*) or a novel (probably to be called *A Novel*), Arnaz marked some of these jottings "Other Book" or "Novel." The notes contain not only many self-revealing moments and juicy gossip (like a list of Lucille Ball's alleged lovers), but also some of Desi's best quips.

Seeing Gary Morton, Lucy's second husband, on a TV talk show, he writes: "About Gary on TV with Lucy: Seems to be suffering from a massive inferiority complex to which he is fully entitled." To his children, Lucie and Desi, Jr., he once remarked: "The only reason you are here is because I woke up one night and couldn't think of anything else to do." About his famous quarrels with Lucy, he says: "Lucy and I had some great battles but at times when someone asked me why we fought, I had to answer, 'I don't know. She wouldn't tell me.'" Most pertinent, perhaps, are his thoughts on being a writer: "Writing a book is, I discovered, not an easy thing to do. It also proves that the brain is a wonderful thing. It starts up when you are born and stops when you sit down at the typewriter."

But my favorite is the simple aphorism "History is made at night." It seems appropriate that the box ended up at a place called the Love Library.

THE BARBER OF LITTLE HAVANA

MAMBO NO. 4

When I first became interested in the mambo some years ago, I was puzzled to find that a well-respected British reference work, *The Faber Companion to 20th Century Popular Music*, gave Pérez Prado's first name as Pantaleón rather than Dámaso. More puzzling still, after describing Pérez Prado's career in accurate detail, the entry concluded, "His elder brother Damos [sic] was also a band leader and composer who specialized in the mambo." Later I discovered that Pérez Prado actually had a brother named Pantaleón, who was also a musician. Still later, while going through some music magazines from the 1950s, I found Pantaleón had actually toured Europe claiming to be the Mambo King, an imposture that ended only when Dámaso threatened to take legal, rather than musical, steps.

For many years there has been a barbershop on Eighth Street in Miami called Barbería Pérez Prado. Its elderly owner bears a striking resemblance to Dámaso; some say he is Pérez Prado's brother, Pantaleón. But when questioned by visitors, the barber of Little Havana disclaims any connection. Will the real mambo king please stand up and grunt?

MIRROR, MIRROR

MAMBO NO. 5

One of the landmarks of Cuban Miami is a restaurant called Versailles, which has been located on Eighth Street and Thirty-fifth Avenue for many years. About the only thing this Versailles shares with its French namesake is that is has lots of mirrors on its walls. One goes to the Versailles not only to be seen, but to be multiplied. This quaint, kitschy, noisy restaurant that serves basic Cuban food is a paradise for the self-absorbed: the Nirvana of Little Havana. Because of the bright lights, even the windows reflect. The Versailles is a Cuban panopticon: you can lunch, but you can't hide. Who goes there wants to be the stuff of visions. Who goes there wants to make a spectacle of himself (or herself). All the *ajiaco* you can eat and all the jewelry you can wear multiplied by the number of reflecting planes—and to top it off, a waitress who calls you *mi vida*.

Across the street at La Carreta, another popular restaurant, the food is the same (both establishments are owned by the same man) but the feel is different. Instead of mirrors La Carreta has booths. There you can ensconce yourself in a booth and not be faced with multiple images of yourself. But at the Versailles there is no choice but to bask in self-reflective glory.

For years I have harbored the fantasy that those mirrors retain the blurred image of everyone who has paraded before them. I think the mirrors have a memory, as when one turns off the TV and the shadowy figures remain on the screen. Every Cuban who has lived or set foot in Miami over the last three decades has, at one time or another, seen himself or herself reflected on those shiny surfaces. It's no coincidence that the Versailles sits only two blocks away from the Woodlawn Cemetery, which contains the remains of many Cuban notables, including Desi Arnaz's father, whose remains occupy a niche right above Gerardo Machado's. Has anybody ever counted the number of Cubans who have died in Miami? Miami is a Cuban city not only because of the number of Cubans who live there but also because of the number who have died there.

The Versailles is a glistening mausoleum. The history of Little Havana—tragic, comic, tragicomic—is written on those spectacular specular walls. This may have been why, when the mirrors came down in 1991, there was such an uproar that some of them had to be put back. The hall of mirrors is also a house of spirits. When the time comes for me to pay for my last *ajiaco*, I intend to disappear into one of the mirrors (I would prefer the one on the right, just above the espresso machine). My idea of immortality is to become a mirror image at the Versailles.

ENGLISH IS BROKEN HERE

MAMBO NO. 6

Some years ago a Cuban radio station in Miami aired an advertisement promoting an airline's reduced fares: "Piedmont Airlines quiere limpiar el aire sobre sus bajas tarifas." "Limpiar el aire?" "clean the air?" This phrase is ungrammatical in two languages. First mistake: perhaps influenced by the Spanish *poner en limpio* (to clean up), the author of the ad must have thought that the English idiom was "clean the air" rather than "clear the air." Second mistake: he then decided that "clean the air" could be translated word for word into Spanish. Third mistake: he rendered "about" as "sobre," which in context sounds too much like "over" or "above." Hence: "Piedmont Airlines wants to clean the air above its low fares." But this sentence does have a certain flighty logic, especially considering that it went out over the airwaves. Piedmont's clean-air act is an interlingual utterance that remains up in the air, that cannot make up its mind whether to land in the domain of Spanish or English.

Another comedy of grammatical errors will bring us back to earth: there is a Cuban-owned pizza chain in Miami called Casino's Pizza. When Casino's was launched (or lunched) a few years ago, its publicity campaign included a bilingual brochure. I quote the first sentence of the Spanish text: "Su primera mirada, su primer olor, su primer gusto le dirá que usted descubrió La Pizza Ultima." Since "La Pizza Ultima" (the last pizza) doesn't make much sense in Spanish (it should have been "la última pizza" anyway), upon first reading this anglicized sentence, I had the impression that the final phrase was an incompletely digested translation of "the ultimate pizza." In order to check out my hunch, I went to the English text: "Your first sight, your first smell, your first taste will tell you that you've discovered La Pizza Ultima."

So what happened to my hypothetical Ultimate Pizza? It seems to have been eaten in translation. The same phrase that sounds like an anglicism in Spanish is offered as a hispanicism in English! Food for thought: the English phrase presupposes a Spanish phrase that presupposes an English phrase that doesn't exist. This is a paradox-lover's pizza, one that consumes itself in the cracks between languages. Like the Piedmont ad, "La Pizza Ultima" refuses to be English but cannot be Spanish. If Beny Moré is the "bárbaro del ritmo," the authors of these ads must be *bárbaros* of barbarism. Sometimes the American dream is written in Spanglish.

ARRIVAL: 1960

❧ Pablo Medina ❧

Snow. Everywhere the snow and air so cold it cracks and my words hang stiffly in the air like cartoons. After that first stunning welcome of the New York winter, I rush down the steps of the plane and sink my bare hands into the snow, press it into a ball, and throw it at my sister. I miss by a few yards. The snowball puffs on the ground. I make another and miss again. Then I can make no more, for my hands are numb. I look down at them: red and wet, they seem disembodied, no longer mine. A few flakes land on them, but these flakes are not the ones I know from *Little Lulu* or *Archie*; they are big lumpy things that melt soon after landing. On closer look, I can make out the intricate crystals, small and furry and short-lived. As if from a great distance, I hear my mother calling. Her voice seems changed by the cold and the words come quicker, in shorter bursts, as if there might be a limited supply of them. I follow the family into the airport building. It is early February. It is El Norte.

The drive into Manhattan is a blur. We piled into a cab and took a wide and busy highway in, most probably the Grand Central Parkway. Once over the East River, my first impression was of riding down into a canyon, much of it shadowy and forbidding, where the sky, steel gray at the time, was a straight path like the street we were on, except bumpier and softer: old cotton swabbed in mercury. It seemed odd that out of that ominous ceiling came the pure white snow I had just touched.

But the snow on the ground did not stay white very long. Nothing does in New York. It started graying at the edges four days after our arrival when my father took my sister and me to school, Robert F. Wagner Junior High, on East 72nd Street. It was a long brick building that ran the length of the block. Inauspicious, blank, with shades half-raised on the windows, it could have been a factory or prison. Piled to the side of the entrance steps was a huge mound of snow packed with children like fruit on supermarket ice. J.H.S. 167 was a typical New York school, a microcosm of the city where all races mingled and fought and, on occasion, learned. The halls were crowded, the classes were crowded, even the bathroom during recess was packed to capacity.

On that first day I was witness to a scene that was to totally alter my image of what school was. On my way from one class to the next, I saw a teacher—who, I later learned, was the prefect of discipline—dragging a girl away by the arm. The girl, trying to tug herself free, was screaming, "Mother-fucker, mother-fucker." He slapped her across the face several times. Most students, already practicing the indifference that is the keynote of survival in New York, barely turned their heads. I, however, stared, frozen by violence in a place previous experience had deluded me into thinking ought to be quiet and genteel and orderly. It was the loud ring of the bell directly overhead that woke me. I was late for English class.

When I entered the room, the teacher, a slightly pudgy lady with silver white hair, asked if I had a pass. I did not know what a pass was but I answered no anyway. It was my first day and I had gotten lost in the halls.

"Well, in that case, young man, you may come in."

She spoke with rounded vowels and smooth, slightly slurred r's rolling out of her mouth from deep in the throat. Years later I was to learn to identify this manner of speech as an affectation of the educated.

"Next time, however, you must have a pass."

Not that it mattered if one was late to English class. Much of the time was spent doing reading or writing assignments while Mrs. Gall, whose appearance belied that she was close to retirement, did crossword puzzles. A few days later, in fact, something happened that endeared me to her for the rest of the term. Speaking to herself, not expecting any of the students to help her, she said, "A nine letter word for camel." Almost instantaneously, as if by magic, I responded, "Dromedary."

She looked up at me. "That's very good. You have a nice complexion. Where are you from?"

"Complexion?" I asked.

"Yes, skin."

Skin? What does skin have to do with any of this? I had never thought of my skin, let alone considered it a mark of foreignness.

"Cuba."

"Ah, I was there once."

Then she went off on a monologue of beaches and nightlife and weather.

Home for now was a two-bedroom apartment in a residential hotel on East 86th Street, which we would not have been able to afford were it not for the graces of the company my father worked for. We had few clothes, little money, and no possessions to speak of, yet I do not remember ever lacking anything, except perhaps good food, as my mother, who as a middle-class housewife had always relied on maids in Cuba, was just beginning to learn how to cook.

If there was no money for expensive restaurants or theater tickets, I always had thirty cents for the subway fare. From this building that glossed our poverty, I set out into the city that lay open like a geometric flower of concrete and steel. Its nectar was bittersweet, but it kept me, us, from wallowing in the self-pity and stagnation that I have seen among so many exiles. After a few months, realizing that a return to the island was not forthcoming, we looked on a future where the sun was rising again. Not the fierce tropical sun that made everything jump with life and set over the palm trees as quickly as it had risen, but a gentler, slower sun that yielded reluctantly to night and promised to renew itself. Constancy. It was blonde.

The New York sun is not ubiquitous. It hides behind buildings until well after eleven, then appears and disappears for a few hours in the grid sky. Eventually one does not see it at all, only its afterglow diffused by smog and its reflection on the windows of the tallest buildings. Manhattan is an island without sunrise or sunset. If you want to witness the former, you go to the Long Island shore and look toward Europe; if you want the latter, you move west.

And so it was. I could go nowhere but into the city. Sometimes alone, sometimes with Sam, the one friend I made at school, I traveled from one end of the city to the other. At first boredom was the motivator, but soon an intense curiosity that my parents not only tolerated but encouraged became the fire that fueled me.

Thus I discovered Washington Square, the source of Fifth Avenue. Elegant, restrained, neo-Parisian, and ebbing southward from it, Greenwich Village, already in decadence but nevertheless glowing with an odd sort of peripheral, rebellious energy. Some seed had sprouted there I sensed, but it was years before I saw its vines spread throughout the land.

North I went, too, to find the Avenue's mouth and realized that this was no river of gold, but a snake that devoured its own and spewed them back to a place beyond light or hope or future. When one sees Harlem at 125th Street and Fifth Avenue, one comes face to face with the worst despair. The people there are fixed in a defeat not of their making, but rather the result of the color of their skins and a heritage imposed on them from the outside. Black you are and poor you shall remain; black you are and damned you shall be. The Avenue begins in Paris and ends in hell.

In six months we moved to 236th Street in the Upper Bronx, this time to a modest apartment in a modest building. The trees on the streets actually looked like trees, not like stunted saplings. They gave shade; there was enough room on their trunks to carve initials and love notes; the streets were not forever clogged with traffic; the sun was more visible, and from our sixth-floor windows the red blood of the sunset spilled over the Hudson a mile away.

Discovering the installment plan, my parents bought furniture and china and pictures to put on the walls. We even got a stereo. We met other families in the building, formed friendships. We were, suddenly, in middle-class mainstream America, Bronx style, and the past released its grip and ebbed far enough away so that only memory could reach it. Somehow luck had graced us: we had circumvented the snake.

NEGRITA

✖ Cecilia Rodríguez Milanés ✖

I couldn't think of a name for her straight-off, so I called her Negrita—an endearment that becomes problematic when translated into English (yet it perpetually surfaces in the salsa music I enjoy, the slang I am privy to and the communities I visit). The black rag doll that Illy, my best old girlfriend and I found at a roadside sale in Western Pennsylvania, needed to be called something right away because my then two and a half year old daughter was with us and we had to establish a relationship with this doll immediately. Her gingham dress and cotton leggings were charming but what most endeared her to us was that she was soft, huggable. Her hair of yarn in thick black braids was, yes, wired to stand up. She is the only black rag doll I've ever seen that wasn't offensive. Illy agreed; a dark-skinned Cubana herself, she thought Negrita was apt. The doll was made by someone who took care not to use the grotesque stereotypes of large lips or red gums protruding; in fact, she had no features but one moving eye and a missing piece of its partner. She was damaged then. And she called to me.

✖✖

I don't and didn't like dolls, not even when I was little. Like Claudia in Toni Morrison's *The Bluest Eye*, I couldn't see what all the fuss was about; baby dolls seemed unnatural to me, especially plastic pink ones with shockingly blonde hair and impossibly blue eyes. Don't misunderstand; I played with them—it's mandatory of little girls, I think—but I really preferred the accessories to the dolls themselves—fashionable outfits for my stiff, absurdly endowed Barbie (mine didn't even have hair but painted grooves along the skull) or the doll house my brother's rich padrinos gave me one Christmas with a working doorbell and lamp. I liked the little high-heeled pumps and handbags, the trappings but not the thing itself.

I gave birth to a daughter, Lilian Luisa, named for a flower and her paternal great grandmother. My partner and I vowed that she would not be a prissy, fragile female. We wanted a woman warrior, independent, who wouldn't be used or pushed around by men or anybody. Both of our mothers served as role models. They came to this country as young women (my mother was single); they struggled through factory jobs, learned English at night school, found—at last—satisfactory jobs here and motivated their children, husbands, friends and family to always do better. Our mothers' feistiness is legendary in their neighborhoods both here and in their native Cuba. Lili inherited some powerful genes.

We received many presents for Lili from family and friends and friends of family. My partner emigrated when he was seven and I was born here. Our parents couldn't buy us los regalitos they and their parientes can now afford to splurge on our child. When the first doll-babies started showing up we both decided to politely accept the gifts but then, echarlos pa' 'lante. Close family could be told, bluntly, no muñecas.

As soon as my daughter began to move on her own and play with her primitas, she discovered dolls and decided she would cling to them whenever we were visiting family. Everyone would look at me with muted insult that I had deprived my child of something essential to her being.

❧❧❧

My daughter and I took Negrita to the store in Indiana, Pennsylvania, to the smaller of two malls, on the outskirts of our small town. I worried about what people might think—a light-skinned woman and child with a Black rag doll whose braids were standing up. Only one per cent of the Indiana County is Black, no Latino natives, but the university manages to draw about 5% minorities into the student population.

What would a Black student who didn't know me think of my doll? Would I need to explain that I am a professor with a specialization in "minority" literature? That I teach African American literature, surveys of American minority writers and the like? If I were confronted, would I be insulted or terrified? My expertise is Black women writers, for god's sake.

I went directly to the notions department, found a package of moving eyes to match Negrita's missing one, sheepishly paid for it and left. I was relieved. I wouldn't have to take the doll out in public again.

❧❧❧

Freshly transplanted from the cold, bitter but familiar soil of el norte, I was thrust into the quicksand of South Florida at fourteen. I learned an expression from las cubanitas in my suburban Miami high school, cubana arrepentida. This label was aimed at any girl who wasn't Cuban enough for their standards which included speaking in Spanish, wearing makeup, dating cubanos and consorting with their grupito. I learned all sorts of delightful slurs and insults in Spanish, terms for which I had perfectly good, perfectly obscene equivalents for in street talk. I was being tutored in Cuban chispa and picardía.

Yet, there was another group that attracted my attention, the African American students—bussed in from Liberty City and Carol City. Since there were more of them than of the cubanitas in my predominately Jewish upper middle class high school, chances were I could sit next to two or three Blacks in each class. Since I received no real guidance about taking "academic" courses in high school (a working class Latina, the counselors didn't think I was college material), I veered toward business; you can guess that many of the underprivileged students took the same route. I met some nice folks who taught me about Overtown, real fighting and language—an English language that was far more lyrical to me than that spoken by the white students; I confess, it was more comfortable than Cuban slang too. I learned to speak Black English and this entitled me to hear stories and absorb dialogue. I got on-the-job training in the dozens; the signifying monkey crept into my consciousness, lurking, waiting.

Now, teaching the literature of Blacks and Latinos, I see the connection clearly—the trickster and picardía—syncretism. What lovely alchemy. That monkey leapt into movement, stirring up stories of Elegguá in the texts of African American writers like Zora Neale Hurston or Ishmael Reed. After meeting Lydia Cabrera's Ochún, I realized that she was the honey goddess dancing through the poetry of many black women I'd read earlier. Maya Angelou, Lucille Clifton, Nikki Giovanni and others may call her by a different name but that sass, salsa and powerful womanhood is all Ochún.

❧❧

One night a former student baby-sat my daughter. At first, Christina was concerned that Lili wouldn't understand her because we speak Spanish at home. I assured her that Lili's watching of Sesame Street and going to pre-school in the morning had completely rendered my child bilingual. The next time Christina came to watch Lili she said, "I have to tell you what Lili told me last time. She looked at my face and said, 'Christina, you have big eyes.' I said, 'Thank you.' She shook her head and said, 'That's not good.'" We laughed. Later I tried to understand why my dark-eyed child would say such a thing to a very blonde, very blue-eyed young woman. Lili isn't yet used to seeing a person with blue eyes. All of us, on both sides, have dark hair and eyes. Christina's eyes were strange to her but Lili doesn't know how to articulate strangeness. She noted difference. Having blue eyes isn't a positive trait for her because none of her loved ones have them. Lili didn't know what Pecola knew, that blue eyes are considered beautiful by mainstream society. How odd that this characteristic, not common of Latinos, creates an opportunity to talk about the racism in Cuban American culture and my upbringing—Latina in North America, so used to people of color now surrounded by fair-skinned, light-eyed people. Soon, soon, I know, Lili will realize that the blue-eyeds outnumber us here. Being far from Miami, New Jersey, New York, Philadelphia even, limits our contact with diverse cultures and people.

The racism betrayed in the Cubans I know, am related to, and observe with dismay, in exile, seems to have moved to another level and draws a great deal from the North American brand of racism. As if these cubanos I know, both dark and light-skinned mind you, never lived next door to people of color, never knew their abuelitas (or bisabuelas), never understood that the blood (culture and history) that allows them to dance or walk, sing or talk draws much, so much, from Africa. North American racism has instructed—hide it.

I wonder what the light-skinned Cubanos like Mas Canosa will do when they return and are face to face with all the dark faces that predominate in Cuba. De Congo o Carabalí? Will they remember that? What shall they do with the prejudice that has been so coddled here on the mainland? How will they vent their fear? I think about this and it scares me. It won't be the homecoming those light-skinned, middle and upper class entrepreneurs imagine because they won't, I fear, think of their dark-skinned brothers as brothers, if they ever did. Perhaps there will be a move to denounce the children of African mothers, those fathered by Cubanos in Angola (there is the precedence set by the Spanish denouncing cubanas because they had taken away, sullied their sons with criol-lo blood). Maybe the dark-skinned Cubanos—now well tutored in North American racism—upon their return to their long-lost island, will say these black, black negros are not true cubanos.

🏵🏵

I am to do a fifteen minute presentation on Cuba for my daughter's school—Montessori school—where they teach the children geography and global awareness. I'm to present something that preschoolers can appreciate and follow. Music, I decide, is the most important thing. Shall I play a little of the Mambo Kings soundtrack I have? Even though I disliked the book and think it ridiculous for fabu-

lous Celia Cruz to be singing in English and Linda Ron-
stadt to be singing in Spanish—but at least there is the
Guantanamera with the children singing backup—definitely, I shall play that one. A song I remember hearing
when I was very, very little.

When I arrive to do my presentation, the children
have been listening to German composers, Bach and Wagner. As soon as I turn on the Cuban music, the children are
bouncing. I laugh and say, "Yes, it makes you want to
dance." Besides the Spanish influence, I tell them about
the sway of Africa, the beat they hear that compels them to
move. I show them a guayabera and a tostonera. I decide
against the machete, though I talk about varieties of plá-
tano and caña. I teach them some steps and to sing the
refrain, "Guajira, Guantanamera." I even talk about José
Martí. I'm a hit, like Celia.

The following week I present a workshop on Latina
Poets at the branch campus of my university in the adjoining county—there are no people of color in this small
town. The elders who came to hear me and participate had
invited me back after I presented a talk some months earlier on the African American women writers Alice Walker
and Toni Morrison. This time, they expect to participate in
some collaborative work. To begin, I talk about Latino
demographics in the U.S. and the difference between Latin
Americans and Latinos; their faces begin to reveal perplex-
ity. I save the Hispanic versus Latino issue 'til later. I speak
about Mexican Americans and Chicanos first (and why
some choose one term over the other)—the largest group
of Latinos in the U.S. When I repeat the names of the states
that were Mexican territory with the correct Spanish pro-
nunciation, I note some nodding heads. I move from the
national Latino populations and a little of their history and

then I aim for something my audience will immediately connect with—their home state. When I say that of the 11 million people in Pennsylvania there are one million blacks, they are surprised. When I tell them there are about 250,000 Latinos, some of whom are Black, their jaws drop. One elder challenged me at the midpoint break—I had mispronounced an English word. He left before the discussion of the Latina poetry.

🙢🙠

Negrita was sitting on the living room sofa when Bettye, a Black student whose dissertation on Harlem Renaissance writer Nella Larsen I directed, came over unexpectedly one day. I was nervous, again, despite Illy's sense about the doll. Because the impact of African American culture on U.S. American culture is as profound as mainstream America's response to it, Bettye's impression mattered in a different way. There was no time to break the ice for Lili immediately grabbed Negrita and planted herself at Bettye's feet. "Let's play" was the command. Bettye smiled tenderly as she embraced the offering; she smoothed her hair and said, "We used to wear dresses just like this."

🙢🙠

When I was about eight the city I grew up in celebrated a Centennial. In Bayonne, New Jersey there were two bodegas, a couple of bars frequented by Puerto Rican men, a Spanish American Club and plenty of my schoolmates had Spanish last names; many were Spaniards. Our church, which meant the people who went to the Spanish language services in the auditorium of a Catholic school

every Sunday, decided to participate in the citywide celebration and parade. My mother, an expert seamstress, was
recruited to help and her effort landed me as la rumbera
cubana in the Latin section of the parade. I had never seen
Carmen Miranda but I thought the long, white ruffled cola
was pretty and I got to show my belly because of the short
puffy sleeved shirt; I wore a turban, red, of course, a
miniature version of the North American image of a Latina. One of the little boys my age wore all white, a frayed
straw hat, red kerchief tied around his neck and a painted-
on mustache, the prototypical macho then. We both
danced our way through the city, me shaking maracas and
him scraping the güiro.

A few years later the members of the Spanish American Club, which included many caribeños, met before a
city zoning hearing about their moving into more spacious
quarters a block away from the original location. Some of
the Spaniards testifying felt compelled to clarify that the
club was a *Spanish* American club and offended los
cubanos, in particular. The new club resembled el centro
español in Cuba with most of the members being
Spaniards or Cuban-born children of Spaniards. Not too
long after, the caribeños distanced themselves for good.

I realized years later that we Cubans were never really
in any large numbers in Bayonne; we just knew one another. More importantly, ethnicity, exile, emigration and
mother tongues were as natural for us as they were for the
Italian Americans, Polish Americans, Irish Americans and
Jewish Americans. In my neighborhood, North American
Blacks filled in all the spaces in between and there was
plenty of room left over for difference.

Illy's caramel color was as normal to me as Yoly's, my
surrogate sister, milky hue. I heard Olga Guillot at home

and Motown outside. I played amambrochato and double-dutch. I had to fight both Black and white girls to be included as a fringemember in either group.

My mother asked me why I studied Black women writers when she read my master's thesis on Morrison. I answered her, as I do anyone who asks me, that I love their work. It goes back to my first Women's Studies course, reading women writers of color who spoke directly to me, for the first time. For the first time, literature meant something to me. After reading *Sula* straight through in one sitting, I decided right there and then that if I could write anything as perfect and profound and beautiful as this then I could die. In Sula and Nel's relationship, I was taken back to my girlhood and lifelong friendship with Illy who showed me her budding breasts when I was still wearing a sleeveless tee shirt and wanted more than life to wear a bra, a training, stretchy bra, anything to show that I too was becoming grown up, womanish.

Delving deeper inside myself, I come up with all sorts of justifications and arguments for my scholarly interests—words that are inappropriate to me but others seem to need to hear them articulated as such—perfectly logical reasons why. There is the philosophical and aesthetic commitment I feel that the writing of black women has influenced in my own work as a writer, as a Cuban American, as a Latina feminist. Concerns such as my otherness or outsider status within the dominant culture and the struggle for identity and survival come to mind. Also, there is the accessibility to ancestors' ancient wisdom and how we, women in particular, use that information.

I was awarded a small grant to do research on Morrison at the Schomburg Center for Research in Black Culture. I commuted back and forth between New Jersey and Harlem. Some friends were alarmed. One asked me if there were a lot of Black people in the library. She was worried I might be in danger because I hadn't called her to pick me up at the train station at the designated time. She said she was ready to call the police and tell them to look for me, telling them about my research—that would be some sort of measure of my character. That because I am a light-skinned Latina doing work on a dark-skinned writer that I should be left alone. I am not the enemy, in other words.

Maybe it is genetic, in the blood? My great grand-mother was one of those mulatas who was so beautiful, shapely and alluring that even though she had two daughters from a previous union, my blue-eyed great grandfather threw himself at her feet in awe, quit medical school and preferred to be disowned by his light-skinned family than to leave her. How much is true? Which part did I invent? The part about her flashing green eyes and sassyness? Or her succulent kisses and supple arms holding that ticket out of her caste so dearly? My grandmother didn't tell my mother much about her and it wasn't until much, much later when I began to understand the significance of this for me, of having una abuelita prieta. Not having known her, my nameless great-grandmother takes shape in my imagination. She who buried, killed or left her man only to be worshiped, coveted and married by another—a prime catch—someone with whom she could mejorar la raza; even if she already had two dark-skinned daughters. It's no use, all the stories are closed off types in and around *Cecilia Valdés*, Maureen Peale, Jadine, or the oh-so-boring tragic mulata. What I need to know about her I know through writers in this country who never knew her, her historical moment. Will I find her someday?

❧❧❧

Here I am reading, writing, concerning myself with people of color in the hopes of discovering more about my self. Though most of the Cubans I know don't consider themselves people of color, most North Americans do, especially outside of Miami. No one in my family sees it that way. They think I'm strange, that it's queer of me. They think that maybe my lifelong friendship con mi amiga prieta somehow draws me to color. Naturally then, I am studying myself, my great-grandmother, my mother. My light-skin is beside the point; there is an attempt at self-explanation/realization (I wonder how many times Lydia Cabrera had to explain herself?). I dream of teaching African American literature in Cuba, not forever, for that isn't my home but my ancestral soil; my people are buried there. My life has been here.

I am not nostalgic for my parents' Cuba. I look to a Cuba where a person's skin-color will not cause one physical, emotional, psychological or even economic harm. I aspire to a Cuba where feminism—defined by bell hooks, Audre Lorde, Gloria Anzaldúa et al as the movement which seeks to dismantle the interlocking systems of racial, sexual and class oppression—succeeds. I yearn for a Cuba where one's sexual orientation, faith, or opinion does not land one in jail. My hopes for Cuba are the same as my hopes for the U.S. Here, my struggles include curriculum transformation for the inclusion of the culture, literature and impact of people of color on our society, the empowerment of the disenfranchised and underprivileged and a radical democratization of all of our institutions.

Dreaming these dreams, empowering myself and others, the greatest thrill is that I am not alone.

ﷺﷺ

At last we came up with a name for Negrita because I couldn't stand the thought of anglos misunderstanding this very Cuban, very old endearment or of perpetuating racism in my own home. We decided on Cachita, the name of one of my partner's beloved great aunts, the dark skinned one. There was one last thing to do—give her a face. Lili excitedly picked out a red button for her nose and I stitched in a mouth. Cachita smiled back at us as we admired her lovely countenance.

BITTERNESS

⊱ Virgil Suárez ⊰

My father brings home the blood of horses on his hands, his rough, calloused, thick-fingered hands; he comes home from the slaughter house where the government puts him to kill old useless horses that arrive from all over the island. On his hands comes the blood encrusted and etched on the prints and wrinkles of his fingers, under his nails, dark with the dirt too, the filth and grime, the moons of his fingers pinked by the residue, his knuckles skinned from the endless work. Sticky and sweet scented is the blood of these horses, horses to feed the lions in the new zoo which is moving from Havana to Lenin's Park near where we live. Dark blood, this blood of the horses my father slaughters daily to feed the zoo lions. I, being a child, ask how many horses it takes to feed a single lion. This, of course, makes my father laugh. I watch as he washes and rinses the dried-up blood from his forearms and hands, those hands that kill the horses, the hands that sever through skin and flesh and crush through bone because tough is the meat of the old horses. Feed for the lions. So my father, the dissident, the *gusano*, the Yankee lover, walks to and from work on tired feet, on an aching body. He no longer talks to anybody, and less to us, his family. My mother and my grandmother; his mother. But they leave him alone, to his moods, for they know what he is being put through. A test of will. Determination. Salvation and survival. My father, under the tent on the grounds of the new zoo, doesn't say much. He has learned how to speak with his hands. Sharp are the cuts he makes on the flesh. The horses are shot on the open fields, a bullet through the head, and are then carted to where my father, along with other men, do the butchering. He is thirty (the age I am now) and tired and when he comes home his hands are numb from all the chopping and cutting. This takes place in 1969.

❧❧

Years later when we are allowed to leave Cuba and travel to Madrid—to the cold winter of Spain, we find ourselves living in a hospice. The three of us in a small room. (My grandmother died and was buried in Havana.) My father, my mother and I and next door is a man named Izquierdo who keeps us awake with his phlegmy coughs. From the other side of the walls, his coughing sounds like thunder. We try to sleep; I try harder but the coughing seeps through and my father curses under his breath. I listen to the heat as it tic-tacs coming through the furnace. My father tries to make love to my mother. I try now not to listen. The mattress springs sound like bones crushing. My mother refuses without saying a word. This is the final time she does so tonight. There is what seems like an interminable silence, then my father breaks it by saying to my mother, "If you don't, I'll look for a Spanish woman who will." Silence again, then I think I hear my mother crying. "*Alguien*," my father says, "Will want to, to…" And I lay there on my edge of the mattress, sweat coming on from the heat. My eyes are closed and I listen hard and then the sound of everything stops. This, I think, is the way death must sound. Then my father begins all over again. The room fills with the small sounds…the cleaver falls and cuts through the skin, tears through the flesh, crushes the bone, and then there is the blood. All that blood. It emerges and collects on the slaughter tables, the blood of countless horses. Sleep upon me, I see my father stand by the sink in the patio of the house in Havana. He scrubs and rinses his hands. The blood dissolves slowly in the water. Once again I build up the courage to go ahead and ask him how much horse meat it takes to appease the hunger of a single lion.

CONTRIBUTORS' BIOGRAPHIES

❧❧❧

JOSÉ BARREIRO

José Barreiro is a writer and Cornell University scholar of Taíno/Guajiro ancestry from Cuba. He is active in linking Native communities in the Caribbean and Central America and has a wide reputation among Native American and multicultural scholars and activists for his work in bringing Native viewpoints to light in the past twenty years. Editor-in-Chief of the *Akwekon*, a Native American press that publishes books and a journal, Barreiro's writings began to appear in anthologies in the 1970s and he has won journalistic prizes for best feature stories from the Native American Press Association.

❧❧❧

RUTH BEHAR

Ruth Behar was born in Havana, Cuba, in 1956. She is the author of *The Presence of the Past in a Spanish Village: Santa Maria del Monte*, published by Princeton University Press, which in 1986 was selected by *Choice* as an outstanding scholarly book. She is also the author of *Translated Woman: Crossing the Border with Esperanza's Story*, published by Beacon Press. Behar is a gifted essayist, poet and editor whose anthologies include *Women Writing Culture/Culture Writing Women* and *Bridges to Cuba*, published by *Michigan Quarterly Review*. Of her own writing, Ruth Behar has said,

"I write creative nonfiction, poetry, and memoir. The themes I explore in my work are travel, intercultural encounters, memory, and the predicaments of living a feminist life. In my poetry I blend together the Cuban and the Jewish sense of exile to try to get at deeper meanings of lost homelands." Currently, Ms. Behar is professor of Anthropology at the University of Michigan.

RICHARD BLANCO

Richard Blanco (Ricardo de Jesús Blanco) was conceived on Cuban soil of Cuban parents and named after Richard Nixon. Richard Blanco has lived in Madrid, Spain, and, since 1968, in the United States. He currently makes his home in Miami. Although he claims to have been writing poetry since age five, he considers 1992 as the official beginning of his writing career, the year after he received his Engineering degree from Florida International University. Since then, he has published in local literary magazines and has won awards from the National Writers Association, the American Academy of Poets, the South Florida Poetry Institute and *El Círculo de Arte y Cultura* of Miami. He co-founded a poetry reading series, Butterfly Lightning, which has won attention for showcasing local literary talent, and a program with the Y.M.C.A., which explores the opportunities of inspiration in poetry by introducing local writers to inner city school children. Mr. Blanco is currently enrolled in the M.F.A. Creative Writing Program at Florida International University, where he is working with the American poet Campbell McGrath.

❦❦❦

RAFAEL CAMPO

Rafael Campo is the author of the prize-winning, highly acclaimed collection of poems, *The Other Man Was Me*. Robert Pinsky has said that "Rafael Campo's poems have passion, technical brilliance and vital, important subjects. His book is a voyage of discovery yet homecoming, where the struggle for understanding uses all the unexpected resources of art. Never oversimplifying, always seeking clarity, this is a strong, soulful work that defies stereotypes. Medicine, Cuba, sex, art, history, the United States—all are seen with a fresh, distinctive eye. *The Other Man Was Me* is a wonderful first book." Mr. Campo is a practicing physician in San Francisco.

❦❦❦

SANDRA M. CASTILLO

Sandra M. Castillo has published poems in many magazines, including the *Appalachee Quarterly*, *Florida Review* and *Polyphony*. Her work is showcased in *Paper Dance: 55 Latino Poets*. Castillo's first book of poems, *Red Letters*, was published by Appalachee Press in 1991. Currently she lives and writes in Miami.

❦❦❦

ADRIÁN CASTRO

Adrián Castro was born in Miami in 1967 of Cuban and Dominican parents. He writes in the rhythmic Afro-Caribbean tradition pioneered by Nicolás Guillén and Luis Palés Matos. Castro lives in Miami Beach, where he often performs his poetry with musicians. He has performed around the country in The Nuyorican Poets Cafe in New York, The Naropa Institute in Boulder, Colorado, The Hemingway Literary Festival in Chicago, the Miami International Book Fair and elsewhere. His poems have been published in various literary reviews, including *Bilingual Review, Conjunctions, International Quarterly* and *Paper Dance; 55 Latino Poets*. Castro is a member of the "Bicycle Poets," who regularly bicycle to public schools to present poetry.

❦❧

SILVIA CURBELO

Silvia Curbelo was born in Matanzas, Cuba, in 1955 and emigrated to the United States in 1967. She has received poetry fellowships from the Cintas Foundation (1991-92), the National Endowment for the Arts (1990), the Florida Arts Council (1989) and Atlantic Center for the Arts. In 1992, she was co-winner of the James Wright Poetry Prize for *Mid-American Review*. A collection of poems, *The Geography of Leaving*, won the 1990 Gerald Cable Chapbook Competition and was published by Silverfish Review Press in 1991. Her work has appeared in *Kenyon Review, Prairie Schooner, Indiana Review, Bloomsbury Review, Yellow Silk, Shenandoah, Mid-American Review, Passages North, Tampa Review* and other publications. Of her work, Ms. Curbelo says, "I think my work reflects the duality of growing up between two worlds, between loss and renewal, the ghost of what is missing and the concrete, physical presence of what lies ahead. *The Geography of Leaving* deals with this duality and the tenuous balance between desire to move forward and the inherent, compelling need to keep looking back." Curbelo lives in Tampa, Florida.

⚘⚘

MARGARITA ENGLE

Margarita Engle was born in Los Angeles, California, to a Cuban mother and an American father, a painter who traveled to Cuba to paint the picturesque city of Trinidad. A botanist by training and profession, Engle has worked as an irrigation specialist in Southern California. Her opinion column on topics ranging from culture and history to personal experience has been syndicated since 1982 to more than two-hundred newspapers. She is a prolific short-story writer whose list of publications include journals and magazines such as *Nuestro*, *The Americas Review* and *Revista Interamericana*. She has also contributed non-fiction articles to national magazines including, *Vista*, *Hispanic*, *South American Explorer*, *Garden* and others. She has written two novels, *Singing to Cuba* and *Skywriting*.

⚘⚘

ROBERTO G. FERNÁNDEZ

Roberto G. Fernández was born in Sagua la Grande, Cuba, in 1951, just eight years before the Cuban Revolution. He went into exile with his family at the age of eleven. His family settled in southern Florida, not in the Cuban community of Miami, but in areas where Anglo-American culture was dominant. The Fernández family nevertheless maintained close ties with the Miami community, and this became subject matter for the writer. In 1978, he completed a Ph.D. in Linguistics at Florida State University; by that time he had already published two collections of stories: *Cuentos sin rumbo (Directionless Tales)* and *El Jardin de la luna (The Garden of the Moon)*. At this point, he also began his career as an academic, teaching linguistics and Hispanic literature at Florida State University. He is the author of four open-formed novels which have created for him the reputation of being a satirist and humorist of the Miami Cuban community. In all four, he is a master at capturing the nuances of Cuban dialect in Spanish and English. *La Vida es un special (Life is on Special)*, *La montaña rusa (The Roller Coaster)*, *Raining Backwards* and *Holy Radishes* are all mosaics made up of monologues, dialogues, letters, phone conversations, speeches and other types of oral performance that, in the composite, make up a continuing tale of the development of the exile community and its younger generations of increasingly acculturated Cuban Americans.

GUSTAVO PÉREZ FIRMAT

Gustavo Pérez Firmat was born in Havana, Cuba, and raised in Miami, Florida. He holds a B.A. in English and an M.A. in Spanish, both from the University of Miami, and a Ph.D. in Comparative Literature from the University of Michigan. He has received numerous fellowships and awards, including a Guggenheim Fellowship. He is the author of several books of literary criticism and essays, including *The Cuban Condition* and *Life on the Hyphen*; and three volumes of poetry: *Carolina Cuban*, *Equivocaciones* and *Bilingual Blues*. *Next Year in Cuba*, a memoir, was recently published to great critical acclaim by Anchor/Doubleday. He currently teaches Spanish American literature at Duke University. In his work, Pérez Firmat examines relationships, sex and Cuban-American life with candor and wicked humor, handling both Spanish and English (and *Spanglish*) with seamless assurance and incredible wit.

❧❧

CRISTINA GARCÍA

Cristina García was born in Havana, Cuba, in 1958 and grew up in New York City. She attended Barnard College and the Johns Hopkins University School of Advanced International Studies. García has worked as a correspondent for *Time* magazine in San Francisco, Miami and Los Angeles, where she currently lives with her husband, Scott Brown, and their child. Her first novel, *Dreaming in Cuban*, was published by Alfred A. Knopf in 1992, and it has since that time become a classic. She is currently at work on a second novel.

❧❧

JORGE GUITART

Jorge Guitart is the author of *Foreigner's Notebook* (Shuffaloff Press). His work has appeared in numerous anthologies including *Los Atrevidos: Cuban American Writers* edited by Carolina Hospital (Linden Lane Press). He Teaches at the State University of New York at Stoneybrook.

❧❧

OSCAR HIJUELOS

Oscar Hijuelos was born in 1951 in New York. He is the author of three novels, *Our House in the Last World*, *The Mambo Kings Play Songs of Love* and *The Fourteen Sisters of Emilio Montez O'Brien*. He won the 1990 Pulitzer Prize for fiction and the heartfelt love and admiration of America's reading public. A major feature film version of *The Mambo Kings Play Songs of Love* was released by Warner Brothers.

Hijuelos is the recipient of many awards, including a Cintas Fellowship.

❧❧

CAROLINA HOSPITAL

Carolina Hospital is a Cuban-American poet and essayist residing in Miami, where she is Associate Professor of Writing and Literature at Miami-Dade Community College. Her essays and poems have appeared in numerous national magazines, newspapers and anthologies, including *Mid-American Review, Caribbean Writer, The Gables Paper, Vista, Caribbean Review, The Americas Review, Rio Grande Review, Haydn Ferry Review, Appalachee Quarterly, Confrontation, Amelia, Linden Lane Magazine, Windhorse, Bilingual Review, Miami Mensual, La Bete, Cuban Heritage Magazine* and in the following anthologies: *Looking for Home: Women Writing About Exile, Paper Dance: 55 Latino Poets* and *Other Voices: Latina Writers*. She has also given numerous poetry readings and lectures on the literature of Latinos in the United States. She was resident scholar for the Florida Center for Teachers, sponsored by the Florida Humanities Council, in 1994, leading the seminar, "Los Latinos: the U.S. and Florida." She is the compiler and editor of the groundbreaking anthology *Cuban American Writers: Los Atrevidos* (Linden Lane Press, 1989).

❧❧

WASABI KANASTOGA

Wasabi Kanastoga (a.k.a. Luis E. López) was born in Santiago de Cuba in 1962. Living in California since 1970, he is one of the few tri-cultural Latino-American writers.

He is a poet and a fiction writer whose poems and stories deal with the absurdities of the day-to-day life of Mexicans and Cubans living and dying in Los Angeles. His work has been featured in many literary reviews and anthologies, including *Iguana Dreams: New Latino Literature* and *Paper Dance: 55 Latino Poets*. He has recently completed a novel, *City for Sale*, and is working on a collection entitled, *On Fire/Me Quemo*. He holds a B.A. in Psychology from California State University at Long Beach and is currently a family counselor for El Centro in East Los Angeles.

❧❧

DIONISIO D. MARTÍNEZ

Dionisio D. Martínez, born in Cuba in 1956, is the author of three collections of poetry: *History as a Second Language* (winner of the 1992 Ohio State University Press/*The Journal* Poetry Award), *Dancing at the Chelsea* and *Bad Alchemy*, published by W. W. Norton. He was the recipient of a Whiting Writers' Award, the *Mid-American Review* James Wright Poetry Prize and a Hillsborough County (FL) Arts Council Emerging Artist Grant. Martínez's work has been widely published in journals and anthologies and was selected for the 1992 and 1994 editions of *The Best American Poetry*. Following his family's exile from Cuba, in 1965, Martínez lived in northern Spain and in southern California. A Tampa, Florida, resident since 1972, he is an affiliate writer at the University of Tampa and a collaborating artist with the Y.M.C.A. National Writer's Voice Project. About his work the poet Stephen Dunn has said, "Dionisio Martínez is one of the most exciting new voices in American poetry. His poems are mysterious and intellectually provocative. The world in them reflects the absurdity that

Kafka and the magical realists have made us understand is ours, a world that Martínez makes ever more recognizable. I love the way his poems show us that one can be both bemused and alienated at the same time; in this sense they are the poems of a survivor."

～･～

PABLO MEDINA

Pablo Medina was born in Havana, Cuba, and has lived in the United States since 1960. He has received graduate and undergraduate degrees from Georgetown University. His poetry, prose and translations from the Spanish language have appeared in numerous anthologies and periodicals, including *The American Poetry Review*, *Visions of America*, *Iguana Dreams*, *High Plains Literary Review*, *Paper Dance*, *The Antioch Review*, *Poetry*, *Kansas Quarterly*, *Linden Lane Magazine* and *Cuban-American Writers: Los Atrevidos*. His *Pork Rind and Cuban Songs* (Nuclassics and Science, 1975) was the first collection of poems written directly into English by a Cuban-born writer. In addition, he has published a second collection of poems, *Arching into the Afterlife* (Bilingual Press, 1991); a collection of personal essays entitled *Exiled Memories: A Cuban Childhood* (University of Texas Press, 1990) and, with Carolina Hospital, *Everyone Will Have to Listen* (Linden Lane Press, 1990), a collection of translations from the Spanish of Cuban dissident Tania Díaz Castro. Medina is also the author of a novel, *The Marks of Birth* (Farrar, Straus & Giroux). He has been awarded grants from the Cintas Foundation, The Pennsylvania Council of the Arts, the New Jersey State Council of the Arts, the National Endowment for the Arts and the Lila Wallace-Reader's Digest Foundation.

❥❥

MATÍAS MONTES HUIDOBRO

Matías Montes Huidobro was born in Sagua la Grande, Cuba, in 1931. He holds a doctoral degree in Pedagogy from the University of Havana and has been writing in a variety of literary genres since 1950, the year he received his first drama award from Prometeo, published his first short story in *Bohemia*, the most influential magazine in Cuba at that time, and his first poem in *Nueva Generación*. He left Cuba in 1961 and joined the faculty of the University of Hawaii in 1964. He has contributed to the field of literary research in the areas of Latin American and Peninsular studies, publishing in journals such as *Hispania* and *Hispanic Review*. His plays have been staged in Cuba as well as in the U.S. and Latin America. Montes Huidobro's novel, *Desterrados al fuego*, received an award from Fondo de Cultura Económica, Mexico, in 1974 and was later translated and published by Plover Press (1982) as *Qwert and the Wedding Gown*. His short stories have been anthologized in *Narradores cubanos de hoy* (Miami: Universal, 1975) and *Veinte años de literature cubanoamericana* (Tempe, Arizona: Bilingual Press, 1988). He has also published a volume of poetry: *La vaca de los ojos largos* (Honolulu: Mele, 1970).

❥❥

GEAN MORENO

Gean Moreno was born in New York in 1972. From age four to twelve he lived in Colombia, his father's birthplace. His poems have been published in *Midwest Quarterly* and *Poetry Forum*. They have also been showcased in *Paper*

Dance: 55 Latino Poets. Presently he lives in Miami, where he attends Florida International University.

✶✶

ELÍAS MIGUEL MUÑOZ

Elías Miguel Muñoz was born in Cuba in 1954 and did not emigrate to the United States until 1969. He attended high school and college in Southern California and earned a Ph.D. in Spanish from the University of California-Irvine in 1984. His published works include two works of literary criticism, *El discurso utópico de la sexualidad de Manuel Puig* and *Desde esta orilla: Poesia cubana del exilio*; two novels, *Los viajes de Orlando Cachumbambé* and *Crazy Love*, as well as two collections of poetry, *En estas tierras (In This Land)* and *No fue posible el sol*. His musical theatre adaptation of *Crazy Love*, entitled *The L.A. Scene*, had a successful run off-Broadway in New York in 1990. His novel, *The Greatest Performance*, was published by Arte Público Press in 1991.

✶✶

ACHY OBEJAS

Achy Obejas is a widely published poet, fiction writer and journalist. Her poetry has been published in *Conditions*, *The Americas Review* and *Beloit Poetry Journal*, among others. In 1986, she received an NEA fellowship in poetry. Her stories have appeared in magazines such as *Antigonish Review*, *Phoebe* and *Third Woman*, as well as in numerous anthologies, including *Discontents* (Amethyst), *West Side Stories* (Chicago Stoop) and *Girlfriend Number One* (Cleis). She writes a weekly column for the *Chicago Tribune* and is a regular contributor to *High Performance*, *Chicago*

Reader and *Windy City Times*, among other publications. Her collection of short stories, *We Came All the Way from Cuba So You Could Dress Like This?* was published by Cleis Press in 1994.

❧❧

ANDREA O'REILLY HERRERA

Andrea O'Reilly Herrera was born in Philadelphia to a Cuban mother and an Irish-American father. "The Homecoming" is the opening sequence of her recently completed novel, *The Pearl of the Antilles*, a work which she describes as a lingual painting of a world that exists only in the collective memory of those who have refused to forget. She currently lives in western New York with her husband and children. There, she continues to write literary criticism, poetry, and fiction and teaches global, multicultural literature, with a special emphasis on contemporary Latina/o writers.

❧❧

RICARDO PAU-LLOSA

Ricardo Pau-Llosa, born in Havana in 1954, has lived in the United States since 1960. Currently, he is an Associate Professor in the English Department at Miami-Dade Community College. He is a prolific writer of poetry as well as fiction. His first volume of poetry, *Sorting Metaphors* (1983), won the national competition for the first Anhinga Poetry Prize, judged that year by William Stafford. He has since published two more books of poetry: *Bread of the Imagined* (Bilingual Press, 1992) and *Cuba* (Carnegie Mellon University Press, 1993). His poetry has also appeared in many journals, such as *American Poetry Review, Beloit Poetry Journal, Black Warrior Review, Caliban, Carolina Quarterly, Colorado Review, Denver Quarterly, Epoch, Iowa Review, Kenyon Review, Massachusetts Review, Michigan Quarterly Review, New England Review, Onthebus, Partisan Review, Prairie Schooner, Seneca Review* and others. Pau-Llosa is also an art critic and curator, specializing in Latin American art.

❄❄

DELIA POEY

Delia Poey was born in Mexico City of Cuban parents and grew up in Miami, Florida. She is currently a doctoral candidate in Comparative Literature at Louisiana State University, where she has taught English and Spanish. She is editor of *Out of the Mirrored Garden: New Fiction by Latin American Women*, published by Anchor/Doubleday, and the co-editor with her husband Virgil Suárez of the anthology of new Latino fiction, *Iguana Dreams*. She lives with her husband and two daughters in Tallahassee, Florida.

❄❄

DOLORES PRIDA

Dolores Prida, born in 1943 in Caibairén, Cuba, emigrated with her family to New York City in 1963. She graduated from Hunter College in 1969, majoring in Spanish American Literature. Her first play, *Beautiful Señoritas*, was produced at the Duo Theater in 1977. Her work has earned her critical acclaim as a playwright of extreme versatility and talent. Her bilingual play, *Coser y cantar* (1981) has been repeatedly produced because of its success in depicting with humor and pathos the cultural and linguistic conflicts of Latinas/os in the United States. In 1990, her play *Botánica* debuted, enjoying a run of several years at the Spanish Repertory Theater. Her collected plays, *Beautiful Señoritas and Other Plays*, were published by Arte Público Press in one volume in 1991. Prida is also a poet of distinction who in the 1960s was a leader of New York's Nueva Sangre movement of younger poets. Her books of poetry include *Treinta y un poemas* (1967), *Women of the Hour* (1971) and, with Roger Cabán, *The IRT Prayer Book*.

❧❧

BEATRIZ RIVERA

Born in Havana, Cuba, Beatriz Rivera moved to Miami at the age of three. Rivera has lived in Switzerland and France, where she obtained her master's degree from the University of Paris IV-Sorbonne. She has worked as a translator, teacher and editor, and currently lives in Union City, New Jersey.

❧❧

CECILIA RODRÍGUEZ MILANÉS

Cecilia Rodríguez Milanés was born in Jersey City, New Jersey, to Cuban parents. In 1982 she received a B.A. in Creative Writing from the University of Miami and in 1985 an M.A. in English from Barry University. She also holds a Ph.D. from the State University of New York at Albany. Her essays, poems and short stories have appeared in numerous literary magazines and reviews. She currently lives in Pennsylvania with her husband and daughter and is a member of the English Department at Indiana University of Pennsylvania.

VIRGIL SUÁREZ

Virgil Suárez was born in Havana, Cuba, in 1962. In 1970 he traveled to Madrid, Spain, where he lived for the next four years, then moved to Los Angeles, California, where he grew up and attended public school. He has a B.A. from California State University at Long Beach and an M.F.A. from Louisiana State University. He studied with Sir Angus Wilson, Edward Abbey, Robert Houston and Vance Bourjaily. Suárez is the author of four published novels: *Latin Jazz* (William Morrow, 1989/Simon & Schuster, 1990, currently distributed by Arte Público Press) and *The Cutter* (Ballantine Books/Available Press, 1991, new edition forthcoming from Arte Público Press), *Havana Thursdays* (Arte Público Press, 1995), *Going Under* (Arte Público Press, 1996) and a collection of stories entitled, *Welcome to the Oasis* (Arte Público Press, 1992). He is co-editor with Deila Poey of the Latino fiction anthology, *Iguana Dreams: New Latino Fiction* (Harper Collins/Perennial, 1993/Quality Paperback Book Club, 1994). He is the co-editor of *Paper Dance: 55 Latino Poets* with Victor Hernández Cruz and Leroy V. Quintana. Suárez is an associate professor in the Creative Writing Program at Florida State University. He teaches contemporary American literature, Latino/a Literature and Latin American Literature. He lives happily with his wife and children, a dog named Mongo and more than one-hundred canaries.

❧❧

OMAR TORRES

Omar Torres is a novelist, poet, playwright and actor whose works and acting have contributed to a boom in U.S. Hispanic literature, theater and film. Born in Victoria de la Tunas, Cuba, from where he emigrated to the United States as a child, he has published five books in Spanish. *Fallen Angels Sing*, published by Arte Público Press, is his first book written in English. The Chilean critic Alberto Baeza Flores has said of his style, "personal, intense, tight and vivid...a style that grabs us, holds us, empassions..."

❧❧

E. J. VEGA

E. J. Vega was born in Oriente, Cuba, in 1961. He was educated at Brooklyn College and Columbia University, and has sailed as a deck hand on tugboats and ocean-going barges. His poetry and fiction have appeared in many literary reviews, including *Parnassus*, *The Americas Review*, *Brooklyn Review*, *River Styx* and *Imagine: International Chicano Poetry Journal*. Among his writing awards are the Irwin Shaw Fiction Prize, the Donald G. Whiteside Poetry Award, and the Grebanier Sonnet Award. He serves on the Humanities faculty of SUNY Maritime College, Fort Schuyler, New York.

❧❧

MARISELLA VEIGA

Marisella Veiga was born in Havana, Cuba. In 1960, her family went into exile, and she was raised in both St. Paul, Minnesota, and Miami, Florida. Her poetry, articles and translations have appeared in numerous publications. Veiga currently lives, writes and teaches in Miami, Florida.

≋≋

JOSE YGLESIAS

Born in Tampa, Florida, of a Spanish father and a Cuban mother, Jose Yglesias is the highly-acclaimed author of numerous novels, works of non-fiction, articles and short stories published in such respected journals as *The New Yorker*, *Esquire*, *The Atlantic* and *The Sunday Times Magazine*. Among his most admired fiction titles are *Break-In*, *A Wake in Ybor City*, *An Orderly Life*, *The Truth about Them* and *Double Double*.

CUBAN-AMERICAN LITERATURE:
A BIBLIOGRAPHY

LITERATURE ANTHOLOGIES

Burunat, Silvia, and Ofelia García, eds. *Veinte años de literatura cubanoamericana*. Tempe, AZ: Bilingual Review, 1988.

Cortina, Rodolfo J. *Cuban American Theater*. Houston, TX: Arte Público, 1990.

González-Cruz, Luis F. and Francesca M. Colecchía. *Cuban Theater in the United States: A Critical Anthology*. Tempe, AZ: Bilingual Review, 1992.

Grupo Areíto. *Contra viento y marea*. Havana: Casa de las Américas, 1978.

Hernández-Miyares, Julio, ed. *Narradores cubanos de hoy*. Miami, FL: Editorial Universal, 1975.

Hospital, Carolina, ed. *Cuban American Writers: Los Atrevidos*. Princeton, NJ: Ediciones Ellas/Linden Lane, 1988.

❧❧

POETRY BY CUBAN AMERICANS

Campo, Rafael. *The Other Man Was Me: A Voyage to the New World*. Houston, TX: Arte Público, 1994.

Castillo, Sandra M. *Red Letters*. Tallahassee, FL: Appalachee, 1991.

Martínez, Dionisio D. *Dancing at the Chelsea*. Brockport, NY: State Street, 1992.

_____. *History as a Second Language*. Columbus, OH: Ohio State UP, 1993.

_____. *Bad Alchemy*. New York: Norton, 1995.

Medina, Pablo. *Arching Into the Afterlife*. Intro. Gregory Orfalea. Tempe, AZ: Bilingual Review, 1991.

Muñoz, Elías Miguel. *En éstas tierras/In This Land*. Tempe, AZ: Bilingual Review, 1991.

Pau-Llosa, Ricardo. *Sorting Metaphors*. Tallahassee, FL: Anhinga, 1983.

_____. *Bread of the Imagined*. Tempe, AZ: Bilingual Review, 1992.

_____. *Cuba*. Pittsburgh, PA: Carnegie-Mellon UP, 1993.

Pérez Firmat, Gustavo. *Equivocaciones*. Madrid, Spain: Betania, 1989.

_____. *Bilingual Blues*. Tempe, AZ: Bilingual Review, 1995.

Suárez, Virgil. *Spared Angola: Memories from a Cuban-American Childhood*. Houston, TX: Arte Público, 1997.

❧❧❧

FICTION BY CUBAN AMERICANS

Barreiro, José. *The Indian Chronicles*. Houston, TX: Arte Público, 1993.

Engle, Margarita. *Singing to Cuba*. Houston, TX: Arte Público Press, 1992.

_____. *Skywriting*. New York: St. Martin's, 1995.

_____. Fernández, Roberto G. *La vida es un special*. Houston, TX: Arte Público, 1981.

_____. *La montaña rusa*. Houston, TX: Arte Público, 1985.

_____. *Raining Backwards*. Houston, TX: Arte Público, 1988.

_____. *Holy Radishes!* Houston, TX: Arte Público, 1995.

García, Cristina. *Dreaming in Cuban*. New York: Knopf, 1992.

Hijuelos, Oscar. *Our House in the Last World*. New York: Persea Books, 1983.

_____. *The Mambo Kings Play Songs of Love*. New York: Farrar, 1989.

_____. *The Fourteen Sisters of Emilio Montez O'Brien*. New York: Farrar, 1993.

Medina, Pablo. *The Marks of Birth*. New York: Farrar, 1994.

Montes Huidobro, Matías. *Desterrados al fuego*. México: Fondo de Cultura Económica, 1975.

_____. *Qwert and the Wedding Gown*. Kaneohe, HI: Plover, 1992.

Muñoz, Elías Miguel. *Crazy Love*. Houston, TX: Arte Público, 1988.

_____. *The Greatest Performance*. Houston, TX: Arte Público, 1992.

Rivera, Beatriz. *African Passions*. Houston, TX: Arte Público, 1995.

Suárez, Virgil. *Latin Jazz*. New York: Morrow, 1989.

_____. *The Cutter*. New York: Ballantine/Available, 1991.

_____. *Welcome to the Oasis and Other Stories*. Houston, TX: Arte Público, 1992.

_____. *Havana Thursdays*. Houston, TX: Arte Público, 1995.

_____. *Going Under*. Houston, TX: Arte Público, 1996.

Torres, Omar. *Apenas un bolero*. Miami: Ediciones Universales, 1988..

_____. *Al partir*. Houston, TX: Arte Público, 1986.

_____. *Fallen Angels Sing*. Houston, TX: Arte Público, 1991.

❧❧

DRAMA BY CUBAN AMERICANS

Acosta, Iván. *Un cubiche en la luna*. Houston, TX: Arte Público, 1989.

Fornes, María Irene.

Prida, Dolores. *Beautiful Señoritas and Other Plays*. Ed.

Judith Weiss. Houston, TX: Arte Público, 1991.

❦❧

ESSAYS BY CUBAN AMERICANS

Medina, Pablo. *Exiled Memories: A Cuban-American Childhood.* Austin: U of Texas P, 1992.

Pérez Firmat, Gustavo. *Life on the Hyphen.* Austin: U of Texas P, 1994.

_____. *Next Year in Cuba.* New York: Anchor Books, 1995.

Suárez, Virgil. *Spared Angola: Memories from a Cuban-American Childhood.* Houston, TX: Arte Público, 1997.